PSYCHOLOGY, RELIGION, AND SPIRITUALITY

# Psychology, Religion, and Spirituality

*David Fontana*

BPS Blackwell

© 2003 by David Fontana
A BPS Blackwell book

THE BRITISH PSYCHOLOGICAL SOCIETY
St Andrews House, 48 Princess Road East, Leicester LE1 7DR

BLACKWELL PUBLISHING
350 Main Street, Malden, MA 02148-5020, USA
9600 Garsington Road, Oxford OX4 2DQ, UK
550 Swanston Street, Carlton, Victoria 3053, Australia

The right of David Fontana to be identified as the Author of this Work has been
asserted in accordance with the UK Copyright, Designs, and Patents Act 1988.

First published 2003 by the British Psychological Society and Blackwell Publishing Ltd

8    2009

*Library of Congress Cataloging-in-Publication Data*

Fontana, David.
  Psychology, religion, and spirituality / David Fontana.
     p. cm.
  Includes bibliographical references and index.
   ISBN: 978-1-4051-0805-8 (hbk. : alk. paper) — ISBN: 978-1-4051-0806-5 (pbk. : alk.
paper)
   1. Psychology, Religious. 2. Spirituality—Psychology. I. Title.
  BL53 .F57 2003
  200′.1′9—dc21

                                                    2002010324

A catalogue record for this title is available from the British Library.

Set in 10/12.5pt Galliard
by Graphicraft Ltd, Hong Kong
Printed and bound in Singapore
by C.O.S. Printers Pte Ltd

The publisher's policy is to use permanent paper from mills that operate a
sustainable forestry policy, and which has been manufactured from pulp processed
using acid-free and elementary chlorine-free practices. Furthermore, the publisher
ensures that the text paper and cover board used have met acceptable environmental
accreditation standards.

For further information on
Blackwell Publishing, visit our website:
www.blackwellpublishing.com

# Contents

# Introduction

## The Family of World Religions

Anyone attempting the daunting task of writing about the psychology of religion and spirituality is faced with an enormous range of material that must be taken into account. Even if we disregard the religions of the ancient world such as those of Egypt, Greece, South America, and Rome, there are some 11 religions that have had a marked impact in various ways upon world history and the history of ideas. India has given us Hinduism, Buddhism, Jainism, and Sikhism; China and Japan have given us Taoism, Confucianism, and Shinto; and the Middle East has given us Zoroastrianism, Judaism, Christianity, and Islam. In addition to what we might call the first 11 of world religions there are numerous smaller groupings that have had a more local, but none the less profound, influence upon the lives of believers. There are also countless more transitory cults and beliefs that over the centuries have attracted adherents and inspired men and women to worship and reverence. No book on the psychology of religion can hope to take account of this extraordinary richness and diversity. Realistically, it cannot even do justice to the 11 major religions, let alone to the various sects and divisions within each of them. A further difficulty is that some of these 11 have not as yet been subject to any significant research by Western psychology. Consequently we know too little about their belief systems, and about the effect of these beliefs upon the behavior of those who follow them.

Thus any book on the psychology of religion and spirituality cannot be other than highly selective. In consequence the present text will focus primarily upon the three major religions emanating from the Middle East, namely Judaism, Christianity, and Islam, and upon three of those that originated from the Indian subcontinent, Hinduism, Buddhism, and

Jainism. For convenience these six religions will be referred to throughout as the *great traditions*. This must not be taken to mean that other
traditions are not equally great, or have less meaning to their followers.
Nor should it be thought that these other traditions do not share much
in common with the six great traditions. Sikhism has great affinities with
both Hinduism and Islam. Taoism has many affinities with Buddhism,
in particular with Zen Buddhism. The shamanic traditions that once
flourished throughout Asia and that are still very much alive and well in
Africa and in Native America hold many beliefs and practices that find
echoes in Hinduism and Buddhism and in the Spiritism of Brazil (whose
adherents also point to some links with beliefs held in the Roman Catholic and other churches).

Within the six great traditions, most attention will be paid to Christianity and to Hinduism and Buddhism. Again not because these three
traditions are in any sense superior to the other three, but because in different ways they have been the subject of most investigation by Western
psychologists, theologians, and philosophers of minds. There are historical reasons for this. Christianity has for centuries been the largest religion
in the Western world, and is intimately bound up with the culture, the
social fabric, the scholarship, the morality, and the levers of power in the
West. Thus it has attracted most attention from Western psychologists
of religion. Buddhism has become particularly open to the West since
the exodus from Tibet of many leading scholars and practitioners. And
Hinduism, initially through the colonial presence in India of the British
from the eighteenth to the mid-twentieth century and latterly from the
presence of Hindu scholars and teachers in Europe and the United States
is relatively well known, at least at a superficial level, in the West.

The psychologist of religion faces other difficulties over and above
trying to do justice to the extensive family of world religions. Each of the
religions to which he or she makes reference requires in reality a lifetime
of study if the complexities of its beliefs and practices are to be fully
appreciated. Furthermore, the differences within each religion mean that
whatever is said about them will be faulted by one or other of their sects.
When one adds to this the difficulty of doing justice to the various
authorities within Western psychology who have shown an interest in
religion it is clear that only a brave – or more probably a foolish person
– would presume to enter this complex area. The aim of anyone who
does so should therefore not be to write anything definitive, but to
provide a broad and where possible a critical survey of the field, to suggest potentially fruitful ways of tackling the many issues involved, to
direct attention to relevant research, and to say enough about religion to
demonstrate how vital a knowledge of it is for our understanding of the
human mind and of human behavior.

The book can thus address only such questions as:

- What is meant by religion, by spirituality, and by religious belief and faith?
- What is the nature of religious experience, and how common is it?
- What forms does the religious life take?
- How does religion influence individual and social behavior?
- Why do people develop religious and spiritual beliefs?
- How do religion and spirituality relate to modern Western science?
- What is the relationship between religion and myths and symbols?
- Do religious and spiritual experiences throw any light on the mind–brain relationship?
- What influence do religious and spiritual beliefs have upon psychological and physical health?

These questions will each recur at various points during the book. To answer them much will need to be said about the belief systems of the great traditions themselves. To date, most work on the psychology of religion has rather avoided going into this kind of detail, but without it, the psychology of religion and spirituality cannot be adequately understood. In the West, the sharp dichotomy between psychology, philosophy, and religion (all of which are concerned with minds and behavior), which began with the seventeenth-century enlightenment, has been to the detriment of all three, and has meant that few psychology courses in Western universities touch more than briefly upon the details of what people believe in any of the great traditions. The result is likely to be ignorance of these details and an impression that religion is little more than a collection of superstitions, of no interest to the scientist of human thought and behavior. Few things could be further than the truth.

## The Predispositions of the Author

Ideally, all texts in psychology should make it clear at the outset where the sympathies and predispositions of the author lie. However much we may wish it otherwise, psychology is still in many ways a subjective exercise. We come to it not only with the knowledge we gain from the literature and from experimental work with others, but also with our own psychological make-up. In fairness to the reader, authors should therefore declare their interests, and allow the reader to keep these in mind when considering what is being said. So I must make it clear that I start from a position of sympathy toward religion. In my view religion and spirituality have brought and continue to bring more advantages than disadvantages (though there are plenty of the latter) both to individual believers and to society in general. I hope that my reasons for taking this position will become clear from what I have to say in the pages that follow, but in the end it is for readers to come their own conclusions on where their sympathies should lie.

It is not of course the task of the psychologist to attempt to arrive at the truth or otherwise of religious and spiritual belief. That is the prerogative of the theologian and the philosopher. The most that can be done while wearing the psychologist's hat is either to acknowledge that there appears to be something intrinsic in us that seeks for meaning in life beyond the constraints of the material world, or to dismiss religious inclinations as a sign of our immature readiness to take refuge in fantasies rather than face the cold fact of human mortality. Psychologists of the eminence of William James on the one hand and W. B. Watson on the other have ranged themselves on opposite sides of the debate between these two points of view. Of one thing we can be sure. The debate is by no means over.

# Why the Psychology of Religion?

## The Breadth and Scope of Religion

Years ago, when I first began to study psychology, the psychology of religion sounded to me like one of the dullest areas of the subject. It suggested dreary sermons, near-empty churches, and earnest individuals talking about their experiences of being "saved". Over the years, I have come to realize how mistaken this view was. Religion has been one of the major formative influences upon human thought and behavior throughout the centuries. It has had a profound effect upon the lives of individuals, and upon groups and cultures. It has inspired some of the most noble acts of self-sacrifice and altruism. It has stimulated much of the world's greatest architecture (including virtually all the monuments of the ancient world), and some of the finest sculpture, painting, and music. It has motivated men and women to develop moral and ethical systems, to philosophize on the nature of self and on the meaning and purpose of life, and to speculate on the destiny that awaits us beyond the grave. It has stimulated the development of techniques for altering consciousness such as meditation, contemplation, ritual, and prayer. It has been associated with mystical states that raise major questions as to the nature of mind, and it has provided countless millions with psychological comfort and solace and with a reason for living. It has been deemed important enough to provide a livelihood for more people than almost any other profession, and has spawned institutions that have become fabulously wealthy and gained political as well as spiritual power. It has, again through its institutions, been the inspirer and the guardian of learning and of scholarship, and has been a powerful force behind business, commerce, and economic development in all its forms, and its legacy to the world includes universities, schools, hospitals, and social welfare.

However, religion has also had a negative side, serving during various periods of history as an ultra-conservative and repressive influence upon scientific development and upon the freedom of thought and speech. It has led to social and cultural divisions, and been the excuse for some of the most barbaric wars in history. It has spawned excesses like the Inquisition, has led to the torture and execution of thousands, to the ruthless repression of whole systems of belief and, through attempts at proselytization, to the virtual extermination not only of many indigenous cultures but also of the innocent people to whom these cultures belonged. It has broken up families and relationships, disrupted lives and ruined careers across sectarian divides. On an individual level, it has led many people to suffer psychological hardship and damage, and been a source of needless guilt, fear, and anxiety. It has taught dogmatic ways of thinking and behaving, hindered many forms of educational development, led to rigid and punitive parental styles, justified social stratification of the most unfair and pernicious kind, led to unnatural and repressive attitudes toward the human body and sexual relations, and hindered creative expression in literature and in the visual and performing arts.

Religious traditions of thought and behavior thus undeniably provide the psychologist with a richness of material well nigh impossible to find in any other area of human activity. If this is not sufficient reason to study the psychology of religion, there are many other, highly contemporary ones. For example, the impact of religious fundamentalism upon the modern world, the growth of cults and supposed "New Age" thinking, the increasingly multi-ethnic, multi-cultural and multi-faith nature of many Western societies including Britain, and the religious conflicts apparent in the Indian Sub-Continent, in the Middle East, in the Balkans, in Northern Ireland and in the Far East. Psychology is not in the business of answering questions posed by religion such as whether or not there is a God or gods, whether or not there is a soul and a life after death (though it has much to say about the nature of mind and human consciousness which impinges upon these questions). But it is in the business of explaining why people believe in such things. Do beliefs spring from coherent inner experiences and from a reasoned appraisal of religious teachings and texts, or from less considered sources such as the desire to conform to cultural and subgroup norms, and the need to seek protection against existential fear and uncertainty?

The psychologist is also interested in exploring whether or not religious belief is rendered irrational by the advances of modern science. Have these advances demonstrated conclusively that religious belief has no grounds for serious support? Science cannot prove that something does *not* exist, but under certain circumstances it is able to provide us with insights into the odds for and against such existence. If science shows the odds against grounds for religious and spiritual belief are near overwhelming, this strengthens the notion that such belief is irrational. On the other hand, if science does not stack the odds against religion and spirituality too heavily, then charges of irrationality might be misplaced, and the psychologist can reasonably ask what light if any does the possible existence of the realities taught by religion throw upon our knowledge and understanding of the mind.

## Why the Current Neglect of the Psychology of Religion and Spirituality?

In spite of these extensive implications for human thought and behavior, the psychology of religion has not attracted the attention it deserves among mainstream psychologists. This does not mean that the subject has been neglected. The literature on the psychology of religion is vast (although there is much less on the psychology of spirituality). An extensive bibliography up to 1970 is given in Eysenck, Arnold, and Meili (1972), and more recent ones appear in Beit-Hallahmi and Argyle (1997) and in Wulff (1997). However, it remains on the periphery of modern psychology. Smart (1996) even considers that the subject is arguably less flourishing now than it was in the years following the birth of scientific psychology, and is relatively neglected when compared to many other areas of psychological investigation. For example, it currently merits no mention in most introductory psychology texts, even one as thorough and well respected as *Hilgard's Introduction to Psychology*. The question is sometimes asked (typically by undergraduate students who are more curious than their elders about such things) why should this be? Commenting upon this question, Houston Clark (1977) observes that "It is a paradox that [in view of the power of religion fundamentally to change lives] modern psychology should be so incurious about the dynamics involved and so neglectful of a force in human nature with the influence religion has for both good and evil in human personality and human history." Further on, he comments that mistakenly "the conventional psychologist still tends to observe [the psychology of religion] warily as a subject that he is not quite sure belongs in his field."

There are four main reasons – in addition to the misleadingly perceived dullness of the subject – for this misguided neglect of the psychology of religion and perhaps particularly of the psychology of spirituality.

1. We have already touched on the first reason, namely that religion and spirituality appear to be contrary to the teachings of science, and to the materialist–reductionist philosophy which arose from the scientific enlightenment of the seventeenth century and dominated

scientific thinking for much of the twentieth century. This philosophy is still seen by many academics and laypeople as the touchstone against which theories of reality must be judged. It dismisses many of the concepts of religion and spirituality as arising variously from superstition, wish fulfillment, and an outmoded and primitive worldview. Religion is seen as claiming the existence of a personal God not far removed from the image of an idealized parent, and spirituality as encouraging belief in a nonmaterial spirit and/or soul for which there is no scientific evidence. Both religion and spirituality, which are defined in due course below, are seen as accepting the survival of consciousness after physical death and as locating this survival in heavenly or purgatorial realms whose existence makes no rational sense. Moreover, they are seen as identified with a form of outmoded dualistic thinking which preaches that mind is separate from brain, and has more to do with an immaterial soul than with a physical body.

Critics argue in addition that the scriptures upon which much of religious doctrine relies is based upon myths, such as those in the Christian bible which claim among other things that the world was created by a divine intelligence in seven days and nights, that human life arose from a man and a woman made respectively from clay and a rib bone in the Garden of Eden, and that physical impossibilities such as raising the dead, walking on water, turning water into wine, and bodily resurrection are all possible for the divine will.

2.   The second reason why the psychology of religion and spirituality has not attracted more scientific interest among mainstream psychologists is that not only does religion appear contrary to science, it has in the Western world at times actively opposed the progress of scientific thinking. A much-quoted example is the hostility the Catholic Church showed toward advances in astronomy in the sixteenth and seventeenth centuries made by Copernicus, Brahe, Galileo, Kepler, and others, an hostility based not upon reasoned argument but upon the charge that these advances contradicted orthodox religious doctrine. Even when Charles Darwin advanced his theory of evolution by natural selection in the nineteenth century, religion was still seen as opposed to free inquiry about the world and the place of humankind within it. Many scientists still retain the fear that such opposition may again become a reality if religion is allowed to reclaim power over hearts and minds. The intolerant behavior of fundamentalist religious sects in both Western and Eastern worlds, together with the dogmatic posturing of various religious cults, is not surprisingly seen as lending substance to this fear.

3.   To work effectively, the psychologist of religion must have a knowledge not only of psychological theory and practice but also of

relevant areas of history, philosophy, theology, and the creative arts. We cannot hope to make sense of the psychology of religion by assuming that psychology is only something done by psychologists, and by seeking to abstract religion and spirituality from the complex matrix of disciplines and patterns of thought within which they are embedded. In these days of increasing specialization, where it is ever more difficult for the scientist to keep up with the exponential growth of knowledge in his or her own subject, few people have the time and energy to achieve more than a cursory acquaintance with the many disciplines essential to an understanding of religion.

In addition, as we discuss in due course, to operate effectively the psychologist of religion must penetrate the esoteric as well as the exoteric side of religion – which often necessitates first-hand acquaintance with certain of the practices used in esotericism, such as meditation and contemplation. Furthermore the psychology of religion requires an ability to tolerate ambiguity and contradiction within the material that is being studied, an openness to the many different ways in which humans express their inner lives and their search for direction and purpose in those lives, and a readiness to approach religion with the respect borne from a recognition of the depth of meaning and reverence with which it is associated by countless men and women from every culture and every walk of life.

4. The fourth reason for the relative neglect of the psychology of religion is that its study presents major methodological problems. Social psychology can investigate the behavior of religious groups and the influence of religious belief and behavior upon cultures and upon the individual, but religion and spirituality are very much more than social behavior. They have to do in large measure with that slippery domain called inner experience, a domain looked upon with great suspicion by many psychologists. The inner experience of others is not directly observable, and our knowledge of it therefore depends upon what they choose – or are able – to tell us about it. The accounts they give depend firstly upon their ability to observe their own mental processes accurately (i.e. to *introspect*), secondly upon their willingness to give a truthful account of this introspection, and thirdly upon their ability to put introspective experiences into adequate language (so important is introspection to the psychology of religion and spirituality that much of Chapter 3 will be devoted to it).

These various reasons – together with comments on the misunderstandings that sometimes surround them – will be touched upon at various points during the chapters that follow. They help to explain why the psychology of religion and spirituality has been neglected by mainstream psychology, but do not in themselves justify this neglect.

# CHAPTER 2

# Definitions and Meanings

## Defining Religion

Beliefs and practices vary so much between the major traditions that any attempt at defining religion can never be wholly successful. This suggests we should be talking of a psychology of *religions* rather than a psychology of religion. Nevertheless, the major traditions do have important elements in common, not least of which is the universal rejection of the notion that men and women are no more than biological accidents, destined to live lives devoid of ultimate meaning and purpose, and to face annihilation when these brief lives are over. As this materialist–reductionist notion is espoused by many scientists (Wilber, 1998, puts it that "modern science gleefully denies virtually all of the basic tenets of religion in general" – a point to which we return shortly), this would seem to place religion and science at the opposite ends of the spectrum of thought. Materialist science holds that the material world is all that there is, religion argues by contrast that the material world is simply the manifestation of much deeper, nonmaterial realities.

The word "religion" comes from the Latin *religio*, which is usually translated as "obligation" or "bond," and the *Oxford English Dictionary* (OED) has it that religion represents the "human recognition of superhuman controlling power, and especially of a personal God or gods entitled to obedience and worship." Such a definition is appropriate for theistic religions such as Christianity, Judaism, Islam, and for certain sects within Hinduism, but it hardly fits others such as Jainism, Buddhism, Taoism, and Advaita Hinduism which all adopt a non-dual approach to spiritual life characterized by the belief that all creation is ultimately one, and that the individual mind is in its essence identical to the essence of all other minds. In the words of an old Buddhist saying, there are many cups, but they are all made from the same clay. It is also doubtful if the OED definition fits Shamanistic and animistic traditions, which are orientated less toward a single supreme being than toward the natural world and an impersonal, all-pervasive cosmic principle (Smith, 1980; Harner, 1990).

A more appropriate working definition of religion is that offered by Argyle and Beit-Hallahmi (1975), namely that religion is "a system of beliefs in divine or superhuman power, and practices of worship or other rituals directed toward such a power." However, it may still sound too orientated toward a divinity for non-theistic religions. Similar doubts attach to Wallace's claim (Wallace, 1966) that the defining characteristic of religion is that "souls, supernatural beings, and supernatural forces exist." The Buddhist *anatta* doctrine, which denies the existence of the enduring, individual "soul" taught by Western theists (a denial also present in Jainism) clearly lies outside Wallace's definition, as does the *Advaitist* teaching in Hinduism that *Atman* (the individual indwelling spiritual essence) and *Brahman* (the absolute essence beyond concepts and definitions) are in reality one. Christian mysticism shows certain similarities with the idea of a unified divine essence rather than of individual souls, a fact recognized both by some Eastern scholars such as Suzuki (Suzuki, 1971) and by some in the West such as Forman (Forman, 1991). Sufi mysticism also appears to move beyond dualism. In the absence of dualistic beliefs, the notion of a soul that is forever separate from its source becomes untenable. Thus while some religions see the individual self as retaining its individuality for eternity, others see it as becoming one with (or realizing itself as) the unity that underlies all the manifest world.

Individual religions not only differ considerably from each other in their understanding both of God or the gods and of the soul (see e.g. Smart 1987 for a survey) but also in a number of other important ways. Theistic religions teach the existence of a creator who brought the universe into being; non-theistic religions either consider that knowledge of a first cause is beyond human comprehension, or that the universe existed from "beginningless time". Even within theistic religions, some belief systems see the creator as eternally outside – though close to and involved in – his/her creation (i.e. as transcendent), while others see him/her as implicit in, and as in fact manifesting this creation as an aspect of his/her own being (e.g. as imminent). And across both theistic and non-theistic religions we find differing views on an afterlife. Some see the nonmaterial dimension (variously thought of as consciousness or soul) in each individual as surviving physical death, and as being subject to some form of reward in a heaven or heavens, or punishment in a hell or hells. Others see this nonmaterial dimension as returning to this world or other worlds to live countless further lifetimes until some form of "enlightenment" (usually described as an awareness of the real nature of existence) is achieved. Some see worship and ritual as important, others see them as of little relevance. Some depend for spiritual development upon other or transcendent spiritual power (the power of God or of the gods which can be called upon through prayer and supplication), while others depend more upon self-power or immanent spiritual power (the power of one's own potentially enlightened mind, which reveals itself through spiritual practices).

These differences are so extreme that we may again question whether all the traditions concerned should come under the one category of religion (a point also stressed by Wulff, 1997). However, they all have in common the belief in a nonmaterial (spiritual) dimension. Without such a belief, we cannot categorize someone as religious. Schoeps (1967) insists on this point, defining religion as "the relationship between man and the superhuman power he believes in and feels himself to be dependent on . . . the theme of religion is redemption from the powers that prevent man from communing with the divine." Can we then use belief in a nonmaterial dimension as our definition of religion? Possibly, though in that case the definition includes individuals (such as some of the adherents of New Age philosophies mentioned earlier) who believe in a spiritual dimension yet follow no recognized religious tradition, never set foot inside a church or temple, and never use techniques associated with religion such as meditation, contemplation, and prayer. Can such individuals be called religious? Argyle and Beit-Hallahmi would appear to think not. In the second half of their definition, quoted above, they consider that religion includes "practices of worship or other rituals directed toward . . . [a divine or superhuman] power." Without such practices, it seems we hardly have anything that we can call religious. Religion also typically entails the acceptance of certain standards of behavior ("doing God's will," as the Christian would put it). These standards will be discussed more fully in Chapter 5 and elsewhere, but they are set out clearly in such things as the Ten Commandments in Christianity, the Noble Eightfold Path in Buddhism, the Five Pillars of Islam, and the Law in Judaism (see Nielsen et al., 1988).

Not surprisingly with a subject as profound as religion, many specialists in religious studies even resist the idea that a definition is possible. For example, Nielsen et al. (1988) put it that "The notion that something called *religion* can be isolated, analyzed or defined is primarily a Western conceit" stemming from the tendency of Western culture to divide the secular from the sacred, and thus to regard nature as an autonomous domain with religion confined solely to spiritual concerns. This tendency, in their view, stems partly from Western theism, which separates God from his/her creation, but is "strongly reinforced by Western science because science in its very essence is an analytical discipline" and most scientists, whatever their personal beliefs, wish to separate religion "as clearly and sharply as possible from nature, which is by definition what physicists and other scientists seek to examine and explain." Accordingly, to the scientist "religion can be no more than a matter of responsible observation and scientific description."

One of the difficulties facing the scientist is that religions characteristically contain an esoteric as well as an exoteric side. The latter is concerned with outward observances, dogmas, and generally accepted beliefs, the former with inner practices and with teachings that are often only imparted to an elite (such as a priesthood) or only discovered through inner explorations by those who wish to penetrate more deeply into the mysteries hidden beneath the surface of things. Esoteric religion can differ markedly from exoteric. Many aspects of the former may be considered "dangerous" in the hands of the mass of the faithful, either because they include meditational and other practices that misused can lead to psychological disturbances, or because they are thought to be too profound for common understanding (e.g. the nature of the divine and the relationship of the individual with and to it; the symbolic meaning of many teachings; the difference between relative truths which apply only to the world of appearances and absolute truths which enshrine eternal verities about creation in all its aspects).

As the truth of esoteric teachings may only become graspable after long study (preferably with a qualified teacher) or after intensive self-exploration, few scientists are sufficiently committed to the study of religion actually to have access to them. In consequence, their knowledge of religion may be confined to the exoteric, a point to which we return in due course when discussing the inner and the outer approach to the psychology of religion.

Nielsen *et al.* make clear that any definition of religion must be extensive and complex if it is to be all-embracing by listing no fewer than 12 characteristics that typically distinguish the religious from the secular, each of which may contain both exoteric and esoteric elements. Briefly summarized, these characteristics are:

1. Belief in a supernatural or other reality beyond, yet basic to, ordinary existence and experience.
2. The presence of a distinction between sacred and profane, or between ultimate and apparent reality.
3. Some emphasis upon ritual or corporate worship or observance.
4. The possession of a moral code or ethical principles, or of a belief that spirits must be "appeased" in some way (by offerings, sacrifice etc.).
5. A striving to attain levels of consciousness beyond normal human experience.

6. The use of sacred texts, prayers, chants, mantras, hymns etc. in an attempt to influence divine will (whether this will is thought of as transcendent or immanent).

7. The presence of a worldview and of the place of the individual within this view.

8. A personal commitment by adherents to this worldview and to the demands it places upon the individual.

9. The presence of formal organization (in the form of institutions, social groupings etc.).

10. The promotion of inner states of harmony with the divine and with one's own true nature.

11. A belief in an afterlife of some kind (in other dimensions and/or through reincarnation in this world).

12. A desire (stronger in some instances than others) to proselytize themselves.

Even these 12 characteristics are not regarded by Nielsen *et al.* as being necessarily all-inclusive or definitive. Nevertheless they are of value, not least because they allow us to make the distinction between the outer or social and objective approach to the psychology of religions and the inner or personalized approach (distinct approaches which we explore in some detail below). It is apparent that although all 12 characteristics may be investigated using both outer and inner approaches, characteristics 3, 4, 6, 9, and 12 are primarily matters for the outer approach, while numbers 1, 2, 5, 7, and 11 are more susceptible to the inner approach (numbers 8 and 10 seem to fall somewhere in the middle).

Looking at these 12 characteristics together with the other definitions quoted above, we can identify three principal factors that seem necessary ingredients for something to be called a religion, and it is these three factors that for present purposes will be taken as a working definition:

- belief in a spiritual dimension;
- observance of a set of spiritual rituals or practices;
- adherence to a doctrine of ethical conduct arising from spiritual teachings.

The first of these factors would seem to be the most important historically. Belief in – and claimed experience of – a spiritual dimension has been the guiding principle behind the founders of all significant religions, and such belief and experience can have a profound effect upon human thought and behavior. Many people in fact accept this first factor while ignoring the other two, which makes it appropriate to distinguish such people from those who accept all three, and from those who accept only two and three. The first group of people we can call *spiritual* rather than *religious,* the second *spiritual/religious* and the third *religious.* This indicates a divide between spirituality and religion, and points to the need for psychologists of religion to define the former as well as the latter.

## Defining Spirituality

Defining spiritual and spirituality is even more difficult than defining religion. Compared with the word religion, psychologists have made few attempts to define spirituality, and there is no denying that it is something of a nebulous concept. In addition, spirituality has many meanings outside the context of religion. We talk of people with spirit or showing spirited behavior, almost as if spirit is a recognized factor of personality. We talk of being in high spirits or low spirits, and even refer to distilled alcoholic drinks as "spirits" (presumably because, at least until the morning after, they may have the effect of raising our spirits). We talk of writing or speaking in the spirit of truth. We talk of people or things being spirited away when they are moved quickly or unexpectedly from place to place. We even talk of sports men and women putting up a spirited performance during competition, and of people taking things in the right or in the wrong spirit.

Used in this way, "spirit" stands primarily for energy, whether physical or psychological. The ancients, who did not share our dualistic distinction between body and spirit, would have been happy with this. The word *spirit* comes from the Latin *spiritus* meaning breath, and is defined by the OED as the animating or vital principle of a person, which links to the idea that God breathed the spirit of life into Adam, the first man ("inspiration," which suggests a sudden infusion of creative ideas, comes from the same Latin word). The *Upanishads* or *Secret Teachings*, written between 600 and 200 BCE and among the most sacred Hindu texts (Goodall, 1996), make no real distinction between breath and spirit, describing the former in much the way that we might describe the latter, namely as "the life of all things" and as "the inner self," the unmanifest. Breath for the writers of these texts is the indrawing of the unmanifest into the manifest, which in the absence of a distinction between breath and spirit implies that the latter is the animating principle sustaining human existence, the reality behind appearances, a reality that is not restricted by the body and that leaves it at death to return whence it came, just as the outbreath appears to return to a nonmaterial dimension.

Thus both in the secular and the religious sense "spirit" originally referred to the force that unified the unseen and the seen dimensions. However, religions now treat the term more narrowly, generally taking it to mean only the eternal, nonphysical aspect of ourselves. Spirituality therefore represents a belief in this nonmaterial dimension, a dimension seen as permeating the physical world and creating other levels of being accessed in mystical experience and in the afterlife. It further implies that men and women are more than their physical bodies, and that human life carries meaning and should be lived in accordance with this meaning. This implication is supported by the findings of a national survey of adult Canadians (Bibby, 1995) that revealed 52 percent of people acknowledged having "spiritual needs" associated either with conventional religion or with a more general desire for wholeness or oneness with the human spirit or soul.

Confusion is caused in theistic religions such as Christianity by the fact that "spirit" is sometimes used synonymously with "soul" while at other times it is taken to mean the universal impersonal principle within us, with "soul" standing for the personal, changing form in which spirit expresses itself in humanity. Where they are taken to be separate, spirit is believed to be ultimately one with God, while soul is separate and bidden to contemplate, obey, and worship God. Spirit is therefore eternal and unchanging, while soul is seen as carrying the imprint of one's behavior during earthly life and subject to rewards, punishments, purgation, and – in some belief systems – to further development in the afterlife.

On the strength of this we can say that "spirituality" also represents the extent to which the individual recognizes his or her spiritual nature, and allows this nature to express itself through the soul and in behavior during material life. The more that spirituality expresses itself, the closer one is to God and to doing God's will. Thus a belief in spirituality, as with religion as a whole, in theory places certain responsibilities upon the individual such as the practice of compassion and understanding toward others, but for the spiritual person these responsibilities are defined by personal conviction rather than by formal religious doctrine. At a deeper level spirituality also means striving to experience the spiritual source of one's own existence. Walsh (1999) describes this experience as a process of inner change and development, and lists many metaphors for it such as *awakening, dehypnosis, enlightenment, freedom, metamorphosis*, and *wholeness*. The clear suggestion is that without this inner change, we are incomplete as human beings, living in only a small part of ourselves, with our deeper potential left untouched.

The term spirituality is also sometimes taken to indicate an openness to the spiritual teachings in all religions and schools of thought, rather than a dogmatic rejection of everything that does not come from one's own favored tradition. Thus although the spiritual person may be a member of a recognized religious group, he or she is less likely to be intolerant of other traditions than are those who are simply religious, and less likely to engage in vigorous or aggressive proselytizing. Of the 12 characteristics of religion identified by Nielsen *et al.* and listed above, spirituality would appear to be involved in the first (belief in supernatural reality), in the second (distinction between sacred and mundane reality), in the fifth (a striving to attain higher levels of consciousness), in the eleventh (belief in an afterlife), and possibly in the fourth (moral code) and the tenth (promotion of inner harmony). Taken together, the term spirituality therefore represents a way of life which combines each of these qualities.

## Defining Materialism

No extended discussion of the psychology of religion and spirituality can ignore the fact that religious and spiritual beliefs are seen by many as in direct conflict with what is commonly known as materialism. And as the term will appear at various points throughout the book, some attempt must be made to define it.

Few informed commentators maintain that what is sometimes called naive materialism or naive realism – the belief that the world and everything in it is composed of solid material building blocks – is any longer tenable. The discoveries of sub-atomic physics, which suggest that matter appears to be a form of energy rather than a form of material, and that this energy may even be susceptible to interaction with human consciousness (a point returned to in Chapter 11), have succeeded in dispelling such a notion. However, materialism, or material reductionism (or physicalism, though we'll stick to materialism for convenience) of a more sophisticated kind informs the thinking of the great majority of scientists. We can define this version of materialism as a theoretical stance that regards reality as in principle capable of a complete and satisfactory description in terms of the current concepts of physical science. As such, it rejects the view, associated traditionally with so-called idealistic philosophies, that what we call matter can be known only through our consciousness of it, and that consciousness is basic and physical phenomena no more than the manifestations of an underlying reality which is intrinsically mental.

The term *monism* is also sometimes used for this form of materialism in that it holds that there is only one form of reality, material reality, and that there is no warrant for any belief in *dualism*, which argues that there are two forms, the one material and the other mental. In the context of this monistic philosophy, materialism places no credence in religious and spiritual beliefs, which it identifies as belonging to the idealist, dualist camp. The sole source of knowledge is sense-experience; reality is directly or indirectly verifiable through observation, and what cannot be verified or falsified through observation is meaningless.

Nevertheless materialism accepts that thoroughgoing empiricism – i.e. basing everything upon experience – is untenable. We have for example no experience of the future, and on the basis of experience therefore have no warrant for making assumptions about it. Yet such assumptions are made all the time, and life as we know it would be impossible without them. Assumptions therefore can be based upon a higher-order reasoning, which is independent of our senses. As Margenau (1959) put it, "Every scientist must invoke assumptions and rules of procedure, which are not dictated by sensory experience. To deny . . . the necessary presence of metaphysical elements in any science is to be blind to the obvious."

However, the materialist points out that scientific assumptions, once made, become testable and verifiable. They can therefore ultimately be accepted or rejected on the basis of experience. Metaphysical assumptions which cannot be put to this kind of test – such as those associated with religious and spiritual belief – are therefore of no obvious credibility. It would probably not be disputed by many materialists that this is in turn an assumption that cannot be put to experimental test, but materialists consider it to be justified by the fact that there is a demonstrable difference between assumptions about the objective world – which can be submitted to repeatable trials – and the assumptions about the subjective world advanced by supporters of religion and spirituality – which cannot.

## Descriptions of God

Carl Jung (1955) speaks of his direct experience of a power of a "very personal nature and an irresistible influence. I call it 'God'." All the great religious traditions with the exception of Buddhism (which nevertheless in some of its sects has many gods) are based upon a belief in God. For the psychologist of religion, "God" is therefore another term that requires clarification. We need to know as much as we can about what it is in which people believe when they speak of God. Similarities and differences between individuals, between sects and between cultures in the form taken by this belief are psychologically revealing. Do similarities reveal a common pattern of religious thinking across traditions? Do differences stem from dogma and from early learning, from inner experience, or from deeply embedded cultural differences in the way in which not only the term "God" but also the world itself is interpreted?

One useful way of identifying the similarities and differences between traditions in their conceptualizations of the Divine is to outline the approach of one of these traditions and then compare it with the respective approaches of various of the others. Hinduism is a vast and extraordinarily complex collection of distinct schools of thought, but there are common themes that run through the most prominent of them, and these provide us with a good starting point.

Hinduism speaks of three levels at which the Divine can be conceptualized. At the highest or third level Hindu sages speak of the Divine as *Brahman,* the Absolute beyond either form or attributes, the Absolute about which nothing can accurately be said, as all attempts at definition only succeed in limiting the limitless, and which can only be known through direct experience. Thus *Brahman* is often spoken of only in negative terms – *netti, netti* – "not this, not that." These negative terms are not taken to imply that the Absolute is none of these things, as such an implication would in turn suggest limitations. Rather they mean that the Absolute is not *just* this, and that your attempts at a description of the Absolute are therefore inadequate. Nevertheless, *Brahman* is sometimes assigned the description *Sat Chit Ananda* – "Being, Consciousness, Bliss," which at least gives the rational mind something at which it can grasp.

The psychologist is likely to ask how we can know anything about the Absolute – i.e. about Brahman, Nirvana etc. – if the Absolute is something about which nothing can accurately be said. The reply we would be given by the sages of Eastern religions is that language is only one way of conceptualizing and communicating, and that we in the West place too much emphasis upon it within the context of religion, philosophy, and scientific explanation (de Riencourt, 1980). It is not that there is anything intrinsically amiss with language; it is simply that it is both limited in what it can express and always indirect, a representation of reality rather than reality itself. We would also be told that an over-reliance upon language can actually get in the way of entering fully into experience, whether it be the experience of the outer material world or of the inner world of the mind. This is a point which has particular bearing upon practices said to lead to spiritual development such as meditation, and more will be said about it in this context at various points in due course.

The Absolute therefore can only be "known" through mystical experience and in the deeper levels of meditative practice (be "known," Buddhist and Advaita traditions would say, by *becoming* it, or by realizing it within ourselves). Such an answer may seem suspiciously like avoidance behavior. If only beings advanced in mystical experience and meditation practice can "know" the Absolute, the rest of us have no way of checking whether what they tell us is true or not. They can avoid our questions rather as the adult avoids those of the child by insisting all will become clear when he or she is older. Wilber (1998) proposes, however, that there are two ways in which checking the validity of this answer is possible; firstly by exploring correlations between the physiological changes evidenced by those claiming to be experiencing deep meditative states, and secondly by looking for consensus between the accounts, however limited and inadequate, they give of these states. Neither of these ways would of itself demonstrate to us the reality of the Absolute, but together they would give us some warrant for attending to what is said by others about this reality. The Buddhist would go even further and tell us that if we are serious in our desire to know more about the Absolute, then this knowledge is open to us (and to everyone else) if we are prepared to undertake the meditative and associated practices, developed and refined over centuries by Buddhist and Hindu teachers and others, that lead to this knowledge.

Below the *Brahmanic* level Hinduism speaks of the Divine with attributes but without limited or individual form. This second level is sometimes referred to as *Ishvara*, the Universal Soul who supports, animates, and is imminent in all creation (Krishnananda, 1969), and sometimes as the Divine emanations (and therefore attributes) of creation, preservation, and change, which are identified by most Hindu sects with the gods *Brahma*, *Vishnu*, and *Shiva* respectively, regarded as essentially formless in that they assume form only for the sake of humankind, and can change this form at will (*Vishnu* for example has manifestations as both the gods *Rama* and *Krishna*, while *Shiva* is frequently shown as *Nataraja*, lord of the cosmic dance, dancing in his circle of flames). The first or lowest level describes the Divine as the active principal, having both form and attributes. Typically, this level is represented by the female consorts (or *shaktis*) of *Brahma*, *Vishnu*, and *Shiva*, respectively the goddesses *Saraswati*, *Lakshmi*, and *Durga* (the last of whom has two other forms, *Parvati* and *Kali*, and is also worshipped as queen of the universe). Also at this level are the many other personalized gods in the Hindu pantheon, some of them with only local followings, who represent various additional Divine attributes such as devotion, martial strength, compassion, wisdom, joy, courage etc. (Housden, 1996). It is through the activities of the consorts of *Brahma*, *Vishnu*, and *Shiva* that the manifest world is created, sustained, and changed (it seems that, much as on earth, the women do the actual housework so to speak, while the men are content with giving instructions – i.e. generating the creative ideas).

A feature of these Hindu representations at the second and first levels is that all the natural forces, beneficent and harmful, are included among the divine attributes, thus avoiding the dilemma faced by other theistic religions of explaining the existence of evil. *Shiva*, as the god of change, is also the agent of destruction. Change, destruction and death are seen as part of the natural cycle of things; and the problem for humanity lies not in these forces but in our reactions to them. Thus change and the challenges that come with change can be seen either as a reason for despair or as an aid to psycho-spiritual development. The circle of flames within which *Shiva*, in his form as *Nataraja*, dances symbolize these natural forces, while his left foot crushes the small figure of *Mujalaka*, the demon of ignorance, and his right foot is raised symbolizing the supraconscious state. The dance itself represents the five activities which life offers: creation, embodiment, preservation, destruction, and liberation.

*Shiva's* consort in her form as *Kali* is often represented in a form that symbolizes destruction and liberation even more graphically. As *Kali* she has garlands of skulls around her neck and waist, and holds a blood-stained sword aloft with one of her four arms and a severed head with another. This image is puzzling at first, since *Kali* is also revered as the divine mother, but in fact it represents time, the destroyer of all created things. *Kali's* black skin and hair represent the future, which is dark and unknown, and the skulls and the severed head represent the false values of the past which the enlightened person has annihilated. With the hand of one of her other four arms she is usually depicted showing the gesture of fearlessness (the empty palm extended toward the observer), and the remaining hand normally holds a disk representing completion. It is said that those who can see beyond the bloodstained image that *Kali* presents will receive the promise offered by her and attain liberation, while those who see nothing but destruction and horror are doomed to repeated lifetimes on this earth until they learn the lessons *Kali* is teaching. Sometimes *Kali* is actually shown dancing on her husband *Shiva*, symbolizing her intention to awake him from his state of transcendent divine consciousness, so that once more he can initiate the processes of change.

Hinduism teaches that as the individual advances on the spiritual path, his or her realization progresses upwards through the three levels of conceptualizing the Divine, though this progression is not taken to mean that the two lower levels are necessarily discarded. In varying circumstances the individual can still think of the Divine at any one of the three levels, though always recognizing that the two lower levels are emanations of the Absolute rather than the Absolute itself. Once at the level of *Brahman*, the trinity of *Brahma*, *Vishnu*, and *Siva*, and all the other Hindu deities are recognized not as separate realities, but as aspects of the formless *Brahman* within the world of form. Clearly the three levels are indicative of increasingly sophisticated levels of conceptualization, from concrete at the first level to formal at the second and abstract at the third.

An obvious similarity between all the great theistic traditions is in fact the way in which the Divine is conceptualized as personifications of supernatural anthropomorphic beings. However, the mystical literature from all traditions insists that Divinity itself is a spiritual force that lies beyond such personalizations.

There are other marked similarities between conceptualizations of God across the major traditions. For example, the Christian concept of God as imminent (within each of us) and as transcendent (above and beyond us), has affinities with the Hindu teachings of *Brahman* as the transcendent, and of *Atman* as the imminent, indwelling divine. Furthermore, like Ekhart and other Christian mystics who speak of ultimate unity, Hinduism sees *Brahman* and *Atman* as in essence indivisible – i.e. there is nothing that is not *Brahman*. The *Advaita* tradition within Hinduism places particular emphasis upon this indivisibility, rejecting the idea of individual existence as having anything other than relative reality (Isherwood, 1963).

There are some similarities between these Hindu concepts of *Brahman* and Aquinas' theory of God which has proved so influential within the Christian Roman Catholic Church. For Aquinas, it is possible to know that God *is*, but not to know *what* God is. Thus in his philosophy it is possible to say for example that God is loving, omniscient, omnipotent, perfect, and divine, but impossible to know what it means to God to be any or all of these things, or in what way it is appropriate for God to be them (Vardy, 1999). Within Christianity, Eckhart refers to this force as the Godhead, the Ground of Our Being, of which the personal God is an emanation ("God and Godhead are as different from each other as earth is from heaven" – see Evans' 1924 translation of Eckhart's work, also Forman, 1991). In Hinduism, as we have seen, the force is known as *Brahman*, from whom *Brahma* (the Creator God), *Vishnu* (the God of Preservation), and *Siva* (the God of Change) emanate. Both the Godhead and Brahman are thought of as the absolute potential from which the world of form arises (Smart, 1968). A somewhat comparable force is recognized in the Jewish mysticism of the Kabbalah, with *Ein Soph*, the Absolute Unknowable, existing as the potential from which the divine emanations of *Kether* (the Crown), *Hokmah* (Wisdom), and *Binah* (Understanding) arise (Matt, 1994). Islam, although strictly forbidding visual representations of God (*Allah*), nevertheless describes him as male and as supreme and indivisible (Denney, 1985), while Judaism, which also prohibits such representations, is unequivocal about the masculinity and fatherhood of God (*Yahweh*).

Buddhism and Jainism, neither of which recognizes the idea of a creator god or first cause, nevertheless both use concepts which bear comparisons with those associated with the Christian Godhead and the Hindu *Brahman*. Thus Buddhism speaks of *Shunyata* (the emptiness that is yet full of infinite potential and from which *Samsara*, the world of form arises and into which it returns). There is also a sense in which *Nirvana*, the indescribable Absolute into which Buddhism teaches that fully enlightened beings can disappear at physical death but yet which is also said to be imminent in each of us, is a further expression of this divine reality (Williams, 1989). The Jainist concept of the *Ishatpragbhara* is very similar to that of *Nirvana* (Dundas, 1992), while *Paramatman*, the divine principle within each of us, has conceptual affinities with the Hindu

*Atman* and with the mystical teaching of immanence in Christianity and the Buddhist teaching of our innate enlightened nature (see Suzuki, 1979, for further similarities between Christian and Buddhist mystical thought in particular).

To summarize, all the great traditions agree that God cannot be "known" through language and the rational mind, only through (or approached through) devotion and direct experience. Nevertheless, if we have to use words, religious traditions tell us that God is that infinite potential (the Absolute) from which all manifestation arises (though Buddhism and Jainism do not use the term "God" for this potential). Theistic religions go further and claim that this Absolute, since it is infinite potential, can also be thought of as personalized into a form or forms which can be more readily conceptualized by the devotee, and even certain branches of Buddhism speak of Celestial Buddhas who, for practical purposes, perform this personalized function.

For the theistic religions, this personalized God is thought of either as imminent and therefore as present in all things (all things are thus aspects of God), or as transcendent and as separate from but omnipotent over his creation. For the non-theistic religions, everything is simply a manifestation of the Absolute, the life force, from the visible world of form to the inner spiritual dimension. Although not touched upon in this chapter, the theistic religions believe that the personalized God can, at some level, be reached through prayer and supplication, and can directly intervene in events. Non-theistic religions also practice prayer and supplication, but teach that these are essentially devices for reaching one's own enlightened mind, which is identical with the Absolute and with the enlightened minds of all other beings.

Both theistic and non-theistic religions believe in some form of rewards and punishments in the afterlife, but whereas theistic religions teach that these arise from divine judgment, non-theistic religions see them as the inevitable (or karmic) consequences of one's deeds during earthly life. We reap what we sow. Both forms of religion therefore believe in a code of ethical conduct to which men and women should conform, whether ordained by God or arising naturally and inevitably from the way existence actually is.

## Belief and "Knowing"

A feature of the 12 characteristics summarized earlier from Nielsen *et al.* (1988) is that all of them involve the presence of belief, which suggests that anyone examining the differences *between* religions must ask five questions of each of them, namely:

- What do those who follow the religion actually believe?
- Why do they believe it?
- What effect do their beliefs have upon their thought and behavior and upon the culture in which they live?
- What influence do their beliefs have upon their psychological well-being?
- What religious experiences have they had in connection with their beliefs?

As religion deals with a spiritual dimension inaccessible to the normal senses, belief in the existence or the possibilities of this dimension obviously has an important role to play. Belief involves trust or confidence in something without having unequivocal evidence to offer in support. But there are many different levels of belief. Beliefs can be deeply held, and abandoned only at the expense of a whole philosophy of life, or relatively superficial and rejected with little consequence for thought or behavior. They can be virtually unshakable or tenuous and tentative. They can be based upon data which, although not meeting strict scientific criteria, would stand up in a court of law, or they may be based upon nothing but anecdote or hearsay. They may be illogical as in the case of superstitions, or they may make theoretical sense. They may be simple or complex. They may involve profound matters such as worldviews and the meaning of life, or they may have to do with trivialities such as the belief that red-haired people are short-tempered. They may be hard won or may come easily. They may be in accord with prior personal preferences and thus be readily accepted, or they may go against such preferences, and be accepted only reluctantly and after much soul-searching. They may be in agreement with the beliefs of the peer group or of the wider culture and lead to social acceptance, or they may go against group and cultural norms and lead to rejection or even persecution. They may be taken over ready-made and unquestioned from authority figures, or they may be arrived at only after careful deliberation and a due weighing of the issues.

Crucially, in the case of religion some beliefs appear to arise from sources within the self, whether these sources are thought of as creative insights, as intuitions (in-tuition), or as revelations from God or the gods. Writing in 1902, William James considered that belief can arise from such intuitions as they "come from a deeper level of your nature than the loquacious level which rationalism inhabits." In his view these intuitions can result in the individual *knowing* that the insights thus provided are "truer than any logic-chopping rationalistic talk, however clever, that may contradict [them]." James goes on to say that "This inferiority of the rationalistic level in founding belief is just as manifest when rationalism argues for religion as when it argues against it." He adds "The truth is that in the metaphysical and religious sphere, articulate reasons are cogent for us only when our inarticulate feelings of reality have already been impressed in favor of the same conclusion. Then, indeed, our intuitions and our reason work together . . ." (James, 1960).

Carl Jung took a similar view, as evidenced by his assertion, quoted in part earlier, that "I don't *believe* but I do *know* of a power of a very personal nature and an irresistible influence. I call it 'God'" (Jung, 1955). These quotations from William James and Carl Jung prompt the psychologist of religion to ask how is it that belief can lead to knowing in this way. Does belief provide the mind with an inner confidence that allows intuitions to arise that otherwise would remain silent, rather in the way that belief that he will succeed allows the sportsman to rise to new levels of physical performance? Or is it that a strongly held belief leads to the delusion that one is having confirmatory intuitions? Alternatively, does this belief perhaps lead one to misinterpret natural events as supernatural, so that for example hypnogogic and hypnpompic images are misconstrued as divine visions, coincidences are wrongly regarded as signs from the gods, and a run of good luck or success in a cherished venture is incorrectly ascribed to divine intervention?

Nevertheless, the psychologist cannot overlook the profound effects this "knowing," whether soundly based or not, has upon behavior (for example the choice by over 300 Cathars during the so-called Albigensian Crusades to be burnt alive rather than renounce their faith – see e.g. Guirdham, 1977; O'Shea, 2000). The founders of all the great religious traditions are said to have experienced "knowing" in the form of revelations which guided or confirmed them in their mission. Moses talked with Jehova, Christ heard the voice of God at his baptism, Mohammed was visited by the Angel Gabriel. Even the Buddha, whose enlightenment is reported as arising from his own Buddha nature rather than from heavenly grace, is described in the early Pali text, the *Ariyapariyesana Sutta*, as having overcome his reluctance to teach others the way to enlightenment – teachings which he considered lay beyond their understanding – only in response to the repeated appeals from Brahma, one of the supreme gods, who came down from heaven for this very purpose. Other, lesser figures, have also claimed knowledge conveyed through divine revelation, sometimes with consequences that have changed the whole course of human history as in the case of Joan of Arc's voices and St. Paul's experiences on the road to Damascus.

Revelations such as the above are said to involve spoken communications from God or the gods. By contrast mystical experience is wordless, but like the former, the latter also leads to "knowing". Much has been written about mysticism (e.g. Underhill, 1942; Stace, 1960; Zaehner, 1957; Staal, 1975; Danto, 1976; Cox, 1983; Grant, 1985), and the similarities across the various traditions between written accounts of mystical experience is of particular interest to psychologists, who are prepared to speculate as to what mysticism may tell us about certain relatively unexplored levels of the mind. Bucke (1923) famously coined the term "cosmic consciousness" to describe the sudden flood of illumination that appears to arise from mystical experience, illumination that leaves the recipient convinced that he or she has seen directly into the true nature of creation (the cosmos), a nature which is typically described as universal harmony, unity, and divine love.

## Belief and Faith

Faith is a word sometimes used interchangeably with belief in religious writings. However, Smith (1963) draws a distinction between the two terms, arguing that the former is only one aspect of the latter. The distinction is certainly appropriate, but in the context of religion it would be more accurate to define faith as a particularly unshakable form of belief, based upon ideas, teachings, and reported historical events which to the individual seem conclusive.

All religions stress the importance of faith, though there are major differences in the use they teach should be made of it. Whereas Western religions – in particular Christianity – tend to see faith as a virtue in itself ("blessed are they who have not seen, and yet have believed" John 20:29), Eastern religions – in particular Buddhism (except Pure Land Buddhism, which in keeping with the *Divyavadana Sutra* holds that faith is more vital even than morality – see e.g. Conze, 1951) – typically teach that faith is only an initial step in the religious life. Nothing should be taken on faith alone. Faith is simply the conviction that a spiritual path is worth following, and must be put to the test by following the practices for mind/spirit development taught on that path. If faith does not metamorphose into the "knowing" mentioned above as a result, one should reject it and look elsewhere for meaning in life.

CHAPTER 3 ——————————————————

# Introspection and Inner Experience

## Psychology and Introspection

As made clear in Chapter 1, introspection is so important to the psychology of religion and spirituality, and has been so neglected by much of mainstream psychology, that it needs to be looked at in some detail.

In ordinary life we trust without much question our own ability and the ability of other people to introspect. Social life would be impossible without this trust, and for the most part it seems well placed. Psychoanalytical psychologists and those engaged in other forms of psychotherapy and psychological counseling also place reliance upon introspection (although accepting that defense mechanisms and other cognitive obstructions may have to be overcome in some cases before sufficient openness is achieved). Why then is scientific psychology so suspicious of introspection, other than the introspection needed to fill in standardized assessment devices that invite stereotypical responses which can be checked for accuracy against Lie Scales and established norms?

In its early days scientific psychology had little hesitation in addressing inner experience through introspection. The German physiologist William Wundt (1832–1920), the initiator of the experimental approach and the first person of any note to call himself a psychologist, defined psychology as "the science of immediate experience" (Wundt, 1904). For Wundt, the subject matter of psychology was the structure of the mind, which he argued consisted of conscious elements such as ideas, memories, and sensations. Under Wundt's direction, *structuralism*, as it came to be called, took as its raw material the descriptions of this immediate experience provided by trained individuals. Referred to as introspectionism, Wundt's method involved exposing these individuals to various stimuli, and recording their descriptions of the reactions and experiences these stimuli evoked. Changes in these reactions and experiences consequent upon changes in the stimuli then enabled inferences to be drawn as to the nature of the mental processes involved. This was a careful and perhaps overcautious approach to the investigation of inner states, but one that appeared to hold promise for extensive future development, and that not only left the way open for the development of the psychology of religion, but also provided it with possible methodologies – for example the recording of subjects' experiences and reactions when presented respectively with religious, sectarian, and irreligious symbols, and with religious and profane texts, doctrines, concepts, works of art, and behaviors.

However, developments in the USA rapidly overtook those in Germany, switching attention from Wundt's structuralism to what came to be known as *functionalism*. William James (1842–1910), with a background in medicine and philosophy and another of the founding fathers of modern psychology, was quick to embrace functionalism, which emphasized not Wundt's structural components of consciousness but the actual functions of conscious activity in daily life, such as perceiving and learning (James, 1890). Such activities were not regarded as ends in themselves, but as mechanisms whose purpose was to produce useful behaviors. This still left open the way for the psychology of religion, in which James himself took a leading and abiding interest, writing what is still regarded as one of the classics on spiritual experience (James, 1902). But functionalism proved to be as short-lived as structuralism, primarily because psychology was under increasing pressure from colleagues in the natural sciences to justify its position as an objective discipline, concerned like physics, chemistry, and biology with recording and studying observable phenomena rather than subjective experience. Thus the impetus was there for the third major development *behaviorism* to emerge, absorbing functionalism in the process rather than supplanting it as functionalism had supplanted structuralism.

Behaviorism, associated in its early days particularly with Nobel prize-winning physiologist Ivan Pavlov (1849–1936) in the Soviet Union (Pavlov, 1927) and with Edward Thorndike (1874–1949) and John B. Watson (1878–1958) in the USA (Thorndike, 1911; Watson, 1919) quickly found enthusiastic acceptance, concentrating as it did upon the overt, public world of behavior, upon what people did rather than upon what they reported was going on in their heads. The structures of consciousness studied by Wundt were finally discarded as far too subjective to lend themselves to scientific investigation, and even thinking was only regarded as worthy of consideration if it was viewed as nothing more than a subvocal (and therefore still behavioral) conversation that one held with oneself.

Behaviorism was and remains an indispensable tool within psychology, but in a few short years it came to be regarded as virtually the only tool worth having (perhaps in part because it focussed attention upon other people as "subjects," and absolved psychologists from the task of self-exploration). In consequence, behaviorism ensured that the study of inner experiences – particularly the inner experiences associated with something so unpopular with scientists as religion – fell from general favor, prompting Sir Cyril Burt (1962) to comment that psychology first lost its soul and then its mind, as both represented aspects of psychological life not subject to direct observation. In the light of this loss, studies in the psychology of religion – where they existed at all – became restricted to the social and ritualistic behaviors arising from adherence to religious groups or traditions. Thus although Watson's groundbreaking *Behaviorism* (Watson, 1930) was written little more than two decades after William James' *The Varieties of Religious Experience* (James, 1902), so different is it in style and content and in its author's conception of what constitutes psychology that the two books might well be separated by centuries.

The mistake made by the early behaviorists was to regard introspection as a unitary process, which is either reliable or (in their judgment) unreliable. But introspection is not this kind of process. It varies dependent upon the nature of the mental events that are the object of introspection. We each carry vast amounts of data in our heads upon which we can introspect with consistent accuracy. If this were not the case, individual and community life would rapidly become impossible. On the basis of their research findings, Nisbett and Wilson (1977) conclude that individuals can accurately introspect in order to give accounts both of the objects of their current attention and of the resultant cognitive activity that prompts behavior. Introspection becomes less reliable when long-term memory is involved, or when verbal accounts are given of nonverbal experience, but even here major differences exist between individuals and as a consequence of the nature and strength of the experiences under report.

The way in which introspection is invited and studied is also rather different now from what it was in Wundt's day. Whereas Wundt (and before him Tichener) used introspection in an attempt to identify the hypothetical structures within consciousness, it is now primarily employed by humanistic and transpersonal psychologists to yield data on the individual's attitudes and beliefs, self-evaluations, self-regard, and worldviews. Even the fact that there may be fluctuations from day to day in the self-reports given by individuals is itself seen as providing important psychological data on the nature of cognition, affect, and inner experience.

Methodologies for studying introspection are also more extensive than they were in Wundt's time. Case studies, structured and semi-structured interviews, and standardized questionnaires all allow the researcher to look for common factors between self-reports, for correlations between these reports and actual behavior, for consistencies and inconsistencies between reports, for developmental patterns and age/sex variables, for the extent of commitment to expressed beliefs, for changes in beliefs and self-concepts consequent upon the use of practices such as meditation, prayer, contemplation, and confession, and for similarities between self-reports of the states of mind experienced during these practices.

A good example of one of the ways introspection can be used in research into the psychology of religion is provided by the work of the Latvian Karl Girgensohn and his colleagues at the University of Dorpat in Estonia. Influenced by the Wurzburg school of psychology, Girgensohn's principal method was to ask his subjects to read little-known religious poems chosen for their perceived usefulness in uncovering the formal characteristics that distinguish the religious life, and then to report on the feelings and images that they had experienced during the reading. In some experiments, they were also asked to free associate to the poems. Publishing his findings in 1921 (*Der Seelische Aufbau des Religiosen Erlebens*), Girgensohn reported that the two essential components of religion appeared to be intuitive thinking (associated less with logic than with feelings) and ego functions (self-surrender to the divine). After Girgensohn's death his work was carried on by a number of his students who continued to demonstrate the viability and vitality of his methods (see e.g. Wulff, 1997, for a summary).

The re-establishment of introspection as a legitimate method within psychology has also been assisted by the fact that, after some 50 years of pre-eminence, the strict behaviorism of Thorndike and of Watson has been largely superseded by a neo-behaviorism which views behavior within the context of the cognitive processes that initiate and are prompted by it. Mental events such as imagery and attention – and even consciousness itself – are thus once more regarded as legitimate areas for scientific inquiry. Verbal reports of this experience, whether the experience takes the form of thoughts or of feelings, emotions, visions, and flights of imagination, although they remain beyond the reach of objective verification (other than possible correlations with physiological measurements), are nevertheless now recognized as playing a vital role in the psychological life of the individual. Caution is still necessary in assessing the reliability of these self-reports, but by looking for consistencies and patterns between them the psychologist of religion can regard the data yielded by them with some confidence. Such data proves an indispensable aid to the inner approach to the psychology of religion.

## Psychodynamic Psychology and Inner Experience

It also proves an indispensable aid to psychodynamic therapeutic practices such as psychoanalysis, and it is therefore not surprising that Sigmund Freud, the founder of psychoanalysis, and his various followers have shown particular interest in the psychology of religion. Many of those in psychotherapy reveal major concerns with religion and sometimes with spiritual experience. Arising from medical and clinical studies rather than from scientific psychology, and with an interest in mental models and a reliance upon techniques such as free association and direct association, psychodynamics in fact places major emphasis upon inner experience and upon the individual's ability, given appropriate help, to introspect upon and articulate this experience. As a result the various psychodynamic movements have always existed uneasily alongside behaviorism, from the pioneering work of Freud (e.g. 1900) and Jung (e.g. 1921) onwards. Nevertheless, as will be made clear in chapter 8, both psychoanalysis and analytical psychology and their various offshoots have made extensive – even if highly controversial – contributions to the psychology of religion (e.g. Freud, 1927; Jung, 1931).

In spite of the variance between the two movements, psychodynamics shares with behaviorism the view that much of the motivation behind human behavior is associated with early experiences, and that this motivation therefore frequently lies beyond our conscious awareness. But here the similarities between the two movements end. While behaviorism largely explains this influence in terms of stimulus–response bonds, psychodynamics proposes elaborate mental models involving id, ego, and super-ego and the formation of a range of ego-defense mechanisms. Not surprisingly the former – and scientific psychology in general – has always been highly suspicious of the latter, regarding both its theories and its practices as beyond experimental verification, and therefore, in spite of their undoubted popularity with the general public, as of dubious value (e.g. Eysenck, 1985).

## Humanistic and Transpersonal Psychologies and Inner Experience

Throughout the years when the prime emphasis of scientific psychology was upon observable behavior and that of psychodynamics was upon unconscious motivation and mental models, there remained a small number of psychologists, identified with neither of these schools of thought, who consistently argued for a more holistic approach to inner experience (e.g. McDougall, 1928), and for a psychology of religion that embraced inner experience (e.g. Thouless, 1971).

During the final decades of the twentieth century the rapid development of cognitive psychology (e.g. Anderson, 1990), which acknowledges that conscious brain processes are indeed a legitimate area for scientific investigation, might have been thought similarly to prove sympathetic to inner experience. But cognitive psychologists typically choose to focus primarily upon the way in which information received through sensory input is codified and stored by brain processes in order to initiate behavior, and show little interest in the spontaneous experiences central to religion such as mystical insights, revelations, so-called enlightenment, and sudden conversion. Even when the existence of these experiences is acknowledged, they are still for the most part regarded as at best a product of imagination or hallucination, and at worst as evidence of a form of psychosis (see chapter 12).

However, alongside cognitive psychology two other forces, humanistic psychology and transpersonal psychology, also gained increasing attention in the last decades of the twentieth century, rendering the climate within sections of the psychological community once again more favorable toward a psychology of religion which attempts to look not only at outer religious behavior but also at inner experience and the influence of religious beliefs, allegiances, and concepts upon subjective as well as objective variables. The starting point for humanistic psychology is that all those states and experiences deemed by individuals important to their humanity are the concern of psychology. It argues that during the twentieth century psychology, by adopting the methodology of the physical sciences, became overconcerned with studying *quantity* at the expense of studying *quality*, and that many important mental and affective states and experiences have to do with the latter rather than with the former. Quality occupies a central role in the development and operation of variables such as self-concepts, belief systems, aesthetic appreciation, emotions and feelings, life goals, existential meaning, personality, self-evaluation, morals and ethics, self-fulfillment, creativity, spontaneity, free will, peak experiences, self-actualization (the achievement of one's true intellectual and emotional potential), and religious belief and a sense of the sacred. Thus humanistic psychology holds that a full understanding of observable behavior is only possible if the inner experiences associated with quality are taken fully into account.

The psychologists responsible for the development of humanistic psychology were not men and women of little consequence. Numbered among them were respected figures such as Gardner Murphy (1947), Erik Erikson (1968), Abraham Maslow (1970a and 1972), Gordon Allport (1961), Carl Rogers (1961), Roberto Assagioli (1975), Karen Horney (1950), Erich Fromm (1965), and Rollo May (1953). In the course of the development of humanistic psychology it also became apparent to

Maslow and others that many humanistic variables represent what he chose to call man's "higher and transcendent nature," and that this nature "is part of his essence" (Maslow, 1971). Thus, although there is some doubt as to who first used the term, Maslow was instrumental in establishing another important movement, namely transpersonal psychology, which focuses upon these higher qualities. In doing so he predicted that it would not only go beyond humanistic psychology but would also subsume it.

A brief definition of transpersonal psychology is that it studies and seeks to understand the nature, varieties, and causes of those human experiences in which the sense of identity appears to go beyond (*trans*) that of individuality and encompasses other people, the natural world, even the cosmos (a state that Allport, 1961, referred to as an "extended sense of self"), together with the behaviors, philosophies, disciplines, arts, cultures, lifestyles, and religions inspired by these experiences (see e.g. Walsh and Vaughan, 1993). It is also concerned with the practices, such as meditation, ritual, and prayer, that assist in the development of transpersonal states, with the body–mind–soul relationship and with the insights, intuitions, altered states of consciousness, and creative inspiration that illuminate these states. As such, the psychology of religion and of spirituality features prominently in its concerns.

From its inception, transpersonal psychology has attracted the support of a number of psychologists and psychiatrists distinguished in more mainstream areas of inquiry. Prominent examples are Wilber (1998), Walsh (1999), Tart (1989), Braud (Braud and Anderson, 1998), Stan and Christina Grof (1989), Vaughan (1985), Murphy (1992), Goleman (1996), and LaBerge (1985). Aspects of the subject have also received impetus from the work of scientists whose findings and arguments have called into question – sometimes tentatively and incidentally, sometimes emphatically – a purely materialistic view of the world and of mind. These scientists include medical doctors (Simonton, Matthews-Simonton, and Creighton, 1978; Benson, 1996; Dossey, 1999 – see also Foss and Rothenburg, 1987; Ornstein and Sobel, 1989; Moyer, 1993; Goleman and Guerin, 1993), anthropologists (Grossinger, 1987), neurophysiologists (Penfield, 1975; Eccles, 1984), philosophers (Searle, 1989), biologists (Watson, 1986; Sheldrake, 1988; Goodwin, 1994), biochemists (Behe, 1996), political scientists (Wesson, 1991), and physicists (Johnson, 1971; Bohm, 1980; Wolf, 1985; Gribbin, 1991; Goswami, 1993; Davies, 1993; Lazlo, 1993; Capra, 1988 and 1996; Ravindra, 2000).

The explosion of interest in Eastern psycho-spiritual systems and models of mind (see e.g. Hopkins, 1971; Parrinder, 1987; Schuhmacher and Woerner, 1989; Powers, 1995; Smart, 1989 and 1996; Goodall, 1996) has provided further impetus to the psychology of religion. Historically,

Eastern thought has generally refrained from drawing sharp distinctions between religion, psychology, and philosophy (Akhilananda, 1948). There are many possible reasons for this, ranging from the important political and educational roles played by religious bodies in Eastern societies, to the presence in the East of a radically different worldview from that held in the West. We shall be returning to these and related issues in due course, but there is no doubt that the exponential growth of interest in, and knowledge of, Eastern traditions and their relevance to Western psychology (e.g. Hayward, 1987; Pickering, 1997) has provided the psychology of religion with new perspectives and a range of additional and stimulating resources. Eastern (particularly Vedantic and Buddhist) models of mind are of a detailed complexity which compares very favorably with those developed in the West (see e.g. Govinda, 1969; Guenther, 1976), while the absence in Eastern thought of abrupt dichotomies between psychology, philosophy, and religion allows a more holistic approach to religious experience. The psychology of religions is now able to take into account philosophy's concern with meaning, epistemology, and ethics, and religion's beliefs and speculations about ultimate reality and the place and role of humankind within that reality – all subjects which are directly relevant to a comprehensive understanding of human thought and behavior.

This potential broadening of the psychology of religion is timely for a number of reasons, not least because it allows us to subject to informed critical exploration the upsurge of interest in what are sometimes loosely called "mind, body, and spirit," or "New Age" philosophies, beliefs, and practices which took place in the last decades of the twentieth century (e.g. Ferguson, 1982; Bloom, 1991) and which still continues. This interest appears to be associated in part with an active search by many people for what is argued to be a deeper and more meaningful philosophy of life than that provided by the materialist–reductionist thinking dominant in the twentieth century, in part with the desire to find ways of exploring, altering, and developing consciousness, and in part with what might loosely be called an innate longing for spiritual certainties. People affected by this upsurge of interest could be described as religious, though their approach to religion may not follow any of the orthodox paths, favoring instead an amalgam variously of Eastern ideas, Western paganism, mystery and occult traditions, and native American shamanism.

It may be protested that the various movements and cults associated with New Age thinking are often too confused and idiosyncratic to be of interest to the psychologist of religion. Such a protest ignores the fact that one of the tasks of science is to find out how things *are*, while another task is to find out how they have *become* as they are, and a third task is to discover the consequences of their *being* as they are. Thus the fact that religious beliefs and practices are now associated by large numbers of people less with institutions than with the discovery of a personal spiritual path, and less with a priesthood than with inner experience and a synthesis of ideas from many sources, is of prime relevance to the psychologist of religion. Important questions demand to be answered as to why these changes have taken place, and as to their consequences for thought and behavior.

Some of the answers that emerge to these questions are unlikely to be as rigorous or as generalizable as the answers sought in other areas of psychology. Nevertheless, if it is to advance on a broad front, psychology cannot avoid investigating areas of human thought and action where precision is not immediately possible. Only in this way can such areas be opened up for more penetrative study, as methodology becomes further refined and appropriate. Provided that conclusions remain guarded and false claims are not made for what may be essentially tentative findings, investigations of this exploratory and provisional kind have been part of legitimate science from the very beginning.

# CHAPTER 4

# Approaches to the Psychology of Religion and Spirituality

## Two Main Approaches

It is apparent from what has already been said that there are two main approaches to the psychology of religion. The first of these, which has been effectively formalized and extensively explored by Argyle and Beit-Hallahmi (1975) and by Beit-Hallahmi and Argyle (1997), is concerned with observable behaviors (predominantly social and ritualistic) arising from formal adherence to recognized religious groups or traditions. We can call this the *outer*, or *social* or *it and they* approach. It views religion as a collection of beliefs and practices of great importance in influencing individual, group, and cultural behaviors, and as linked to such readily measurable psychological variables as needs, social conformity, group pressures, and articulated fears and fantasies.

The second approach, which we can call the *inner* or *introspective way*, seeks to explore the nature of religious experience *per se*, together with the activities of mind within the individual that give rise to this experience and sustain the beliefs associated with it. It thus studies self-reports of the nature and importance of religious experience and belief, of so-called ineffable or mystical experiences, and of spontaneous events (such as supposed communications from divine sources or from the deceased) which affect the percipients' belief systems. It also explores the models of mind and the intricate systems for psycho-spiritual development contained in the teachings of Western and Eastern spiritual traditions – for example in the Hebrew *Kabbala* (Scholem, 1974) and the Buddhist *Visuddhimagga* (Nanamoli, 1991) – together with the descriptions provided by these traditions of inner states such as "enlightenment" and "salvation," and the methods of meditation, contemplation, prayer, and ritual said to lead to these states. The classic early example of this approach is William

James' *Varieties of Religious Experience*, mentioned earlier and based upon his Gifford Lectures (James, 1902), a book rarely out of print and still one of the most widely and consistently quoted of all books on the psychology of religion and spirituality.

## The Outer Approach

The outer approach is more concerned with what we earlier called the exoteric side of religion, while the inner is more concerned with the esoteric. Both approaches are essential for the psychology of religion, but – and the point is vital – neither can replace the other and neither should be mistaken for the other. An example to illustrate this point is the two ways in which a sample of people participating in an act of religious observance such as church attendance can be studied. The outer approach would concern itself primarily with observing the function that church-going has for the individuals and groups involved and for the community at large, while the inner approach would question each sample member on the meaning that churchgoing personally has for him or her. The outer approach would probably conclude that churchgoing assists group cohesion, gives a sense of belonging, leads generally to more ethical behavior on the part of group members, and to their greater readiness to support charities and other good causes, and is correlated with question-naire reports of less than average substance abuse, marriage breakdown, individual loneliness, and sexual promiscuity. The inner approach might conclude that churchgoers feel the act of collective worship heightens their sense of the sacred, provides them with confirmation of individual existential meaning, lifts their spirits through an awareness of divine love and protection, and honors God and brings them into what they regard as a closer, more deeply felt relationship with Him.

The outer approach either takes no position as to the reality of a spiritual dimension within religious observance, or actively seeks to ex-plain this supposed dimension in terms of known psychological variables such as wish-fulfillment. The inner approach accepts as a working hypo-thesis that such a dimension may exist, and at the least may point to levels of mind that remain to be explored by modern psychology. The outer approach is scientific in intention and in practice. It emphasizes objectivity, adequate and appropriate sampling, rigorous measurement and analysis of data, and peer evaluation. It employs surveys, question-naires, exploratory and illuminative investigation, makes use where pos-sible of experimental and control groups, specifies variables and if appropri-ate hypotheses, and controls contaminating variables. Properly conducted, it produces findings that are reliable and, if circumstances permit, replicable.

## The Inner Approach

The inner approach relies primarily upon self-reports, whether historical or contemporary. As discussed in chapter 3, the advent of new movements and methodologies renders the inner approach increasingly effective and valuable for the psychologist of religion, and the findings it generates appear to approximate to the real meaning that religion has for those who adhere to its beliefs and practices. It is thus appropriate that the psychology of religion utilizes both outer and inner approaches, keeping in mind the strengths and limitations of each. Consequently this is the procedure adopted in the present book. Its aim is to help readers recognize the part that religion plays in human thought and behavior at both the individual and the social level. This is not to argue that psychology should usurp theology's role and attempt to answer questions as to the existence and nature of God or of the gods. Instead, its role among other things is to focus upon why men and women need to ask these questions, at how they arrive at answers to them, at the status of these answers, and at the reasons why some people find them acceptable while others do not.

Its role is also to draw attention to the fact that when approaching fundamental issues of mind, body, and soul and their possible relationship to each other, the psychologist's own belief system must be taken into account. The idea that the psychologist, in religion or in any other area of investigation, is a completely objective observer, detached from whatever is being asked and observed, is unrealistic. The questions that we pose, the way in which we pose them, the answers we receive and the way in which we interpret these answers are all influenced by the perspective from which we view the world. This is analogous to the way that students, although following the same program in psychology, will variously be drawn to behaviorism, to cognitive psychology, to psychodynamics, to social psychology, and to humanistic/transpersonal psychology. Where we are at the start of any journey inevitably helps determine where we will be at the end of it.

## Religion as Myth

In approaching religion and spirituality, we are bound to ask whether the historical accounts upon which religious traditions place great reliance are factually correct or are simply evidence of the myth-making capacities of the human mind. If the former, we must accept among other things the reality of the miracles and other supernatural happenings associated with these traditions and which contradict the known laws of science. If the latter, then we must take the accounts concerned either as symbolic or as pure fiction. However, acceptance of the latter explanation does not necessarily allow us to dismiss these accounts as of no importance. In Jung's view, psychology is not concerned with the truth or falsity of religious ideas, but with the fact that such ideas exist (Jung, 1969).

Nevertheless it is significant that many theologians and students of comparative religion seem bent upon stripping from it all those elements that seem at odds with modern scientific understanding. This so-called "de-mythologizing" of religion tends for example to reduce Christianity largely to a set of socio-ethical principles (Cupitt, 1980 and 1987), and Buddhism to a collection of psychotherapeutic techniques (Epstein, 1995). In the process, gone is the idea of a spiritual dimension in any readily recognizable form, and in its place there remains only an approach to human behavior – i.e. only the lowest of the three factors listed in chapter 2 – as constituting the necessary ingredients for something to be called a religion.

Regardless of whether the miracles and other wonders associated with the lives of the founders and saints of the great religions are historically true or not, belief in them implies a belief in spirituality, since like them spirituality lies outside what we understand as science. Furthermore, they provide the basis for some of the influential moral and ethical teachings associated with religion. For instance the reported miracles of Christ emphasize in a graphic and compelling way such qualities as his compassion for others, his sensitivity toward human grief and suffering, his readiness to heal men and women shunned by their fellows, and his spiritual power over natural laws. Without such emphasis, it is questionable whether these qualities would have attained such an enduring place in Christian doctrine, and have influenced so profoundly the behavior of those who adhere to this doctrine.

Supernatural events in fact play such an important part in religious belief that their implications for the psychology of religion must be left to a more appropriate place later in the book. And even when such events are known to be mythical (as in the case for example of Greek legends of gods and heroes), their enduring appeal still has a great deal to tell us about human psychology (Campbell, 1973; Campbell and Moyers, 1988). Psychodynamic psychologists in particular have urged that these myths help us to understand unconscious processes (e.g. Jung, 1968), and to recognize the influence that these processes have upon motivation and behavior, all issues that will be returned to in chapter 9. But true or not, supernatural events seem so integral to the spiritual essence of religion that it is doubtful if the latter can survive *qua religion* without them. Buddhism is a good example of how spirituality and the supernatural appear inseparable. Starting as a revolt against the ritual, the concepts of divine grace and of a pantheon of spiritual beings central to Hinduism, it proceeded to restore each of these over the centuries (particularly in the Mahayana Buddhism of Tibet, India, China, and Japan). And its founder, who steadfastly refused to be drawn into speculation on the existence or otherwise of a personalized god, has himself been transformed by his followers into something which, in practice if not in theory, resembles just such a god himself.

Irrespective of whether divine truths are in fact communicated through revelation and mystical experience or not, humankind seems to have a consuming need for belief in a spiritual dimension and in the supernatural events which help lend it credence.

## Religious Symbolism

Much as it makes use of what modern science and much of modern theology regard as myth, religions make extensive use of symbols. Carl Jung (1978) defines a symbol as:

> a term, a name, or even a picture that may be familiar in daily life, yet that possesses specific connotations in addition to its conventional and obvious meaning. It implies something vague, unknown, or hidden from us (p. 3).

Jung also distinguishes between *symbols* and *signs*. In contrast to the profound connotations of the former, the latter (e.g. sets of initials, business logos, and trademarks) do no more than denote familiar objects, often in an arbitrary way. In contrast to signs, he explains symbols as arising readymade from the unconscious, and often as possessing universal, cross-cultural appeal (e.g. as in the case of geometrical shapes such as the cross, the triangle, the crescent, the star, the square, the pyramid, and the circle). As they originate from the unconscious, symbols act as keys back into the unconscious, unlocking in the process some of its mysteries (Jung, 1956). This Jungian explanation accords with the religious belief that meditation upon, or contemplation of, religious symbols (including allegedly divinely inspired works of arts such as icons and rupas) help take the worshipper into that altered state in which revelations, spiritual insights, visions, and mystical experiences inaccessible to conscious awareness arise.

In meditation, these revelations and experiences arise spontaneously into the mind. Thus for example in Christianity the cross may, in addition to Christ's sacrifice, bring an awareness in the devotee of the descent of the divine (the perpendicular line) into the world of matter (the horizontal line), and then deep down into the human heart. Subsequently the perpendicular line may arouse a sense of the ascent of the devotee to the divine. The Celtic cross, with the cross halloed by a circle, may evoke a profound recognition of the completeness of the divine (the circle) illuminating the four-fold dimensions of the physical world (the cross). On a different level it may prompt a realization of the mystic union of male and female, the union of Christ with his church, and the union of spirit and matter. In this way these and other traditional religious symbols lead to felt levels of awareness in the devotee which carry more psychological power than mere verbal teachings (see e.g. Jung, 1964; Cooper, 1978; Barber, 1979; Fontana, 1993).

All the Hindu gods are typically shown carrying symbolic objects, which serve as powerful psychological devices for reminding devotees both of the functions of the divinity and the devotees' own obligations toward him or her. For example *Brahma* is often shown with four faces which represent the four aspects of human personality, and as seated on a lotus, which is the symbol for the blossoming of higher consciousness from the mud of ignorance. *Vishnu's* four hands carry a mace (to destroy evil and ignorance), a conch shell (to call the listener to the spiritual life), a disk (to symbolize the inevitable karmic consequences of each human action, and the cycle of death, rebirth, and death that arises from these consequences), and a lotus (to symbolize higher consciousness). *Shiva* typically has a serpent around his neck to symbolize the destructive ego which he has conquered, a trident in his hand to represent the three ways of thinking (knowledge, action, and ignorance), each of which must be transcended in order to go beyond the deluded conscious mind and reach final unity, and a crescent moon in his hair to symbolize auspiciousness – the good fortune that comes to the enlightened mind which is able to see all things as opportunities for spiritual development.

As a consequence of their extensive use of symbols – in particular of images of deities – Eastern religions have sometimes been accused of fetishism and idolatry by those who misunderstand the psychological processes concerned, and who suppose the worshipper believes the symbol actually to be the deity (similar accusations are sometimes leveled against Roman Catholicism). Such a belief is expressly warned against in the Hindu/Buddhist traditions, for example in the well-known admonishment that one must never mistake the finger pointing at the moon for the moon itself. However, the risk that the worshipper may nevertheless make this mistake is one of the reasons why Jainism, Judaism, and Islam all forbid images of the Divine (and one of the reasons for the beautiful abstract, geometrical art that is such a feature of Islam).

Music also performs some of the functions of religious symbolism in that it is used as a way of altering the consciousness of worshippers in the direction of the divine. Tibetan Buddhism even insists that its temple music is not intended for sensual enjoyment, but as a way of cutting through the habitual illusions of the senses. Chanting and plane song in Buddhist, Christian, and other traditions is particularly designed to induce altered states, and sacred choral and orchestral music in the West is also intended to have this effect, sending the mind soaring to contemplative heights where the worshipper becomes absorbed in love for the divine. Furthermore, many of the composers responsible for this sacred music – and for other forms of classical composition – report their work to have been inspired by some spiritual force outside themselves. Beethoven put it that "music is a higher revelation than all wisdom and philosophy" (Von Arnim, 1810).

Some religions make extensive use of animal symbolism (see variously Cooper, 1978; Barber, 1979; Fontana, 1993). Christianity for example speaks of Christ not only as the lamb of God, but as the Good Shepherd. Three of the four evangelists are traditionally represented by the three beasts in Ezekial's vision (Ezekial 1:10), thought by some to prophesy the writing of the gospels themselves. Thus St. Mark is symbolized by the lion as his gospel emphasizes Christ's courage, St. Luke by the bull as his gospel lays stress on Christ's strength, and St. John by the eagle as his gospel is concerned primarily with Christ's spirituality. (St. Matthew is symbolized by the fourth figure in Ezekiel's vision, man himself, as his gospel emphasizes Christ's humanity and compassion.) Elsewhere in Christian symbolism the Holy Spirit is represented by the dove, and those who accept and those who reject spiritual teachings by sheep and by goats respectively. Satan is symbolized as the lord of the flies, and in medieval texts as horned and cloven-footed (symbolism probably borrowed from that of the Greek nature god Pan). In Hinduism, *Hanuman*, the god of courage, intuition, and spiritual devotion is depicted as a monkey, and *Ganesha*, the god of wisdom, spiritual strength, and leadership who overcomes all obstacles, as an elephant. *Vishnu* is sometimes symbolized by the fish (symbol of the fecundity through which life is sustained and preserved), a symbol that also appears in Christianity.

For the Hindus, the cow symbolizes fertility and motherhood, and is sacred throughout India, and many of the gods and goddesses are frequently depicted with an accompanying animal. The goddess *Saraswati* rides upon a swan or a peacock (symbols of purity and beauty), the goddess *Durga* (or *Kali* as she becomes in her more fearsome aspect) rides upon a lion, the god *Shiva* upon a bull (symbol of power), *Vishnu* sits upon the great many-headed serpent *Ananta* (symbol of the numerous aspects of the human mind) and is halloed by hooded cobras (symbol of protection), and *Krishna* (one of the incarnations of *Vishnu*) is shown bringing the cows (the faithful) back to their rightful home. In Jainism, *Parshvanatha*, one of the most prominent of the 24 *jinas* or saints is also shown protected by a snake, the seven-headed serpent king *Dharanendr,* while the first of the *jinas, Rishabhanatha*, is often shown with a bull, and *Mahavira*, the last in the line, with a lion.

The religion of Ancient Egypt made particular use of animal symbolism (Budge, 1972). *Thoth*, the God of Wisdom had the head of the seemingly grave and stately ibis; *Horus*, the son of *Osiris* and *Isis*, had the head of the high-flying and far-seeing falcon; *Anubis*, who was thought to conduct souls from this world to the place of judgment, was depicted as the jackal known to frequent burial grounds; *Bastet*, protectoress of the gods, was shown initially as a fierce lion and later as a cat; *Seth*, the sinister god of chaos, was always given the head of a mythical creature with a long beak and high pointed ears, presumably because no known animal was thought adequate to symbolize such a power of evil. The human immortal soul (the *Ba*) was symbolized by a bird, with its ability both to rest upon the earth and to soar into the heavens.

The psychological function of this animal symbolism is relatively clear. The gods and saints were not thought to be animals or dependent upon protection by animals (although for many of the cultures that spawned these early religions far less distinction was made between humanity and the animal kingdom than is now the case). Instead, the animals were and are seen as representing some of the qualities embodied by the gods (or, in the case of the saints, the qualities expressed through their writings or their actual deeds) – serving even as memory aids to help worshippers remember these qualities. Animal symbolism allows abstract concepts such as wisdom, courage, strength, and devotion to be concretized into forms well known to the faithful. We are thus presented not with a form of primitive animism, but with a relatively sophisticated understanding of the power of symbols to serve as teaching devices and mnemonics. In addition, animal symbols serve – in Hinduism in particular – as devices for inducing desirable states of consciousness in devotees in that intensive meditation upon these symbols is considered to arouse the potential for the quality concerned within the worshipper him or herself.

## Religion and Sexual Identity: God as Male

The great majority of the scriptures revered by the great traditions is written by men. More men take up the monastic life than women, and the priesthood in most religions tends to be male. Similarly, deities are more often thought of as male than female. Psychologically this is of particular interest, especially in the West where more worshippers are female than male. This point will be returned to later in this chapter, and a discussion of the way cultures may use religion to suppress femininity will be dealt with in chapter 12. But for present purposes the concern is with the sexual identity assigned to God and the gods and with possible reasons for the imbalance.

Christianity, Judaism, and Islam typically speak of God as male. This may reflect the dominance of a patriarchal ethos in the cultures concerned rather than inner experiences that point unequivocally toward masculinity. In the cultures that grew up around the Mediterranean basin from 3,000 BCE onwards, female goddesses figured as prominently as male, and often took more subtle roles. For example in Egypt the goddesses *Maat* (goddess of justice, truth, and order), *Hathor* (goddess of love, music, and dance), *Isis* (queen of the gods and of magic), and her sister *Nephthys* (guardian of the dead) all attracted particular attention (Spence, 1986). Female goddesses were also well represented in the Greek (Guerber, 1994) and Norse and Celtic traditions (MacCulloch, 1991), in both cases playing a highly influential part in events, sometimes as the instigators of discord. The cultures concerned also laid great stress on the role of the priestess. At the Oracle of Apollo at Delphi in Greece, it was the priestess (the python) who – probably in trance – received the answers to questions put to Apollo, while the priests simply relayed these to inquirers, interpreting where necessary. In both actuality and mythology, it was the feminine principle that represented mystery and access to the deeper secrets of life, while the masculine stood for direct action in the outer world.

## Religion and Sexual Identity: God as Female

In the Hindu pantheon, the female is also possessed of great spiritual power, though the roles of male and female gods are reversed from those thought to obtain in other pantheons in that the male is seen as the initiatory spiritual force and the female as the power that gives material expression to this force. Thus, as already made clear, each Hindu god is accompanied by a female consort goddess (his *shakti*), who complements him by giving birth (form and substance) to his creative spiritual energy, and who is also worshipped in her own right as representing divine properties. So indispensable to each other are god and goddess that they are sometimes represented as aspects of a single force rather than as separate divine beings (hence the erotic embraces in which they are frequently depicted in Indian sacred art and temple architecture).

## Male and Female Principles

These fundamental differences in the way in which various religions conceptualize the sexual identity of the spiritual dimensions in which they believe give some insight into the way in which the cultures concerned view the sexes. God or the gods may be created in the image of worshippers, and the self-image of worshippers may be partly created by the concepts they have of God. Western mystical traditions (Godwin, 1981) long held that each individual is composed of both male and female, and that spiritual development consists of unifying these two principles. Jung (1968) laid much emphasis upon this unification, focussing particularly upon alchemy which he saw not as a naive attempt to turn base metal into gold but as an inner teaching designed to bring this unification about. The alchemists' description of the creation of the hermaphrodite from the union of sulfur (the red king) and mercury (the white queen) Jung saw as symbolizing the whole inner psychological process, and also identified the symbolism of the male–female unit in the two-headed eagle of the Eastern Orthodox Church and in mythical creatures such as the unicorn. We find further symbolism of this kind in the story of Adam and Eve in which Eve literally was created from Adam's body, a division into sexual opposites, which could be seen as representing the divided nature of the human individual.

Unlike ancient Greek, Egyptian, and Eastern traditions, the theistic religions of the West, Judaism, Christianity, and Islam have no female representations of the God, but in Christianity at least this is partly rectified by assigning femininity to the Holy Spirit, and by the elevation in the Roman Catholic and Eastern Orthodox churches of the Virgin Mary (as the Mother of God), in practice if not in theory, to the role of divinity. It could be argued that this indicates a human awareness that religion is incomplete without a female aspect to the Divine or, if one takes the Freudian view that religion is a way of facing the fact of human powerlessness when confronted by the realities of life and death, that this is a desire for the nurturing security of an ever-loving mother.

In all probability, the respective roles of male and female in the spiritual dimension developed partly from simple observation. By giving birth, the female gives form and substance to male creative energies, as emphasized in the Hindu pantheon. However, the male procreative organs are apparent and visible, those of the female are secret and hidden, and taken together with the differences in behavioral characteristics between male and female this contributes to the fact that in many traditions the male is seen as the extrovert, active, conscious, rational element, and the female as the introvert, passive, unconscious, mysterious element. The female role is also seen as nurturing and supportive and the male as belligerent and violent, thus identifying the female role with compassion and mercy and the male with leadership and conquest. Jung (1968) considered that these differences are in fact archetypal, that is innate psychological structures deeply embedded in the human psyche which help determine the way in which we experience the world and ourselves.

## Conclusion

Some understanding of the way the terms religion, belief, and God are used is crucial for the psychologist of religion. In spite of the differences in approach summarized in this chapter, adherents of the great religious traditions would probably broadly agree that religion involves a belief in a creative, spiritual dimension, and a conviction that the individual can have a personal relationship with this dimension, whether the dimension is seen as transcendent to the self or as imminent within the self. The existence of this dimension is associated with a belief in the survival of personality in some form after physical death, and seen as imposing certain behavioral obligations upon the individual.

The psychological implications of these behavioral obligations are considerable. Religion is a powerful moral imperative. If one believes that only certain kinds of behavior are acceptable to a divine being, that this being knows one's every action however private and one's every thought, and that rewards and punishment (whether in the form of atonement or actual suffering) await one in the next life, then one has a strong motivating force for principled action.

The psychological implications of the comfort and condolence of religion in times of suffering and bereavement should also not be underestimated. Equally important is the sense of meaning and purpose that religion offers to believers. Again the nonbeliever may reject all this and urge that everyone faces the "facts" of existence, but we can both look at the foundation for these "facts" on the one hand, and the effect of this philosophy of nonbelief on the other.

If there are phenomena that appear inaccessible to the scientific method as at present constituted, this does not mean either that the phenomena do not exist or that the scientific method is wrong. They simply demonstrate the limits of this method, and call for its further development. Science cannot ignore things, whether in the natural world or in human activity because they present particular problems of exploration. Genuine science is driven by a desire to know, and the humility to recognize the limits of our present knowledge and its provisional nature. Thus although psychology may wish to recognize that certain categories among its data are more securely based than others, the acquisition of new data remains always a challenge and an excitement to the genuine researcher. Psychology certainly is and I imagine always will be about observable behavior, but it is also about the processes that prompt this behavior, about the accounts that people give of their own mentation, and indeed about all aspects of human experience. Only by acknowledging this can we put ourselves in a position so to refine and develop our methodology that ultimately we may feel assured that more and more of this experience can be explored and discussed with confidence.

# CHAPTER 5 —————————————————————

# Religious Beliefs and Practices

## The Contents and Origins of Belief

We cannot understand the psychology of religion and spirituality unless we have an idea of what it is in which religious people believe, of the origins of this belief, and of the effect it has upon the way in which they live their lives. As with the concepts of God and the gods touched on in chapter 2, we also need some idea of the similarities and the differences between these traditions in their approach to belief and practice.

Due to problems of semantics (each of the great traditions is identified particularly with certain races and cultures), some at least of these similarities and differences may be more apparent than real. Language influences not only expression and communication, but also thought and conceptualization. Later, when we look at mysticism (chapter 10), we will find it is said that only at the mystical level, where language is transcended, true similarity of religious experience becomes apparent. However, even here language is still the medium of information and explanation, and its role as a means both toward understanding and confusion must never be overlooked.

## Belief in Rewards and Punishments

All the major religious traditions claim that devotion to the spiritual path changes the lives of adherents in a number of positive ways. These changes are claimed to have profound consequences for future lives, whether these lives are said to be lived in a next world or in further incarnations here on Earth. Failure to recognize the spiritual dimension to existence or to live life in accordance with the moral teachings of the religious path is said to lead to unpleasant consequences in the afterlife, whether spent in hell realms or in another incarnation in the present world (which some Eastern traditions claim might as punishment be as an animal). Not surprisingly, such teachings concentrate the minds of believers as little else could, and act as powerful incentives to remain on the spiritual path.

Emotive terms such as "salvation," "enlightenment," "self-realization," "liberation," and being "born again" are variously used by the traditions to designate men and women who not only remain on this path but also pass significant spiritual milestones. Such progress is said to lead not only to the promised rewards in the afterlife but also to benefits in the present life – for example the development of a compassionate and joyful heart, and the ability to face the challenges, hardships, and suffering of this world with equanimity. The Hindu *Maharamayana* describes this realized state as "full of unfailing rapture [in which the individual] reigns supreme over the empire of his mind. He turns his attention to nothing either sweet or bitter . . . Whether his body is . . . broken on the wheel . . . or exiled in a desert land, the believer in *Brahman* remains inflexible" (Shastri, 1971). Even though breaking on the wheel and exile to desert lands are infrequent experiences these days, the prospect of this unfailing rapture serves as a further attraction for believers.

In the case of theistic religions such as Christianity, Islam, and some Hindu traditions, the benefits said to accrue from the spiritual life are thought to arise not from personal merit but from the divine grace consequent upon surrender to the divine will. Islam, for example, stresses that God is all-merciful and all-loving, and that He welcomes into the ranks of the blessed all who turn to Him. Christianity teaches that divine grace arises from the vicarious atonement given to us through Christ's sacrifice on the cross, a teaching based in part upon St. Paul's Epistle to the Romans 5:8–9 (". . . while we were yet sinners, Christ died for us. Much more then, being now justified by his blood, we shall be saved from wrath through him"). What is required from us is that we place our faith in Christ as the Son of God, and follow his teachings on how we should live our lives.

By contrast, non-theistic religions such as Buddhism and Jainism teach that enlightenment comes about primarily through our own efforts to remove the veil of ignorance that dominates our habitual ways of seeing the world and ourselves. By removing it we are said to allow ourselves to recognize the all-embracing unity which is ultimate reality, and to acknowledge the illusion of our separation from this reality. However, the concept of "salvation" through the belief in a higher being is not absent from Buddhism. The Pure Land School, popular particularly in Japan, holds that by placing faith in Buddha *Amida*, who personifies both the Buddha of Boundless Light (*Amitabha*) and the Buddha of Boundless Life (*Amitayus*), the unenlightened can be spared rebirth in this world and can instead be reborn in *Amida's* Western Paradise (*Sukhavati*), where with his help final enlightenment is easier to attain than it is in the material world. Buddhists who are unhappy with the idea of reliance upon "other power" rather than upon "self-power" insist that *Amida* is simply another expression of the boundless potential within each of us, but in Freudian explanations of the psychology of religion, to which we turn in detail in due course, reliance upon *Amida* is a further indication of the universal human need for protection by a father substitute from the terrifying helplessness engendered by the uncertainties and perils of existence.

## The Nature of a Future Life

There are significant differences between the descriptions given by the great traditions of the heavens and hells said to await us in the afterlife. In Islam, heaven takes the form of a paradisiacal state in which individuals are rewarded with many of the sensual delights that they have denied themselves in this life, while hell contains a range of highly unpleasant punishments reminiscent of the medieval torture chamber. Christianity has traditionally portrayed heaven and hell in similar physical terms (although the main pleasure in the Christian heaven is traditionally portrayed not as sensual gratification but as the singing of God's praises, ideally as members of a celestial choir), and over the centuries preachers and many artists have taken particular pleasure – an aspect of their behavior not without interest for the modern psychologist – in illustrating in graphic detail the nature of the tortures which the wicked can expect. Worse still, these tortures have traditionally been described as eternal, a description whose only warrant in the Gospels is the reference in St. Matthew to the "everlasting fire" (Matthew 18:8) that awaits those who do not cut off their offending hand or foot or pluck out their offending eye (a warning that sounds more symbolic than realistic) and to the "everlasting punishment" in store for those who refuse to give to the poor (Matthew 25:46).

Even today some fundamentalist Christian sects consider that the unjust can expect no pardon and no remission of their eternal damnation. Eastern religions have always taken a more merciful approach, with Buddhism perhaps presenting us with the most coherent example. Although Buddhism even outdoes the West in depicting the awful things that await wrongdoers – in some Buddhist literature 18 hells of graduated nastiness are described, some noted for their extreme heat and others for their extreme cold – in none of these is the sentence eternal, since nothing below the level of Nirvana, entered only after final enlightenment, is permanent (or rather, beyond concepts such as permanence and impermanence).

When the weight of one's bad *karma* (a term for the consequences of one's actions in supposed past lives) has been duly lifted by anything up to and including aeons of suffering, there is release and the opportunity for rebirth in this or other worlds where one can try to make a better showing of things. In addition, one of the many Buddhas ("Buddha" simply being a term used to designate a fully enlightened being), Buddha *Tsitigarbharaja*, is said to visit the various hells in order to help those who repent of their transgressions qualify once more for rebirth.

The downside of the Buddhist teaching of impermanence is that one's sojourn in the various heavenly realms is also said to be temporary. Merit gained in this life ensures access to the heavens, but only for the length of time earned by that merit. Thus, as with the consequences of transgression, the consequences of a righteous life are destined to become exhausted in due course, at which point one has to return for another birth in this world, where the search for full enlightenment must recommence. The inhabitants of the heavenly realms – referred to as the gods – are therefore not to be particularly envied. As everything is harmonious in heaven, and consequently there is no challenge and no choice between good and evil, there is no opportunity for further spiritual growth. Only on this earth, where we are constantly confronted by decisions between proper and improper conduct, is full enlightenment possible. A single human life, with all its suffering and its many difficulties, is therefore considered more precious than aeons of time spent in the luxuries and the beauties of the heavens. Heaven and hell are both aspects of the realm of form, and thus for the Buddhist are something of a waste of time. Only the formlessness of Nirvana is beyond the so-called wheel of becoming, the wearisome cycle of birth, death, and rebirth to which the unenlightened are subject.

For Buddhists therefore, the goal of the religious life is not to reach heaven, but to attain Nirvana (or *PariNirvana*, i.e. final Nirvana, since it is said that the enlightened person can experience a form of Nirvana within his or her own being while still on Earth). The Buddha himself, beyond assuring his followers that Nirvana *is*, would not be drawn into any positive statements about its nature. Instead, he defined it in terms of what it is not or what it lies beyond, just as the Hindus define Brahman. Nirvana is beyond birth, origination, creation, and form. Those who enter it can neither be said to exist or not to exist, because Nirvana is beyond all existence as we know and understand it. The *Theravadin* school of Buddhism, the oldest school and prominent in Sri Lanka and South East Asia, tends to view Nirvana as an escape from life attained by overcoming the attractions of the material world, while the *Mahayana* schools (dominant in Tibet, China, and Japan) regard it as the fruition of life, achieved through the unfolding of the infinite possibilities innate within our own Buddha-nature (i.e. within our intrinsic enlightened mind). Once Nirvana is entered after death, there is no return to the world of form; there is indeed no individual *to* return, since concepts like individuality and even unity no longer have meaning, confined as they are to this world where in our ignorance and our preoccupation with form our minds are dominated by the kind of oppositional thinking which recognizes only individuality *or* unity, life *or* death, self *or* others.

Not everyone who is fully enlightened and able to enter Nirvana, however, chooses to do so. In *Mahayana* Buddhism, the ideal of the *Bodhisattva*, who refuses to enter Nirvana until all other beings can enter with him or her, is held in greater esteem than the *Arhat*, the ideal of *Theravadin* Buddhism, who passes alone through the veil that separates Nirvana from conceptual existence, never to return. For the *Mahayana* Buddhist, the *Bodhisattva* is the highest possible expression of pure altruism. The *Bodhisattva* has nothing more to gain for him or herself, having already gained entry to the ultimate state of Nirvana, and having passed beyond the "self" that desires personal gratification. Yet for lifetime after lifetime, the *Bodhisattva* returns to the hardships of physical existence, purely in order to teach and to serve fellow human beings.

For the psychologist, pure altruism – absolute unselfishness – is unobtainable. Early conditioning means that even if we think we are doing good solely for the benefit of others, there is still the subtle reward stemming from the conviction that we are doing the right thing. The internalized parent is still there to praise us for our unselfish actions or, in the case of the religious person, there is the sense of reward that comes from doing God's will. However, the *Bodhisattva* ideal gets around this, if only at the theoretical level, by positing that the small limited self, the ego that thinks of itself as a separate individual capable of receiving personal reward, no longer exists for the *Bodhisattva*. He or she has passed beyond such self-delusion.

## The Intermediate Afterlife State

Certain Christian traditions – Roman Catholicism and the Eastern Orthodox Churches – also teach that certain afterlife states are impermanent, in this case the intermediate level between heaven and hell known as purgatory, where those not yet ready for heaven but not bad enough for hell can purge themselves of their transgressions and, in the fullness of time, become worthy of entry into heaven. There are echoes in this belief of that of the ancient Greeks, who held that there are three afterdeath states: the Elysian Fields, which are the destination of the blessed; Tartaurus, which is the place of the damned, and where the punishments meted out are tailor-made to suit the crimes of the individual concerned; and Limbo, a shadowy, intermediate state between the two where those unsuited to the Elysian Fields but not bad enough for Tatarus live out a listless, joyless existence.

Christian mystical traditions have also hinted at the impermanence of some afterlife states and referred to what is sometimes described as a return to the source (Griffiths, 1982). Instead of spending eternity praising God, the individual soul is said eventually to become one with Him, with the very source of all being. This suggests there is potential for further work and development once heaven is attained, a concept clearly at odds with the Buddhist notion that progress can only be made in this world, but in keeping with more esoteric religious traditions which draw upon both Western and Eastern ideas, such as Theosophy. More recently, some Christian thinkers, in another alternative to the notion of eternal happiness or eternal damnation, have suggested that heaven and hell are essentially of our own making. Heaven is the ability to be at peace with the divine and with ourselves in the afterlife, while hell is alienation from God and a consequent inability to find peace. Such thinkers also suggest the possibility of redemption. Once the individual is able to go through the process of repentance – which may be long and difficult – he or she is able to leave this alienated state behind. In the course of this process the individual has to experience, at first-hand, the pain and suffering he or she has caused to others, and only when this pain and suffering have been fully borne, and genuine regret is felt and expressed, does further progress become possible.

For many psychologists the idea of an afterlife, in particular an afterlife which redresses the injustices of this life and repays in kind both the righteous and the wrongdoer, looks suspiciously like an instance of wish-fulfillment. There are obvious attractions in such an afterlife for the believer. It allays some of the fears of death (both one's own death and the death of loved ones), offers hope of realms where all striving and suffering are left far behind and where the theist comes close to the divine, and may lead to a sense of superiority over unbelievers. For those in positions of religious authority, the threatened torments of the hell realms also offer a powerful weapon for asserting control over followers, and for exacting their obedience.

This may make theoretical sense to many psychologists. But before we dismiss ideas of an afterlife out of hand (thus consigning much of religious belief to the realms of self-deception) it is worth remembering that physical science has not disproved the reality of survival after death. Indeed it is not easy to see how it could do so, since the concern of physical science is with material phenomena, and any survival of death would involve, by definition, the existence of some meta-material state.

Similarly we should remember that we cannot dismiss belief in survival because it supposes the existence of this state. Belief in survival is common to all the great traditions and to most of the lesser-known ones, and although it may be associated with early attempts to explain events outside human understanding, it can also be traced to the mystical certainties said to be experienced by the founders of these traditions and even by a number of laymen and women who even without prior interest in a spiritual dimension have been precipitated into altered states of consciousness which leave them with a conviction of the immortality of aspects of being (see e.g. Abhayananda, 1996; Bucke, 1991; James, 1960). As these altered states (which may include the peak experiences described by Maslow, e.g. 1970b and 1976) can occur in the absence of any symptoms of psychotic disturbance, they may suggest the existence of a common mental process which has as its function either removal of the fear of death or, as religion insists, the provision of assurances that human beings are more than just their physical bodies. Either way, it is difficult to see how belief in an afterlife can be explained in terms of the Darwinian struggle for existence, since it is unlikely to contribute much to survival in the physical world.

## Near-Death Experiences

As with much of religious experience, a major concern of the psychologist is with the effect that these altered states have upon subsequent behavior and beliefs. Recent research into this effect has focussed particularly upon so-called near-death experiences (NDEs). NDEs are associated with episodes during which the subject is either briefly clinically dead (i.e. manifesting an absence of the vital signs regarded as medical evidence of life), or in extreme danger of clinical death. Findings vary (see chapter 11 for more details), but in a significant percentage of cases subjects report a continuation of consciousness during these episodes, and sometimes provide details of clinical interventions and other procedures that took place during them and of which they could not have been normally aware. On occasions they even report leaving their physical bodies and experiencing "paradise" conditions from which they return to their bodies with reluctance (Bailey and Yates, 1996). Research by Ring (1985) into the subsequent behavior and belief systems of a sample of the individuals concerned revealed that approximately 75 percent of them showed a significant increase in:
- appreciation of ordinary things and of nature;
- concern and compassion for others;
- patience and tolerance of others;

- love for and insight into others;
- acceptance of others;
- the desire to search for meaning and purpose in life;
- self-understanding.

They also showed a significant decrease in their interest in material things, a greater orientation toward religion and spirituality, and a very significant decline in fear of death. In his review of the literature, Ring shows that his findings are consistent with those of other researchers, and that the changes concerned appear to be long term.

It is possible that these changes came about from a sense of relief at emerging from a close brush with death rather than from the content of the NDE itself. Such a brush would be a reminder of mortality, and might well serve to turn the mind toward more spiritual things. However, the verbal accounts given to Ring by his sample suggest otherwise. Clear convictions were expressed in these accounts that the NDEs were real, and that they provided insights not only into a life after death but also into some higher spiritual reality behind existence.

No matter how we explain the NDE or what it may tell us about the activity of the mind (points returned to in chapter 11), the important thing is that typically it brings conviction of survival to those who encounter it, and profoundly changes their belief systems and significant aspects of their behavior. Whether we see these changes as beneficial or not depends largely upon our own value systems, but for the most part the individuals concerned seem in no doubt that they are. A number of popular books by those who claim to have had NDEs have been published in recent years (e.g. Brinkley and Perry, 1994; Atwater, 1994), while more scholarly analyses of the incidence and content of these experiences appear in works by Sabom (1982), Grey (1985), Zaleski (1987), Forman (1988), Moody and Perry (1988), Morse and Perry (1991), Fenwick and Fenwick (1995), Kellehear (1996), Bailey and Yates (1996), Osis and Haraldson (1997), Rhodes (1997), Wilson (1997), and others. Recently Ring and Cooper (1999) have explored NDEs in those who have been born blind, and report that the accounts given to them of these NDEs include apparently visual experiences, some of which appear to be veridical, though Ring and Cooper are suitably cautious as to the interpretations they place upon these experiences.

One of the many interesting features of NDEs is that they are reported to occur to those without religious belief as well as to those with such belief. This suggests that they cannot readily be accounted for by expectation. Nor, as we discuss in chapter 11, can they be effectively explained away as vagaries of the dying brain, although attempts have been made to do so. At face value, and judging by the accounts and convictions of those who have actually had the experiences concerned, they would seem to provide some support for the belief that physical death may not lead to the termination of consciousness. If consciousness is considered to be a product exclusively of brain function, there are obvious difficulties in such a belief. But if, as religious teachings would have us believe, mind (or soul) is distinct from and works through brain, then these difficulties do not arise (some of the evidence for each of these conflicting views is summarized in chapter 11).

## Implications for Daily Living

The codes of conduct urged by religious traditions as leading to propitious experiences in an afterlife are typically expressed through a series of commands or injunctions believed to have originated from a divine or enlightened source. Judaism and Christianity have their Ten Commandments said to have emanated from God Himself. Judaism in addition has Mosaic Law and the rabbinical decisions about the Law derived from the *Torah* and the *Talmud*, while Christianity has the sayings of Christ and of his more notable followers. Buddhism has its Noble Eightfold Path, first taught by the Buddha, and the five precepts (injunctions against killing, stealing, lying, illicit sex, and intoxication) followed by the laity, and the *Vinaya* which governs the monastic life. Islam has its Five Pillars, namely *Shahadah* (belief in Allah and in Mohammed as his prophet), *Salat* (the five daily prayers), *Zakat* (the giving of alms), *Sawm* (fasting in Ramadan), and *Hajj* (pilgrimage to Mecca). All Muslims are expected to uphold *Shahadah*, and at the very least not to repudiate the other four pillars. In addition, Islam has *Shari'a*, a code for both spiritual and temporal life based upon the *Koran* and the *Sunnah* (the sayings and doings of Mohammed). Taoism has the *Tao Te Ching*, thought to have been written either by Lao Tzu or by Chuang Tzu (sixth and fourtth century BCE teachers, respectively), which emphasizes particularly the concept of *Wu-wei* (non-interference with the natural order of things), and Confucianism has the *Ssu-chu* (the "Four Books") written by Confucius and his followers, which enshrine among other things the doctrine of *li* (the rules of proper behavior in social, political, and religious living). Hinduism has the *Manu-Samhita*, the Law-Books of Manu, dating from the second and first centuries BCE and based upon the *Vedas*, twelfth–eighth century BCE sacred texts said to originate with the *hotars*, mental beings thought to stand between the divine realms and the human realms. The *Manu-Samhita* present a judicial system still serving as the basis for religious and social behavior among Hindus.

The longevity of these various codes is of great psychological interest. Enduring over many centuries, they have come to form the basis not only for religious law but also for much of the civil law in all the cultures concerned. The authority of their supposed authors, together with the belief that adherence to them will lead to advantages in the afterlife, provide some explanation for their endurance, but their appropriateness for the maintenance of the social order is another important contributory factor. In addition, there are many similarities between them. The five Buddhist precepts are reflected in most codes, as are the instructions to give alms and to protect the poor, the elderly, and the sick. Also universal is the teaching that the "self", perhaps best understood in terms of the self-constructed Freudian ego, must in some way be changed or transcended if spiritual progress is to be made.

Some differences exist regarding the role of the self however. In the theistic traditions such as Judaism, Christianity, and Islam, this self is an active obstacle to salvation or spiritual progress because either through weakness or willfulness it sets itself up against God, for example by failing to follow divine law, or – worst of all – by denying the very existence of spiritual realities. In Christianity such denial is regarded as blasphemy against the Holy Spirit (Mark 3:29), the one sin for which there is said to be no forgiveness (logically because reconciliation with God cannot take place so long as one denies His very existence). Thus for the theist the goal of the religious life is to subordinate oneself and become a servant of God by doing His will and following His path.

At times this concept of a servant/master relationship can lead to feelings of guilt and worthlessness – seen as their most excessive in the self-negation apparent in the flagellations and other mortifications of the flesh practiced by various holy men and women in medieval times. More properly it is seen as the need to humble oneself before God in order to be exalted, to cast oneself down in order to be lifted up, and to confront, confess, and repent one's wrongdoings in order to be granted absolution. The theistic traditions regard their commandments and codes as given to man by God in order that His will be done on Earth, and the individual self become purified and perfected through a combination of personal effort and divine grace.

By contrast, Buddhism sees its codes as arising primarily from the direct experience of the Buddha (a man and not a god) during his enlightenment under the Boh tree some 500 years before the birth of Christ. By way of further contrast between theism and Buddhism, the latter has no wish to give the self to God or to the gods, because it sees the self as an illusion which tricks us into believing we are separate from the rest of creation and from the source of all being. For Buddhism there is nothing permanent about this self (to which it assigns the term *anatta*, "no-self" or "not-self"), which is viewed as nothing but a constantly changing process. Only when freed from a deluded self-view is the person able to recognize the truth about his or her own being, and the way to this freedom is by keeping the precepts and following the Buddha's Noble Eightfold Path of correct understanding, thought, speech, action, motivation, livelihood, meditation, and mindfulness (i.e. direct awareness of the moment-by-moment experience of being alive).

Hinduism is in some way poised between this Buddhist interpretation of the self and the interpretation given by the theistic religions. Like the latter it accepts that there is an enduring substance in each of us, the *Atman*, which underlies the purely conditioned ego. However, the *Atman* is regarded as ultimately one with *Brahman*, rather than as an expression of eternal individuality. Hinduism frequently refers to the impermanent ego as the "self," and the *Atman* as the "Self". (Somewhat confusingly Buddhism sometimes uses the same convention, for example in the *Dhammapada* where we are told that the "the Self is lord of self"; but it does not dwell on the nature of this "Self".) As with Buddhism, Hinduism considers that enlightenment is impossible until the practitioner recognizes that the barrier to its attainment is quite literally self-delusion.

There are other important differences between theistic and non-theistic ways of regarding the self, but the common feature is the recognition that the self, however it is conceived, is something that must be mastered rather than indulged, whether we master it through our own efforts or with the help of grace. This common feature generates in practitioners of all the major traditions – in theory – a humility and an unselfishness that leads to a readiness to serve not only spiritual realities but also fellow human beings. Self-aggrandizement, self-seeking, self-gratification are all seen as direct obstacles to spiritual progress. Buddhism places further emphasis upon this by its teaching that since we are all fundamentally one, harming others is the same as harming ourselves (a teaching of some subtlety, as even if the idea of fundamental unity is hard to accept, it is easy to recognize that personal spiritual progress is harmed if we harm others). The Buddhist teaching on reincarnation also provides a further incentive to treating others well, for it is argued – somewhat improbably unless taken symbolically – that so innumerable are our past lives that everyone now on Earth has at one time or another been our own mother.

## Religious Practices

There are also many similarities – and some differences, many of which are more apparent than real – between the religious practices taught by the different traditions. Hinduism and Buddhism – and even more so Jainism – place particular emphasis upon *ahimsa*, nonviolence. In these traditions, *ahimsa* is to be practiced not only toward fellow men and women (in marked contrast to the warlike behavior of certain other faiths), but also toward all living things. In fact the Jains lay such stress upon *ahimsa* that they eschew agriculture (on the grounds that cultivating the soil destroys small life forms), and avoid root crops by taking from plants only those parts which can be surrendered without compromising survival. In addition, Jain monks wear mouth masks to prevent breathing in (and destroying) flying insects, and brush the ground ahead as they walk in order to avoid treading on any life form. In one of the two major Jain sects, the *Digambharra*, the monks even eschew clothing, both because clothes crush small insects on the skin and as earnest of their complete renunciation of worldly possessions. Buddhism counsels its adherents to avoid what it sees as the three main hindrances to enlightenment, namely attachment (particularly in the form of greed, grasping, and acquisitiveness), aversion (especially in the form of hatred, but also in that of fear, distaste, and dislike), and delusion (in particular the ignorance already mentioned several times that leads us to mistake the world of form for ultimate reality, and to mistake our individuality for separateness from the rest of creation).

Without going to such lengths as the Jains, Buddhism lays great stress upon *metta*, loving kindness, which should be extended not only to family and friends but to all sentient beings, including animals and those people antipathetic toward us. Christianity similarly lays great stress upon the importance of love, and Christ's teaching that God is love and that we should love even our enemies and pray for those who ill-use us is one of the defining (though regrettably one of the most frequently ignored) features of his message.

Despite these similarities, differences are apparent between the traditions in their attitudes to society. The most obvious example of this is the Hindu *varnas* (literally "colors" – commonly known in the West as the caste system), which because of its uniqueness in human behavior requires some detailed description – and an attempt at psychological explanation. The *varnas* system, which has endured for many thousands of years, divides individuals into a hereditary hierarchy of occupational groups. Although probably pre-existing in a loose fashion, the system is explicitly set out in the *Rigveda* (the oldest of the four *Vedas*). The *Rigveda* describes humanity as arising from the dismemberment of *Perusa*, the cosmic man, whose mouth became the *Brahmins* (the priestly caste, sometimes spelt *Brahmans*, showing the link with *Brahma*, the creator god), whose two arms became the *Rajanya* or *Ksatriyas* (the warrior caste), whose thighs became the *Vaisya* (the traders and farmers), and whose feet became the *Sudras* (the manual worker caste).

The Laws of *Manu* further formalize the *varnas* system by teaching that below the *Sudra* come the *Dalit* or outcasts (devoted to occupations such as hunting, butchering, fishing, working with leather workers, and handling corpses), often referred to as unclean or as untouchable, who are not regarded as part of the system at all. In addition the Laws make reference to more than 50 hereditary (originally non-Aryan) groups of workers in important manual occupations who do not fall under one of the four main *varnas*. These groups, who make up the basic units of the working population, are known as *Jatis*, and although they are regarded as subdivisions or extensions of the *Sudras*, each group is given its own *varna*, governed by its own laws.

Strict guidelines are laid down on how the divisions between the *varnas* are to be observed. The *Brahmins* are supreme in purity and rank, and crimes against them have traditionally been punished more severely that those committed against members of the lower *varnas*. The role of the *Brahmin* is to perform sacrifices, to study and teach the *Vedas*, and to protect the *dharma* (the sacred truth). *Brahmins* have a right to call upon the services of the *Sudras* at any time, and if in economic difficulties are permitted to take up one or other of the livelihoods associated with the *Ksatriyas* and the *Vaisyas*, provided these livelihoods are among those classified as ritually pure. The *Ksatriyas* are the protectors of society, and provide the kings and rulers, although they must heed the counsel of *Brahmins* in everything related to the *dharma*. Under no circumstances must they take over the duties of the *Brahmin*, but if need be they can follow the livelihoods of the *Vaisyas* and the *Sudras*, and the *Vaisayas* may take over those of the *Sudras*.

There is, however, a great religious and social gulf between the three higher *varnas* (who are described as *dvijas* or twice-born, as the males undergo initiatory re-birth rites) and the *Sudras*, and between all four *varnas* and the outcast *Dalit*. The *Dalit* are forbidden to assume the work of any of the *varnas*, to marry a *varnas* member, to study the *Vedas* (presumably because this may give them ideas above their station), or to accumulate wealth (which would give them power). Their role is one of service to those above them, who in turn have a duty to protect them from starvation. Technically they are not allowed to live within a town or village, or to enter towns or villages at night without permission. Members of the higher *varnas* may leave food for them (placed on the ground in broken dishes), but are not permitted to teach them the scriptures. The role of the *Dalits* is to perform all the unpleasant tasks beneath the dignity of the *varnas*.

Although not all *varna* members now follow their traditional roles and there are civil laws forbidding discrimination against individuals on the strength of *varna* (untouchability was also legally abolished in 1949 and its practice forbidden in any form), the *varnas* system is still a dominant feature not only of the Hindu religion but also of the Indian social system. *Varna* membership is still hereditary, and movement (or marriage) between *varnas* is not formally sanctioned. Even after centuries and the opposition of civil law, the system therefore still shows no real sign of withering away. It is said that the reason for this is not only religious but also the contribution of the system to the social stability of a vast, multicultural, and economically impoverished country which, it is claimed, would be very difficult to control by other means.

One of the most interesting features of the *varnas* system for the psychology of religion and for psychologists studying behavior is that it places the *Brahmins*, the priestly *varna*, at the head. Most *Brahmins* do not practice their priestly functions on a regular basis, and follow instead one of the ritually pure professions (e.g. law, business, and the ownership of land), but only they can carry out these functions, all of which remain crucial to Indian society. On all matters of religious belief, doctrine, and observance *Brahmins* remain the supreme arbiters, and as such occupy a privileged place in society, though one which also carries great responsibility for ethical conduct. The question is why should they have continued to enjoy such eminence for so long? Unlike in Europe, where wealth and authority accompanied military power and where the clergy rapidly lost their status once the spread of literacy rendered redundant their function as civil servants to monarchy and aristocracy, the priestly class is still seen by Hindu India as having access to levels of wisdom and scholarship which are beyond the reach of the rest of the population.

This suggests the enormous importance still attached by nearly a billion Hindus to religion as a way of life. There has never been any major uprising, intellectual, political or social, against the *varnas* system, even though the majority of people belong to one or other of the lower two *varnas*, or as *Dalits* are excluded altogether from the system. Even Buddhism, which was born in India and at one time attracted widespread support partly because of its opposition to the *varnas* system, subsequently lost its hold over the people and has all but withered away in the country of its birth. There are a number of possible interconnected reasons for the continuing general acceptance of *varnas* even by the underprivileged.

1. The almost universal belief in an afterlife leads people to attach only limited importance to their lot in the present life.
2. The acceptance of reincarnation prompts people to accept that their present lot is a consequence of their behavior in past lives, and that hard work and meritorious conduct in this life will lead to more favorable rebirths.
3. The Hindu teaching that this life is *Maya* – i.e. is illusory, or rather is experienced by the unenlightened mind in an illusory way – and that ultimate reality lies beyond, lends further strength to the belief that material conditions are of relatively little importance.

4.   The belief that material reality is created, sustained, and destroyed by the gods produces what Westerners may call an attitude of fatalism – the order of things is planned by beings beyond humankind and there is therefore no point in struggling against it.
5.   The belief that the ultimate aim of human life is in any case to escape the cycle of birth, death, and rebirth, and become one with the ineffable Brahman.
6.   Continuing acceptance of the powerful creation myth that humanity arose from the dismemberment of *Perusa*, with each *varna* arising from a specific part of his body and thus inheriting the function of that part.

We can speculate that poor education and economic hardship rob people of both the political will and the physical energy to fight against an elitist system, but historical events in other European and Asian countries lend little support to this. Perhaps more convincingly we may argue that an elitist system like the *varnas* that consists of several well-defined hierarchical levels is more stable than a system with only rich and poor. Each level in a multi-hierarchy gains its political and economic satisfaction from its superiority over the levels below, while in the case of India the situation is further stabilized by the powerless *Dalits* who perform all the unpleasant menial tasks in society and have few educated leaders or sympathizers in the levels above them.

Nevertheless, the persistence of the *varnas* system demonstrates the extraordinary psychological power of religious belief, a power which the various explanatory models developed by Western psychology may have difficulties in explaining satisfactorily.

## Further Differences in Codes of Behavior Between the Traditions

Many of the other similarities and differences between the commandments and codes taught by the different tradtions may, although acquiring religious significance over the years, have had their origins in local preferences and prejudices and social necessity. For example, the embargo upon intoxicants in Buddhism may have arisen from the recognition that drunkenness inhibits the clarity of mind and physical self-discipline demanded by the spiritual life, in particular the spiritual life followed by the monastic communities once so widespread in Tibet and elsewhere. Islam, which has no monastic traditions or priesthood (the Iman is a scholar and teacher who leads the community in prayer, but there is no ordination or its equivalent in Islam, although Shi'ite Moslems believe in a succession of 12 Imans who were gifted with exceptional spiritual authority and intercessory powers between God and the faithful) also forbids alcohol, so here the reason may stem in part at least from a recognition of the drug's ability to reduce social and moral inhibitions. However, intoxicants do sometimes feature in the imagery of the Moslem paradise, where it seems individuals are able to enjoy their benefits without suffering their disadvantages (a state of affairs drinkers here on Earth might envy). The strict rules and taboos in the Judaic tradition governing the selection, preparation, and serving of food may also have had their origin in sensible hygiene practices rather than in spiritual revelation.

Some of the major differences between traditions lie, however, in their treatment of other faiths. Islam professes tolerance toward Jews and Christians on the strength of their adherence to Moses and to Christ, both of whom are recognized by Moslems as prophets in the line preceding Mohammed, and on their possession of scriptures recognized in the Islamic tradition. However, those who follow other faiths, in particular faiths thought guilty of idolatry in any of its forms, do not enjoy the same dispensation. Although times are changing, Christianity has traditionally claimed for itself a supreme revelation through Christ, and has therefore felt itself justified in engaging in persecutions, both martial and cultural, against all other traditions; an intolerance which has also been apparent between the various Christian sects themselves and toward any who profess unorthodox views. Judaism also claims a special status for itself, on the grounds that Jews are the chosen race of God, though (possibly for reasons of historical weakness) it has not engaged in warfare on the strength of this status.

In general, the Eastern traditions have been much readier not only to tolerate those with different faiths, but also to recognize the validity of many of the teachers and teachings within these faiths. For this reason, they have also shown little inclination to proselytize. In addition, there has generally been less rivalry and hostility between the various sects within these traditions. In both Hinduism and Buddhism, the emphasis is often placed more upon the quality of the teacher than upon the sect to which he or she belongs. Thus the aspiring young man or woman can go from teacher to teacher, without censure by members of his or her own sect. It is also often recognized that the variations in approach and emphasis practiced by the different sects cater for individual differences. Thus the varying emphases placed by sects and by teachers upon ritual, intellectual study, devotion, meditation, and other practices are seen as ensuring that a suitable path is available to everyone.

Links between religions and temporal power, and the use of religion as an agent of social control, are widely apparent. Organized religion has historically been more authoritarian than democratic in its structures, and frequently more identified with the political and social status quo than with radicalism. The most obvious example in modern times is Tibetan Buddhism, which invests both spiritual and temporal power in the Lamas, the religious leaders. From the seventeenth century CE pre-eminence among the Lamas has been given to the Dalai Lama, the head of the *Gelupa* sect, which overcame the ambitions of other sects with the support of the powerful Mongol invaders in 1621 (Powers, 1995), but who also carries authority as the claimed reincarnation of *Chenresi* (Sanskrit *Avalokiteshvara*), the Buddha of Compassion and the Supreme Protector and Spiritual Patron of Tibet.

The link between spiritual status and temporal power is also still evident in the Roman Catholic Church. During medieval times, the status of a bishop and the church which contained his throne (or *cathedra*) depended in part upon the prestige of the saints whose relics (bodily remains or associated objects) the church possessed. The more exalted the saint, the higher the status. Thus the Basilica of St. Peter in Rome, erected by the Emperor Constantine in the fourth century CE on the supposed site of the crucifixion of St. Peter – the apostle upon whom Christ had declared he would build his Church (Matthew 16:18) – became particularly revered. Together with a fortuitous combination of political and religious events, this led to the recognition of its bishop, the Bishop of Rome, as the Father of the Church (*Il Papa*, the Pope – a title which previously had been applied to all Christian Bishops) – and thus as the supreme spiritual and judicial head of the Church.

Constantine's policy was in fact to identify the Church with the secular State, hence his designation of Christianity as the official religion of the Roman Empire. The subsequent removal of the Imperial Capital from Rome to Byzantium (renamed Constantinople) in 330 thus left the Bishop of Rome as the most prominent figure in the Western Roman Empire in both religious and secular terms. In the centuries that followed, the Church, with its virtual monopoly of literacy and scholarship, its religious authority, and its territorial and other wealth, became essentially a civil power, gaining what amounted to control not only over religious doctrine but also over all theories and discoveries concerning humankind and the natural world. Such control was used to suppress any movements of thought which questioned the Church's teachings and thereby challenged its hold over the levers of state. Inevitably this led to the bitter conflict between the Church and natural philosophy (the latter fast developing into what was to become modern science), a conflict which still contributes to the hostility that many contemporary scientists evidence toward religious beliefs and ideas.

The alliance between religious and secular power worked to the benefit of both groups. With the help of religion the secular powers were able to create a civil service essential to the administration and control of the state, while with the help of the state religion was able to exercise control over the expression of beliefs and ideas and to amass and retain great possessions. A further convenience for the state was that it could get rid of those whose power it considered a threat or whose possessions it coveted by aligning itself with the Church in accusations of heresy (accusations used to destroy the Knights Templar in 1312), while an added convenience for the Church was that anyone convicted of heresy by the ecclesiastical courts could be handed over to the civil authorities for execution, thus protecting the Church from staining its hands with blood.

# CHAPTER 6

# Approaches to Spiritual Development

## The Different Paths

Little work has as yet been done by psychologists of religion into categorizing the various different paths toward spiritual development followed in the major religious traditions. In consequence we must rely upon attempts from scholars within the traditions themselves, and in particular upon Hindu scholars such as Aurobindo (e.g. 1957) and Ghose (1970), as it is they who have given such categorizations most attention. Hindu thinkers identify five major developmental paths (each of which contains various subdivisions which lie outside our present concerns), usually referred to as five different forms of *yoga*, a Sanskrit term meaning "yoke" – that is yoke or union between humankind and the divine. The five paths (all of which except *Hatha Yoga* are described in the *Bhagavad Gita*, one of the most revered Hindu scriptures) are present in all the major religious traditions, though the relative emphasis upon each may vary from tradition to tradition. These paths are not mutually exclusive, and adepts such as Aurobindo have followed and synthesized all five. However, it is said that each path appeals primarily to a particular kind of person, which indicates that through direct observation over the centuries Hindu sages have identified what might be called five distinct religious personality types. The five paths are described and discussed below.

## Hatha Yoga

*Hatha yoga* is the yoga of union with the divine through physical practices and physical transformations. Regarded by many in the West as primarily a set of techniques for physical well-being, *Hatha Yoga* is in essence based upon the belief that by gaining control of the body and its appetites the individual can transmute physical energies into spiritual energy (Wood, 1962). There are two ways in which this belief is justified by practitioners. In the first, as in the Western monastic and aesthetic traditions, the gross appetites of the body for sex, food, and other sensual pleasures are seen as major distractions on the spiritual path – at times even as actively degraded and repulsive – because they focus upon material existence instead of freeing the mind to turn toward the divine. Therefore the flesh must be subdued through chastity, fasting, and deliberate abstinence from creature comforts. Certain similarities are apparent in the methods used by some shamanic traditions (forms of spiritual observance practiced by the indigenous peoples of the Americas, Siberia, and parts of Africa and Asia) where fasting again is practiced, along with voluntary submission to tests of physical endurance involving great physical pain said to distance the spirit from the body and allow visions of other worlds and of spiritual helpers to arise (see e.g. Halifax, 1979). In Hinduism, comparable practices, often with the reported demonstration of extraordinary insensitivity to pain and of control over bleeding and over the speed of wound healing are a feature of some of the devotees of Shiva (Hartsuiker, 1993).

The second (and not incompatible) way in which *Hatha Yoga* is justified by its practitioners is that the actual physical energies of the body can, by a series of *asanas* or postures (which bring pressure to bear upon internal organs) helped by detailed visualization practices, be transmuted into spiritual energies. The most powerful of the physical energies is thought to be sexual energy, and sexual abstinence is therefore practiced, not because the sex act is bad in itself but because it is thought to dissipate this precious energy. The physical, meditative, and visualization practices are thought to open the subtle channel (*sushumna*) which is said to run from the sexual organs up the spinal column to the crown of the head, thus allowing *kundalini* energy to ascend through each of the seven so-called *chakras* (subtle energy centers of increasing purity and refinement said to lie within the body from just behind the sexual organs to the crown of the head) until it arrives at the principal *chakra* at the crown, where it explodes into what is referred to as the thousand-petalled lotus of spiritual enlightenment. Yogic philosophy tells us that the god *Shiva*, the essence of consciousness, slumbers in the crown *chakra* while his *Shakti* or consort (who brings his creative energy into physical existence) resides in the base *chakra*. By means of the *kundalini* practice, *Shakti* rises up through the body to be united in an embrace with *Shiva*, thus merging material with spiritual energy and awakening *Shiva* within the human mind.

This second of these justifications sounds of course like nonsense. Modern Western medicine has no way of measuring this supposed *kundalini* energy and its movement, or the *chakras* through which it is said to ascend. However, the physical and psychological effects of *kundalini* have been graphically described by practitioners, who also insist that its ascent is fraught with many dangers for the unwary. For example Krishna (1970) tells us in harrowing detail how, after arousing *kundalini* without the guidance of an experienced teacher, he was tormented by agonizing physical and psychological problems which took him 12 years to resolve. Sanella (1987), approaching the subject as a psychiatrist, notes a range of similarities between the various accounts given by individuals of their *kundalini* experiences. Sensations to which they typically refer include tingling and excessive heat in the body, an awareness of bright lights moving up the spine and inside the head, and sensations as of space or holes opening at the crown. Sleep patterns are sometimes described as badly disrupted, while parts of the body are apparently hot to the touch of others. Frequent and prolonged meditation is said to be vital if these various symptoms are to be contained and prevented from overwhelming the practitioner both psychologically and physically.

Clearly therefore *kundalini* experiences have a degree both of subjective and objective reality. Sanella suggests that they may be explained by the unusual surges of energy felt along the axes of the body which, together with the psychological confusion arising from the breakdown of old expectations and habits, occur when people are undergoing life crises. Nevertheless, some psychologists and psychiatrists who have researched the subject extensively consider that *kundalini* experiences, however we explain them, are an exceptional opportunity for psychological and spiritual growth (Grof and Grof, 1989).

Many other systems involving physical movements – some of which have become very popular in the West – can also be thoughts of as forms of *Hatha Yoga* in that they are claimed to enable the dedicated practitioner to gain control over a subtle energy in the body known as *chi* in Chinese and as *ki* in Japanese (and probably analogous to the *prana* energy said in yoga to be inhaled with each breath and to pervade and sustain the whole body), and by doing so to enhance both physical health and spiritual development. Most of these systems had their origins within Eastern religious traditions, and many of them are associated with the so-called martial arts, practices of self-defense which are also said to be paths to spiritual growth. One of the most widely practiced, *Tai Chi*, a series of slow and highly ritualized physical movements, is said to have been developed by a Taoist hermit, *Chan San Feng* (Horwitz, Kimmelman and Lui 1982). The related *Chi-kung* exercises incorporate elements of both Taoist and Buddhist spiritual practices (Hwa, 1980).

The Shaolin monastery in Honan province in China is in fact the claimed birthplace of practices from which most of the subsequent forms of the martial arts such as *karate* and *aikido* are derived, all of which at one level or another are claimed to serve spiritual ends (Payne, 1981). Particular forms of archery and swordsmanship are used as meditative and spiritual practices in Zen Buddhism (Herrigel, 1953), and a Japanese legend has it that *judo* was first taught to mortals by the gods *Kajima* and *Kadori*. Even in modern times, when the spiritual purposes associated with these various systems and practices may not be particularly acknowledged, it is still insisted that they serve as an invaluable form of mind training. The practitioner is taught, during a lengthy period of intensive practice under an experienced teacher, to pay single-minded attention to the arousing and direction of *chi* energy within the body so that he or she can allegedly direct it outwards at an opponent with stunning force and without muscular exertion, and to develop a sharply focussed awareness that allows lightning-fast reaction at the first hint of the latter's attack. Along with these skills goes an essential ethical philosophy that allows their use only in defense of others and of self when all peaceful methods for settling disputes have failed.

Most religious traditions practice a form of *Hatha Yoga* in that they prescribe certain physical self-disciplines, particularly in relation to sexual matters (one reason why sex and the body are still surrounded legally and culturally by so many taboos in most countries in the world). In Christianity, lust – sexual desire – is regarded as one of the seven deadly sins, along with gluttony and five more psychologically orientated failings (pride, covetousness, envy, anger, and sloth). Underlying this whole approach is the notion that too much attention paid to bodily appetites distracts attention from spirituality, and in medieval times in particular the afterlife punishment for such attention was to endure the all too physical torments of hell. For the Buddhist, the goal of the religious life, *Nirvana*, is seen in fact as the cessation of all material cravings, the extinction ("blowing out") of the desire for physical existence, a desire which is seen as the root cause of the individual's return, lifetime after lifetime, to further experiences of the material world.

Islam also has physical prohibitions that the faithful are expected to observe, particularly – as mentioned earlier – abstention from alcohol and from other intoxicants at all times, and avoidance of all food and drink between sunrise and sunset during the weeks of Ramadan. As already indicated, the observance of Ramadan is in fact one of the five pillars of Islam. Ramadan, the ninth month of the Islamic lunar calendar and the time when the first book of the *Koran* was revealed to Mohammed, is in fact a time of restriction from all the things of the flesh. The teaching is that carnal desires threaten to dominate our lives, and that by abstaining from tobacco and sexual activity as well as from food and water during the hours of daylight throughout Ramadan, the Muslim replaces these desires with the wholehearted desire for God and for the moral and ethical conduct associated with God. In addition, abstention of this kind is also thought to have an important social function in that it allows Muslims to gain insight into the plight of the poor, who go hungry by necessity rather than by choice, and thus to develop social sensitivity and an awareness of personal responsibility for alleviating the sufferings of those less fortunate than oneself.

Psychologically, abstention is also thought to strengthen will power, and to remind the faithful to appreciate more fully the divine gifts of food and drink. Judicious fasting is also thought in all religions to purify both the body and the mind (a claim which is now given some guarded support by modern Western medicine), and Jung went further by suggesting that over-nutrition is one of the reasons why modern Westerners have less access to the mystical experiences reported in medieval times (see e.g. Zum Brunn and Epiney-Burgard, 1989) and is still not uncommon in the East. In Judaism, the prescriptions for conduct, the *Halacha* (literally "the way to walk") compiled by the rabbis, regulate sexual relations and virtually all other important daily activities, any of which, incorrectly performed, is said to profane the name of God. Although the emphasis is not laid so squarely upon the need for fasting or other forms of denial, the faithful are instructed to remain always aware of the actions of the body, and to ensure that at no time do these actions involve anything considered unacceptable to God – that is anything which transgresses the Commandments and the Law, and which thus distances the created from the creator. Again, this discipline of self-awareness has psychological value. The individual is made conscious of his or her actions, thoughts, emotions, and motivation, and in consequence strives to maintain those which bring spiritual development and offer support to those in need.

In the religions of both East and West, there is therefore a powerful current of rejection toward the undisciplined and licentious use of the body and the gratification of its desires and functions. In effect, each religion insists that humankind has a choice, either to follow the ways of the flesh or the ways of the spirit. Orthodox Christian doctrine lays particular emphasis upon this choice, holding that God is separate from His creation, and that the souls of humankind have "fallen" from divine grace through the original sin of Adam and Eve, which gave birth to the human capacity to develop systems of knowledge and belief independent of those of God, and that men and women must therefore strive to renounce materialistic philosophies ("the world"), carnal desires ("the flesh"), and self-aggrandizement ("the devil"). This approach is somewhat different from the Eastern traditions, where absolute reality is regarded as expressing itself not through a single act of creation but moment by moment through all existence. Physical life, with its choices and challenges, is seen as a path toward the realization of this reality, a realization which depends crucially upon the recognition that physical life and the material world in which it takes place are not and must not be mistaken for ultimate reality.

The psychologist is bound to ask whether the popularity of *Hatha Yoga*, *Tai Chi*, and other similar practices over the centuries is due to their demonstrable physical and psychological benefits rather than to any spiritual effects. These benefits are claimed to include improved physical health, greater suppleness and reduced incidence of physical strains and sprains, increased body awareness and mind–body coordination, relaxation, stress reduction, improved sleep habits, enhanced self-confidence, reduced blood pressure, weight loss, increased mental, physical, and sexual energy, equanimity, serenity, improvements in mood, increased alertness and object awareness, and greater self-control (see e.g. Leonard, 1986, 1991; Weller, 1998; Kent, 1999). Such benefits may persuade the practitioner that he or she is making spiritual progress, but there could be no real warrant for this. The reinforcement that arises from group membership and from teacher approval, the feelings of elitism and of personal power that may come from following practices perceived as exotic and esoteric, and the desire for the paranormal powers said to arise from certain of the methods of breath control associated with yoga, may also play a significant role in sustaining commitment to practice.

On the other hand, there is always a danger when those who have not followed certain spiritual practices attempt to tell those who have what these practices mean. This danger is particularly apparent in the psychology of religion. Clearly much more research is needed into the various practices themselves – which can only be fruitfully done in full partnership with the practitioners concerned – before we can reach realistic conclusions as to their benefits. And while it is true that Western medicine has not been able to measure so-called subtle energies like *chi* and *prana* (Benson, 1996), doctors in the Far East trained in Chinese and Indian medicine are in no doubt both of its existence and of its important role in healing body, mind, and spirit. Western doctors who have studied the methods of their Eastern colleagues also express conviction that, measurable or not by modern medical technology, *chi* does appear implicated in certain successful medical interventions (Moyer, 1993).

## Karma Yoga

*Karma Yoga* is usually described as the yoga of selfless action in the world or as the yoga of good works. Such action can be of either a spiritual nature (e.g. as a religious teacher) or a physical nature (e.g. as a worker among the poor and needy). Christ's instruction to St. Peter (John 21: 15–17) to "feed my lambs" and to "feed my sheep" is an example of references to the spiritual importance of this service. One of the most revered Hindu texts, the *Bhagavad Gita* (see e.g. Zaehner, 1966), presents the moral dilemmas and challenges – within oneself as well as in relationships with others – that the desire to perform meretricious action in the world often involves, and stresses that these must be faced rather than avoided if spiritual development is to take place.

In all religious traditions there is in fact something of a dichotomy between those who seek a solitary life of prayer and meditation, as hermits or as members of closed monastic communities, and those who choose to stay in the world and work with and for others. Buddhism demonstrates this in the distinction it makes between the *arhat*, who seeks personal enlightenment and is said after death to disappear into Nirvana and be lost to the world, and the *bodhisattva*, who seeks enlightenment for the benefit of all, and who vows to return to the earth in successive incarnations until all sentient beings can enter Nirvana together. *Karma Yoga* is very much the province of the *bodhisattva*. Some traditions, in particular some Zen Buddhist teachers (e.g. Thich Nhat Hanh, 1995), insist that full enlightenment is only possible if the aspirant practices both *Karma Yoga* for the well-being of all sentient beings, and the inner work associated with meditation (referred to under *Raja Yoga* below) designed to reveal one's own true spiritual nature.

*Karma Yoga* has historically been central to both Western and Eastern religious traditions. In the West the first hospitals, the first organized attempts at work in the community, and some of the first teaching institutions were established by religious orders. Until the state took over many of these functions, monasteries, friaries and the parish churches provided what were relatively effective social services, supported by tithes, donations, and endowments from the laity. Travelers were assured of hospitality at monasteries, and in lawless times the churches provided sanctuary for those in physical danger.

As with *Hatha Yoga*, the psychologist may wish to question whether the motives behind *Karma Yoga* have more to do with psychological than with spiritual rewards. For example, the admiration and gratitude that one can receive as a spiritual teacher may reinforce feelings of self-worth, which are further sustained by material rewards such as hospitality and donations from the faithful, in some cases by sexual favors offered by adoring devotees, and by the availability of physical care from devotees in infirmity and in old age. Similarly, involvement in charitable works might have more to do with obtaining peer group approval, with enhanced social status, and with guilt reduction than with a spiritually driven desire to serve others. Even when performed in a sincere attempt to follow religious teachings, the underlying (or unconscious) motive might be less to help others than to secure the rewards of virtuous self-esteem and of better prospects in the afterlife.

Against this must be set the fact that all the great traditions teach psychological techniques intended to combat the self-aggrandizement that may arise from the performance of *Karma Yoga*. Contemplation of Christ's sacrifice upon the Cross, particularly when performed with the emotional intensity associated with for example the *Spiritual Exercises* compiled by St. Ignatius Loyola, the founder of the Jesuits (Corbishley, 1973), is said to develop corresponding selfless emotions in oneself, as is reflection on Christ's teaching that alms giving should be done in secret if it is to be a spiritual act, and that public alms giving wins only the reward of social approval. Buddhism not only teaches the *bodhisattva* ideal (which many Buddhists make solemn daily vows to emulate), but also has the *metta* or loving-kindness practice, which involves meditating lovingly and compassionately on those especially dear to one's heart, then progressively extending the emotions thus aroused to people increasingly remote – i.e. from friends to acquaintances, strangers, those one dislikes, and finally to the "whole world".

Essentially, *Karma Yoga* involves altruistic behavior, and the constant self-monitoring and self-knowledge that enables one to recognize each instance where good deeds are ego-driven rather than performed selflessly. When such recognition takes place, another psychological technique, the practice of nonattachment, is recommended by the Eastern traditions. Thus one deliberately puts the good deed concerned out of mind, and refuses to own it as "mine". And in one's daily devotions one repeats prayers which "give" all merit gained from *Karma Yoga* to the rest of the world. Similar injunctions are laid upon Christians when they are told by Christ to go the extra mile, to "love your enemies," and to "pray for those who despitefully use you." The skeptical psychologist may insist that in spite of all these attempts at selflessness, elements of what we might call the "do-gooder syndrome" remain. So they may, but it has to be conceded that if selflessness is thought to be important, these various techniques are not a bad place at which to start with its cultivation.

## Bhakti Yoga

*Bhakti Yoga* – the Yoga of Devotion to the divine or to some spiritual principle – is a universal feature in all the major traditions, and takes many forms. For example praising God or one of the gods through hymns chants, and prayers, through music and ecstatic poetry, and through the repetition of devotional mantras (short sayings in honor of or in supplication to the deity concerned).

The love and devotion expressed through *Bhakti* is sometimes so intense that it may appear to have sexual overtones. A devotee, whether male or female, may speak of being bodily possessed by the divine, as if in a sexual embrace. Female Christian mystics such as the sixteenth-century St. Theresa of Avila (St. Theresa of Avila, 1974) were particularly given to these ecstatic utterances, as if their great love for the divine could only be expressed in sexual imagery. Male poets from the Sufi tradition (a mystical movement within Islam) such as Rumi (Harvey, 1996) were similarly ecstatic, sometimes even casting themselves in what appears to be the female role. In each case, it seems as if there is a yearning for total union with, or absorption by, the divine, and it would appear as if sexual union provides the most graphic symbol through which such unity can be expressed.

The theme of sexual union, in this case the union of the god with his consort, is graphically portrayed in many of the sculptures adorning Hindu temples, providing devotees with meditative objects which help them imaginatively experience something of the sense of becoming one with the god. Similar ecstatic embraces between divine beings are portrayed in Tibetan Buddhist iconography. The sexual theme, though in a rather more discreet form, is also apparent in the romantic poetry of the fourteenth-century French troubadours – poetry which is said to have given birth, through misinterpretation, to the whole concept of romantic love, as it is typically addressed to a courtly lady who the poet loves from afar. There is evidence that this sudden outpouring of troubadour verse symbolized devotion to the Holy Spirit, and sought to keep alive the gnostic Cathar heresy suppressed with great savagery in the Languedoc area of France during the Albigensian Crusade (Nelli, 1968; Guirdham, 1977).

In Freudian terms, *Bhakti* would be interpreted as further evidence of the craving by men and women for a parental figure as an antidote to existential feelings of helplessness. Love and adoration lavished on such a parental substitute might also reflect Oedipus and Electra complexes, hence the sexual imagery, and also the childish belief that the remote uncaring parent can be wooed through elaborate demonstrations of affection and obedience. From a sociological perspective, *Bhakti* might be interpreted as an expression of the need for allegiance to some higher power whose perceived greatness lends vicarious status to devotees, thus compensating in many ways for the disappointments and hardships they may experience in real life (cf. exaggerated allegiance to football clubs, pop stars, political parties, and dictators). In addition, the very act of *Bhakti* may arouse pleasurable feelings. Durkheim (1915) saw all religion as arising from what he called "collective effervescence," an intense outpouring of emotions which strengthen social bonds. Membership of groups engaged in such collective effervescence also appears to increase the self-esteem of the individuals concerned (Carlton-Ford, 1992), and may induce a sense of euphoria not dissimilar from that produced by mood-altering narcotics.

Plausible as these various explanations are, we must once again introduce a note of caution. External similarities between patterns of behavior do not necessarily mean that the behaviors stem from the same source. Thus although the outer approach to the psychology of religion may see little real difference between the behavior of the *Bhakti* and that of camp followers everywhere, the inner approach may reveal that in at least some cases the motivation is quite different. Mention can be made again of the spiritual autobiography of St. Teresa of Avila, and we can also draw similar attention to the autobiographies of other holy men and women such as St. Therese of Lisieux (1977). Such writings can be dismissed as the work of authors driven to displace their human wish for love onto imaginary spiritual beings, but once again this raises the danger that those who have not had the profound and unusual experiences described by the respective authors nevertheless claim superior expertise in understanding and explaining them – and in understanding and explaining the compassionate and saintly behaviors to which the experiences give rise.

## Jnana Yoga

*Jnana Yoga* is the yoga of knowledge (cf. Western *gnosis*), and in particular the yoga of intuitive knowledge, of insights into the meaning and nature of reality and of the spiritual dimension. *Jnana Yoga* typically requires two things from followers, firstly assiduous study of sacred writings, and secondly profound contemplation of the themes contained in these writings, thus opening the way for the appropriate insights to occur. Although religious movements may be looked upon by skeptics as naive and misguided, there is in fact a powerful tradition of scholarship running through the best known of them. This tradition was one of the mainstays of learning in Europe and Asia for many centuries, giving rise not just to metaphysical speculation but to many of the leading strands in philosophy from Plato to Whitehead. It also played an important role in the development of the various esoteric and mystery movements that flourished in the Mediterranean basin during the Hellenic period and, often in disguised form, still persist into the present day (see e.g. Meyer, 1987). With their intricate models of the Cosmos and of the human personality, with their esoteric hierarchical systems of contemplative practices – for example those of the Hebrew and Christian Kabbalists (Scholem, 1974) – and with their secretive studies into astrology and alchemy, these movements provided insights into the workings of the mind which are still of interest to many modern psychologists (e.g. Jung, 1968).

Hindu practitioners of *Jnana Yoga* insist that one of the insights to which it gives rise is that the entire manifest universe is transitory and unreal, and that behind, above, and beyond it there is an absolute reality which is permanent and knowable. Ordinary factual knowledge of the material world tells us only about things that are impermanent, and nothing about this absolute reality. Those who wish to follow the *Jnana* path (the *Jnanamarga*) are thus instructed that the intensive study and contemplation necessary must be undertaken with detachment from this manifest world, and with the clarity of thought needed to overcome every form of ignorance (Vivekananda, 1955).

A second insight is that this absolute reality (*Brahman* for the Hindus, *Sunyata* or emptiness for the Buddhists, *Ain Soph* for the Kabbalists) is the essence of all that exists, from the gods to the smallest grain of sand. Therefore it is also the fundamental reality of our own being. The *Chandogya Upanishad* contains a refrain that is much revered in Hinduism, namely "That is reality, That is the self (the *Atman*), That are you." The *Brihadaranyake Upanishad* puts it even more directly, "I am the *Brahman*," a statement which bears comparison with that of Christ "I and the Father are one" (John 10:30), and with the sayings of Christian mystics such as Eckhart ". . . God is nowhere so truly as in the soul, and . . . in the inmost soul, in the summit of the soul" (Walshe, 1979).

Hume (1971), one of the translators of the Hindu scriptures, observes that when a culture has attained a certain stage of mental development, it must undertake to "construe the world of experience as a rational whole". This undertaking is behind not only *Jnana Yoga* but also the whole of Western scientific inquiry. Thus although the methods used in *Jnana Yoga* are different from the scientific method, their aim is similar, namely to discover the reality behind the world of appearances. Both *Jnana Yoga* and scientific rationalism recognize that the world as experienced by the senses is not the "thing in itself" and must be probed and dissected if we wish to find this "thing". In addition to exploring the outer world in an attempt to find the divine reality from which the world of appearances arises, those who follow the *Jnana Yoga* path endeavor to discover the real person (the *Atman)* behind the physical form. The physical form manifestly ages and dies, and the search is for that something that is unaffected by this physical decay.

Failing to find this "something" by observing the physical form, the early *Jnana* sages turned the search for the nonphenomenal constituents of the self inwards, using the method of introspection. Generally Hindu thinkers (and others from Eastern traditions) have regarded the findings of inner experience as equally valid to the data yielded by external observation – in some ways even more valid, as introspection provides direct experience of mental phenomena whereas external observation yields only sensorially modified information of the phenomena of the outer world. The result of their introspection was the conviction that our real nature is not the physical form in any of its manifestations – nor is it the mind, the intellect, or the ego as a whole. Not only can it not be perceived by the senses, it cannot be known in states of ordinary consciousness. They took the view that although consciousness is a characteristic of the *Atman*, and that wherever consciousness exists the *Atman* is present, the *Atman* cannot be *known* through ordinary consciousness. It can only be directly experienced by stripping away the transitory levels of consciousness by which it is normally obscured. Thus when, as in meditation, the individual remains conscious without being conscious of any particular thing (a state described in Buddhism as "content-less awareness"), then consciousness is experienced pure and complete in itself, without the limits imposed by conceptual thought and by space-time. At this moment, the *Atman* is one with *Brahman*, the very ground of its being and its own absolute nature.

Such ideas as these raise a particular problem for the psychologist of religion. If the *Atman* (which we might translate by the rather vague term "spirit") can only be experienced through introspective methods – in particular deep meditation – then it lies beyond the reach of normal inquiry. *Jnana Yoga* thus appears to be asking those who have never experienced these deeper levels of consciousness to accept the existence of the *Atman* on trust. The practitioner of *Jnana Yoga* would counter this problem by insisting that through the contemplation of sacred writings and through meditation everyone can experience, even if only momentarily, their own consciousness free from the presence of thoughts. This experience, they insist, leads to a realization that the statement "I am conscious therefore I am" contains more truth than does the Cartesian "I think therefore I am" (Nielsen *et al.*, 1988). It is true that in these brief thought-free moments we may still be conscious of physical sensations, so such moments cannot be said to represent the "content-less awareness" that is supposedly the full experience of oneself as *Atman* or as pure spirit. Nevertheless, they help us recognize the ever-shifting nature of normal conscious experience, and demonstrate to us that we are not our thoughts, and that consciousness is still present even when empty of thinking.

After many years of virtual neglect, psychology is once more taking an interest in consciousness (e.g. Velmans, 2000), as is philosophy (e.g. Searle, 1989). One aspect of this interest has been an extraordinary upsurge of research into meditation. Murphy and Donovan (1990) list no fewer than 1,300 research reports on meditation produced between

1931 and 1990, and in subsequent years much further work has been reported (e.g. Tart, 1989 and 1994; Murphy, 1992; Benson, 1996; Murphy and Donovan, 1997; Fontana, 1998; Andresen, 2000). The purpose and consequences of meditational practices will be looked at in detail later in the book, but the reports given by long-term meditators of their psychological experiences show remarkable consistency, a fact which it is claimed renders the area increasingly susceptible to scientific analysis and comment (Wilber, 1998; Andresen, 2000).

In the course of their own investigations over many centuries, *Jnana Yoga* sages claimed to identify four states of consciousness. Firstly there is what is called the ordinary waking consciousness, in which we carry out our dealings with the outer world. Secondly there is dreaming consciousness, an inward state in which we continue to experience an apparently physical world, but one which is in fact subtle and phantasmal. Thirdly, there is the state of dreamless sleep, in which our consciousness of worldly things vanishes, and in which we experience none of the limits or boundaries imposed by the world of form. Finally, there is the ultimate state, which is blissful consciousness of and in itself, without awareness of any object, and in which there remains only the total peace of the *Atman*.

The sages who tell us these things also claim it is possible to remain conscious not only during the first state of consciousness but throughout each of the remaining three. That is, they are conscious of the fact that they are dreaming when dreaming (an ability now recognized by Western dream researchers and referred to as "lucid dreaming" – see e.g. LaBerge, 1986 and LaBerge and Rheingold, 1990), conscious of the fact they are dreamless when dreamless (i.e. conscious that I – the sleeper – am aware of feelings of bliss – the object), and conscious in the fourth and ultimate state, where all sense of "I" as subject and of anything else as object disappears and there is only the unity of the true Self. This unbroken flow of consciousness is also reported by practitioners of Western mystical systems such as the Kabbalah (Regardie, 1972) and by experienced meditators (Wilber, 1999).

The first three levels of consciousness are seen by *Jnana Yoga* as in effect veils which obscure from individuals the experience of the fourth state, which is who we really are. The aim of *Jnana Yoga*, and of the spiritual life in general, is said to be to remove these veils. This does not mean the abolition of the three more superficial levels of consciousness. Normal waking consciousness, dreaming and nondreaming consciousness are all still required, but these states can be entered with the knowledge that they are simply ways of allowing the real self, the fourth state, to operate in the material world.

The experience of the *Atman* in this fourth state is said by those who claim to have experienced it to bring not only total peace, but also actual awareness of the fact that *Atman* and *Brahman* are one, an observation analogous both to that of Eckhart and other Christian mystics when they speak of the oneness between the soul and the Godhead (Forman, 1991), and to the unity between the Buddha mind and Nirvana expressed in the *Nirvana Sutra* (Suzuki, 1979).

The similarity in this respect between the mystical teachings of these three traditions is of particular interest to the psychologist. In a letter to Freud, Rolland described the fourth state as an "oceanic feeling," and considered it to be the true source of all religious sentiment. Freud, who failed to find evidence of this feeling in himself, attributed it not to any innate religious disposition but to a regression to "an early phase of ego-feeling" (Freud, 1930), specifically regression to the experience of the infant at the breast in the days before the ego is distinguished from the external world. Thus memories of the feelings of unity and bliss experienced by the child during breast feeding resurface in the case of mystics, and are misinterpreted by them as an experience of unity with the Absolute.

There are several problems with this Freudian interpretation. In the first place it is unsupported by research evidence, even by that arising from introspection. We have no idea what the infant is actually feeling while at the breast. His/her behavior suggests a contented, survival-related response, but this gives little warrant to suppose a parallel with the reported experiences of fourth-state unitary consciousness. Secondly, there is even less warrant for supposing that when the mind reaches this fourth state, a state whose attainment reportedly requires long and dedic-ated practice, it experiences an automatic identification with an early, prelinguistic experience at the maternal breast. Wilber (1998) refers to this kind of supposition as the "pre/trans fallacy," that is as a confusion between the undifferentiated experience of the infant (who has never experienced differentiation), and the unified experience of the meditator and the mystic (who have experienced differentiation and now reportedly recognize it as illusory). He points out that "Freud tended to take all genuine transrational (i.e. unitary consciousness) experiences and reduce them to prerational infantilisms (to primary Narcissism, oceanic dissoci-ation, preambivalent oral stage, and so on)." Incidentally, Wilber also notes that the pre/trans fallacy can operate in the opposite direction, by naively elevating prerational childhood experiences and mistaking them for the transrational level.

The third problem with the Freudian explanation is that if fourth-state unitary consciousness is identified with the feeling enjoyed by the infant at the breast, then we have once more preferred an explanation offered by someone who on his own admission has never experienced an "oceanic feeling" to the explanations given over many centuries by those who have. It might be said that since both sets of explanation are unscientific in the sense that they do not arise from public events, then we are free to plump for whichever we prefer (or to reject both). However, collecting reports of their experiences from subjects and analyzing them for differences and similarities is legitimate science. Science is concerned with the systematization of ascertained knowledge, and in the case of fourth-state unitary consciousness experiences this means assembling a database from extant reports and studying them for similarities and differences. Should there be sufficient similarities, explanation, however tentative, can be attempted.

In addition, science has at its disposal physiological measurements of the brain states of those who report themselves able to reach the fourth state. Results (Wallace, 1970; Wallace and Benson, 1972) suggest that a range of physiological changes take place while in this state, and that each of the four states of consciousness, from the normal waking state to state four, show characteristic brain signature patterns. These and more recent findings are dealt with more fully in the next section, but the evidence is at least sufficiently strong to demonstrate that meditation is distinct from ordinary fantasizing, from daydreaming, and from hypnotic trance. It can rightly be argued that the physiological changes registered by the EEG do not and cannot confirm that the meditator is indeed experiencing the claimed fourth state. But the same can be said for all the states correlated with distinctive EEG signatures. Having observed these signatures, the scientist relies upon the reports given by subjects of their mental states at the time. This is not regarded as a major difficulty in most circumstances. Consensus among the reports can be regarded as indicative of a significant level of reliability.

Taken together with the findings from EEG research, it seems that at the very least the consistent reports offered by *Jnana Yoga* practitioners over the years of the nature of fourth-state consciousness merit attention by the psychologist. Rolland may or may not have been correct in suggesting to Freud that this state is the basis for all religion, but the emphasis placed upon the attainment of this state by *Jnana Yoga* and by *Raja Yoga* (which we look at next) indicates that religious belief and behavior cannot be adequately understood without taking it into proper account.

## Raja Yoga

A discussion of *Raja Yoga* follows logically from what has just been said, as *Raja Yoga* is the yoga specifically directed toward the control of the mind in order to attain the fourth state. It is sometimes said that all the yogas considered in this chapter begin at the level of *Hatha*, the yoga of the body, and end with *Raja*, the supreme yoga of the mind (Slater, 1968). The principles of *Raja Yoga* were set out in the *Yoga Sutras* around the second century BCE, reputedly by the sage Patanjali, although authorship remains uncertain. The *Yoga Sutras* claim that *Raja Yoga* allows the practitioner progressively to master the various elements of his or her own nature, particularly and progressively the physical body, the active will, and the observing mind. Once mastery is achieved, the practitioner attains the spiritual perfection of the fourth state.

Patanjali's *Yoga Sutras* comprise one of the most sacred texts in the Hindu tradition. Various acceptable English translations exist (Prabhavananda and Isherwood, 1953, and Goodall, 1996, are among the more accessible). They are still held by scholars of Eastern religions to constitute one of the most comprehensive courses of spiritual development extant, although other Eastern spiritual traditions also have systems of yoga involving body work, breathing exercises, and concentration/meditation practices (Luk, 1970; Anderson, 1979; Chang, 1980). Based, tradition has it, upon his own first-hand experiences (Whiteman, 1993), Patanjali's *Sutras* set out eight graded *ashtanga* (limbs – usually translated as "steps") on the path of spiritual development, and these are worth listing for their psychological content, together with brief descriptions as to their meaning.

Step 1:  *Yama* – Self-restraint, control over the appetites and desires of the physical body, allowing the practitioner to turn more attention toward the mind.

Step 2:  *Niyama* – Self-discipline, which includes the moral and ethical restraints said to be essential if the higher levels of yogic practices are to be attempted in safety.

Step 3:  *Asana* – Physical discipline, including the postures of *Hatha* yoga, and in particular postures that allow the body to remain balanced and centered during meditation.

Step 4:  *Pranayama* – Control of the breathing. The tradition has persisted that life came into being through the breath of the Creator, and that the act of breathing therefore brings one close to one's own essence. Certain rhythmic practices of breath inhalation, retention and expulsion (warned as highly physically and psychologically dangerous unless performed under the direction of an experienced teacher) are said to give rise to luminous inner experiences, seen as a positive step toward the fourth state of consciousness.

Step 5:  *Pratyahara* – Control of the senses. The senses are withdrawn from the external world, so that consciousness can be focussed exclusively and intensively inwards.

Step 6:   *Dharana* – Control over the powers of concentration. The attention is steadied so that it can be focussed inwardly for long periods on a chosen object (e.g. a sacred image or an imaginary lotus within the heart).

Step 7:   *Dhyana* – Control over the powers of meditation. In the Hindu yogic tradition often a mantra – a sacred sound – is used as the focus, and the meditation is developed until the awareness of individual selfhood nears extinction.

Step 8:   *Samadhi* – An untranslatable term which refers to the fourth state of unitary consciousness in which the practitioner experiences what is described as his/her oneness with – or identity with – what is variously referred to by such terms as the Divine, the Absolute, *Brahman*, the Ground of Our Being, the Source, the Self, Infinite Potential, Unitary Consciousness, Emptiness, the One, the Godhead, Nirvana. The experience is said to be beyond the conceptual thought of the other three states of consciousness, and therefore impossible to put accurately into words.

The eight steps thus progress from physical and ethical restraint, body work and breath work to an increasingly focussed form of inner concentration. The psychologist may propose that what happens during this inner concentration is that the practitioner progressively excludes all external stimuli and enters, in *samadhi*, a state of extreme dissociation. In this state he or she becomes highly suggestible to the fictional being believed to be symbolized by the sacred image or mantra which is the focus of concentration, and experiences, through association, something of the ecstatic emotions thought to be a feature of this being. The weakness in this proposal is that whereas dissociation is relatively easy to achieve, *samadhi* is said to be attained only after many years of intensive practice. A further weakness is that *samadhi* is accompanied by physiological changes that are much more striking and unusual than those associated with dissociation. A number of studies using fMRI, PET, and SPECT, as well as EEG under well-controlled conditions testify to these changes and to the extraordinary control over both body and mind which appears to be associated with them (see e.g. Murphy, 1992 for a summary; also Murphy and White, 1995; Murphy and Donovan, 1997; Newburg and d'Aquili; and Andresen, 2000). One of the most interesting of these changes is the continuous production of delta brain rhythms. Wilber (1999) refers to evidence that demonstrates his own ability to produce continuous maximum delta rhythms (normally associated only with deep dreamless sleep) in both brain hemispheres while in *samadhi*, and continuous delta and theta (the latter normally associated with dreaming sleep) rhythms in both hemispheres on switching to a mantra visualization practice.

There are three things of particular interest about these physiological changes. Firstly they suggest that deep levels of inner concentration with attendant changes in mentation are indeed taking place. Secondly, they seem to indicate that, without the aid of biofeedback equipment, it is possible for impressive levels of control to be achieved over the autonomic nervous system and over brain and body functions. Thirdly, they place on record the extraordinary levels of commitment, typically with little or no material reward, that the individuals concerned are prepared to demonstrate in order to acquire these levels of concentration and of physical and mental control. This must raise questions as to the motivation of these individuals, and as to the identity of the reinforcers that sustain this motivation over long periods of time, and in the face of highly demanding physical practices on the one hand, and low levels of obvious mental stimulation on the other. Wilber, one of the few Western researchers who has reported first-hand experience of fourth-state consciousness, tells us that it was achieved only after 25 years of dedicated and consistent meditation practices (Wilber, 1999). It would thus seem that the practitioners concerned have a very strong desire for spiritual progress, and obtain high levels of reinforcement from the inner experiences that arise as a result of their efforts.

One thing is seemingly clear. Interesting and potentially very important psychological states are reported – and accompanied by measurable physiological changes – to take place as a result of following Patanjali's eight *ashtangas* or similar practices. These cannot be ignored by psychology, in particular by the psychology of religion. In view of this, it is appropriate to gather data from those who have experienced these states, using person-centered research methods. These measures should include, as Wilber suggests (Wilber, 1998):

- recording the physiological changes that accompany reported fourth-state experiences;
- looking for consistency in these changes across the practitioners who report these experiences;
- seeking correlations between types of experience and attendant physiological changes;
- establishing the level of agreement among practitioners on the nature of these experiences;
- interpreting conclusions in the light not only of Western theories of mind but also in that of the theories advanced by the traditions that developed the practices leading to these experiences.

# CHAPTER 7 ⸺

# Spirituality and the Brain

## Frontal Lobes and the God Spot

In recent years, advances in brain research involving in particular the detailed mapping of functions of large areas of the cerebral cortex, have also led to insights into the claimed spiritual dimension. Following on from earlier work by Persinger (Cook and Persinger, 1985; Persinger, 1996), Ramachandran has demonstrated that when individuals are exposed to evocatively religious or spiritual words or ideas, the electrical activity in their temporal lobes increases to a level comparable to that experienced during epileptic seizures (Ramachandran and Blakeslee, 1998). Epileptic seizures are known to be associated with subsequent reports that appear similar to some mystical experiences if not to actual fourth-state consciousness, experiences such as visions of what are described as divine lights, insights into incommunicable ultimate truths, feelings of oneness with the Creator, and moments of intense rapture. Ramachandran also shows that stimulation of various areas of the temporal lobes with magnetic field activity appears to evoke a range of these mystical-type experiences in normal subjects. Reports of these experiences include accounts of quasi shamanic journeys to otherworlds, experiences with UFOs, supposed regressions to past lives etc., and Persinger, Ramachandran, and their colleagues have rather fancifully labeled this area of the temporal lobes the "God Spot" or the "God Module".

This research is still controversial, and requires extensive replication by others before we can say that temporal lobe activity is involved in the experiences reported across cultures and through the centuries and labeled as spiritual. Even then, use of terms such as the "God Spot" and the "God Module" does not mean in any sense that the research proves the existence or nonexistence of God or of the gods, or the possibility or impossibility of communion between the human mind and divine consciousness. Nor does it prove that spiritual experiences originate in the brain as opposed to a nonmaterial mind, which then works through the brain. But if the "God Spot" (to persist with the term) has indeed evolved to serve some spiritual purpose, as the researchers suggest, then we are bound to ask what is this purpose, and why should the brain have evolved the capacity for it?

Persinger (1987) concludes that "the God Experience is an artifact of transient changes in the temporal lobe," and that it represents an adaptive mechanism that compensates for the human capacity to anticipate future aversive stimuli, such as death. The answer suggested by Zohar and Marshall (2000) is that the God Spot appears to be linked to what they call "spiritual intelligence," which they describe as the ability to be creative, to alter the boundaries of current thought and of situations, to recontextualize experience and to transform our understanding of it, to temper existing laws and rules with understanding and compassion, to allow the mind to create and contemplate infinite possibilities, to address problems of good and evil, to exercise extended choice, to seek for higher meaning in life, and to transform both the self and life situations in positive ways. Certain of these abilities do not appear to have evolved in the service of species survival, yet their very ubiquity implies that they have a function of some value to human psychology.

## The Concept of Spiritual Intelligence

Zohar and Marshall take the view that the God Spot may help us to make choices between life paths, to place our actions and our lives in a wider, richer, and more meaningful context, and to "plug us into meaning and value in an accessible way, cause[s] us to strive, give[s] us a sense of purpose, a sense of context." As such they see spiritual intelligence as complementing cognitive intelligence quotient (IQ) and the emotional intelligence quotient (EQ) popularized by Goleman (Goleman, 1996), and are even prepared to talk of a spiritual intelligence quotient (SQ). For followers of religions this view may well be an attractive one, but Zohar and Marshall have not as yet demonstrated any direct link between the God Spot and spiritual intelligence. In particular there is no hard evidence that the forms of thinking which they include in their spiritual intelligence activate those areas of the brain associated with the God Spot.

Even if the thesis of spiritual intelligence proves sustainable, this still does not tell us what evolutionary advantage SQ actually confers upon the human race. It is known that the frontal lobes, where the God Spot is located, evolved at a very late stage of human development, which indicates that the human race survived well enough without them. In other mammals these lobes are still only rudimentary, which provides further indication that they play no obvious role in physical survival. From the description given by Zohar and Marshall, the God Spot would seem in fact to be concerned more with the *quality* of human life than with the fact of physical survival, and to be closely linked to the generation of altruism. Evidence for the existence of altruism does in fact coincide with the very earliest archaeological evidence for spiritual beliefs. Neanderthal hominids some 60,000 years ago buried what have been identified as joints of food and flint weapons beside their dead (Hawkes, 1965), indicating not only some conception of an afterlife but also concern for the safe passage of those entering into it. In addition, they appear to have cared for members of the group after their physical incapacity. Solecki (1971 and 1977) reports discovering in excavations at the Shanidar Caves in Iraq the bones of two Neanderthal men who had apparently been kept alive by their fellows after suffering severe disabilities. One had a spear wound in his rib cage which would have required nursing care in order to ensure his survival, and the other was so severely crippled by arthritis and by advanced years (for a Neanderthal) that he could have been in no position to make a working contribution to the life of the group. Both men appear to have been sustained by their fellows out of what looks very like simple concern. Solecki also describes floral tributes and medicinal herbs, identified through pollen analysis, placed in the grave of another of the deceased, together with evidence that a feast (ritual or celebratory) had been held around the burial.

## Altruism and Neurology

Altruism is a quality which Darwinians accept presents problems of explanation in the context of evolutionary theory (Dawkins 1979). It may lead to a readiness to sacrifice one's own life in the service of the community, which is obviously of value to species survival. But the problem is that a propensity for self-sacrifice does not enhance the survival prospects of the individual concerned. Quite the contrary. Thus his or her chances of living long enough to pass their genes on to descendants are less good than the chances of their more selfish kinsfolk for whose safety they sacrifice themselves. This being so, it is difficult to see how those with the genetic mutations that led to the evolution of the proposed God Spot and to the altruistic and other qualities associated with it (including Persinger's alleged ability to compensate for future aversive stimuli such as death) could have survived in sufficient numbers significantly to influence the gene bank of what we must assume is the entire human race.

Attempts to trace the diverse manifestations of religious belief, experience, and practice to a common set of neurological processes have in any case certain dangers. They exemplify the reductionist approach to human psychology so vigorously challenged by post-modern thinking (see e.g. Wilber, 1998, for an effective summary). They also make the assumption that if neurophysiological states in the brain correlate closely and consistently with psychological states, this demonstrates the latter states are caused by the former. This is not the place to enter deeply into the mind–brain controversy (returned to in chapter 11), beyond stressing that whatever the origins of religious experiences, we would expect these experiences to be linked to brain activity and thus to show up in physiological measurements, since even the most extreme dualistic theories have never sought to deny that the brain is the physical receptor and mediator of mental (or, in the case of religion, spiritual) input. Whether brain produces mind or mind works through brain, we would expect correlates between neurophysiology and psychology. The correlations, in and of themselves, tell us nothing conclusive about the mind–brain relationship beyond the fact that it exists.

For the scientific materialist, who theorizes that all things arise from matter, any talk of a nonphysical mind is of course anathema. Yet we still have no evidence that thoughts, imaginings, and other nonphysical activities of mind can arise from the electrochemical activity of the brain. At the level of surmise, one is still free to see mind as more than neurophysiology. Wallace (2000) reminds us that even if neuroscientists can manipulate brain processes directly to induce the perception of (for example) the color red, the red thus perceived is not the same as the red one sees when perceiving a rose. The first "is an hallucination created by an internal manipulation of the brain, with no objective referent," whereas the second "is a valid cognition of the color of something external to the brain." We could also add that the quality attaching to the two experiences is fundamentally different.

After a professional lifetime spent exploring mind and brain, the leading neurobiologist Sir John Eccles proposed that the theory that conscious experience is merely a byproduct of neural activity accounts for neither the emergence of consciousness nor its evolutionary development. Eccles (Eccles and Robinson, 1984) reminds us that according to the principles of biological evolution "mental states and consciousness could have evolved and developed *only if they were causally effective* in bringing about changes in neural happenings in the brain. . . ." Equally evident in his view is the illogicality of postulating a thoroughgoing physicalistic determinism that reduces cognitive activity (including of course the cognitive activity of the materialist scientist him or herself) to self-deception. Eccles' own preference was for a dualistic–interactionist theory which sees mind and brain as distinct from – though interactive with – each other.

The Canadian neurosurgeon Wilder Penfield, another leading expert on brain science, after many years spent espousing the monistic assumption that mind is the product of physical brain, finally arrived at the view that "It is simpler (and far easier to be logical)" if one adopts the hypothesis that mind and brain are two fundamentally different elements, each with its own energy. In his view the brain somehow "switches on" the mind during wakefulness and switches it off again during sleep. His conclusion was that "Whether there is such a thing as communication between man and God," and whether the mind can be energized by an outside source after death "is for each individual to decide for himself. Science has no such answers" (Penfield, 1975). The last sentence reminds us of the humility with which science should (but does not always) approach the mind–brain problem.

Finally, a good way to demonstrate for ourselves the distinction between mind and brain is to experience our own mind, and then try and experience our own brain. The first kind of experience is open to us all. I have yet to meet someone who claims to be able to experience the second kind.

# CHAPTER 8 ───────────────────

# The Origins of Religious Belief

## Religion as Need

Whether or not we accept that the God Spot in the frontal lobes of the brain may have evolved to facilitate spiritual experiences, historical and cross-cultural evidence suggest that humankind has a consistent and seemingly innate need to search for what might be called a higher meaning in life, that is a meaning that explains how and why we exist, whether or not we have free will to determine our own actions, and what happens to us when we die. Some indication of this need manifests itself at an early age. Piaget's work on early cognitive development (e.g. Piaget, 1967) has been criticized in recent years, but there is little disagreement with his finding that young children typically show the need to make sense not just of their personal experience but of the world itself, and manifest particular interest in questions of causality and purpose. Religion is one of the ways in which men and women have satisfied and continue to satisfy this need.

## McDougal and Religious Belief

McDougal, one of the founders of social psychology, whose interest in religious belief encompassed both inner and outer aspects of the subject, considered that the reason people find the answers supplied by religion to be satisfying is that they appeal to the three emotions of admiration, awe, and reverence (McDougal, 1950). Admiration was analyzed by McDougal into a fusion of wonder and negative self-feeling, awe into a fusion between admiration and fear, and reverence into a blend of awe and tenderness. Thus McDougal considered that the impetus – which he saw as innate – to search for meaning and to find satisfaction in religion arises from a combination of wonder, negative self-feeling, fear, and tenderness. Drawing upon historical and anthropological data, McDougal saw fear as one of the first of these emotions to manifest itself. In fact the search for meaning – in the form of curiosity – arises in his view when primitive societies develop sufficiently to manifest a concern with those experiences that arouse fear. Beneficent and familiar natural processes such as rain and sunshine are accepted without much questioning by such societies, but irregular and apparently capricious events such as floods, famine, and death initially arouse fear and subsequently the desire to identify the forces and the reasons responsible for them. From this desire it is a relatively small step to personifying these forces and to experiencing negative self-feeling in the face of their power and grandeur, and to attempting to propitiate them and gain their favor through ritualized customs such as prayer, sacrifice, and material offerings of various kinds.

The thoroughness and scholarship of McDougal's approach means that his analysis of religious belief, although completed very many years ago, remains of relevance to the psychologist of religion (it is a mistake to assume that all theories in psychology over a decade old have been either disproven or superseded). He further proposed that once belief in higher forces becomes established, it serves as a powerful agency of social discipline. Any breach of the customs and observances associated with these forces is seen as bringing grave risks to the whole community, which therefore becomes collectively concerned to prevent and to punish any such breach. In the course of time, however – prompted, believers would claim, by the teachings of those who have experienced inner spiritual revelations – religious belief also comes to satisfy the individual's higher emotions, which McDougal identified as wonder, admiration and tenderness. In addition, those societies who survive in the face of famine, plague, natural disasters, and conflicts with rival societies come to see themselves as favored by the god or gods, which in turn leads to feelings toward divinity of gratitude and devotion. When nonbelievers from alien societies are observed to prosper, and when wickedness within one's own society is seen to go unpunished, the belief develops that retribution will nevertheless be meted out in the afterlife in the form of hellfire and its attendant demons.

Along with hellfire comes the belief, McDougal argued, that one must observe religious teachings not only to benefit the community but also to benefit oneself. Even actions performed in private – including eventually one's unspoken thoughts – are perceived as known to the divine intelligence, and therefore become part of the record upon which one will be judged after death, thus making this judgment a very stringent affair. For example, the ancient Egyptians represented such judgment as the act of weighing the heart of the dead person against a feather. Those who passed the test were admitted into the presence of Osiris, and proceeded into the divine world to adore the gods. Those who failed were given to Ammit, the crocodile-headed god who devoured their sin-laden hearts (Faulkner, 1985). McDougal saw this process – firstly of duty to the community and society in general, and secondly of duty to oneself – as the foundation of moral and ethical behavior, which he defined as the control of impulse in accordance with accepted patterns of conduct and in obedience to the strictures and sanctions of human and divine law.

If McDougal was correct, we must suppose that the reason that religious belief has persisted even after science has provided material explanations for those natural phenomena that aroused fear in earlier times is in part the need to identify some sense of meaning in life and death, and to satisfy emotions of admiration, awe, and reverence. The combination of cognitive and affective satisfaction offered by religious belief thus appears to be a compelling psychological mixture. Many people seem able to satisfy these cognitive and affective needs through the adulation of earthly celebrities such as political, media, royal, and sporting personalities, and even through such nebulous concepts as country and nationhood and even scientific dogmas. Nevertheless, despite the decline in formal religious observance among Western cultures, many in the West still find religious answers to be the most satisfying. For example, Gallup and Proctor (1983) produce figures indicating that in the United States religious belief holds steady at around two-thirds of the adult population, while a major survey by the Princeton Religion Research Center (1996) reveals that 96 percent of the population of the United States sampled in 1994 believed in God or a higher power, 90 percent believed in heaven, and 79 percent in miracles. In addition, 90 percent admitted to praying, often more than once a day, while 43 percent had attended church in the last seven days. Figures such as these hardly suggest that religion is in decline, at least in the United States. Interestingly, the figures suggest that religious belief and practice is by no means confined to those who go to church, which may indicate that this belief is based in their case more upon inner conviction than upon outer doctrine.

Finally, McDougal drew attention to the fact that throughout the development of the various religious traditions there have always been men who, without rejecting the notion of a spiritual dimension, have taken their search for meaning outside orthodox boundaries. Such men, who he refers to as the wizards, the medicine-men, the alchemists, and the astrologers, have been consistently persecuted by the purveyors of orthodoxy, but they have sought not only to increase their understanding of natural forces, but actually to discover ways of bringing a direct influence to bear upon them.

## Psychodynamic Theories and Religious Belief

With their interest in the deeper workings of the mind, psychodynamic psychologists have also taken a keen interest in the psychology of religion and spirituality. Freud (e.g. 1930, 1959; Freud and Pfister, 1963) and Jung (1934, 1955, 1969, 1978) in particular recognized the great importance that religious beliefs, for whatever reason, played in the lives of many of their clients. In the light of their concern with the archetypal and myth-making quality of mind, they also considered that the need for religious belief appeared to be innate, arising from deep unconscious levels of the mind.

Freud (1927) took a negative view of this belief, arguing that all forms of religion are the expression of an illusion, a wish-fulfillment of "the oldest, strongest, and most urgent wishes of mankind," a response to the feeling of human helplessness which has its origins in ". . . the terrifying impression of helplessness in childhood (which) aroused the need for protection – for protection through love – which was provided by the father." As this feeling of helplessness endures throughout life, it makes it necessary for adults "to cling to the existence of a father, but this time (of) a more powerful one," namely God. The religious emotions that serve further to bolster this belief are nothing more than regressions "to an early phase of ego-feeling". Freud went further, identifying similarities between religious rituals and the rituals practiced by obsessional neurotics, concluding (1907) that this identification allows us to "regard obsessional neurosis as a pathological counterpart of the formation of a religion, and to describe that neurosis as an individual religiosity, and religions as universal obsessional neurosis."

Freudians consider that the fact people also turn to a god in their search for meaning is simply another example of their need for a substitute father, with all the authority and the supposed wisdom of a father, to help them cope with life's many uncertainties. However, Freudian suppositions leave us no wiser as to why people should find the answers supplied by religion not only emotionally satisfying but also existentially convincing, nor does it approach the question whether or not the things which religion teaches have any truth in them. To argue that people believe in things for the wrong reason does not demonstrate that there are no right reasons for such belief. Freud's theory also fails to address the question why illusory feelings of comfort are sufficient to motivate the extraordinary deeds associated with religion, from art, architecture, literature, and music to self-sacrifice, martyrdom, warfare, and elevated moral philosophies. The God-as-infantile-father-substitute theory has in any case been tested by a number of authorities and found wanting. Nelson and Jones (1957) and Nelson (1971), looking for correlations between concepts of God and those respectively for father and mother, found greater correlations with mother than with father, while Vergote and Tamayo (1981) established that among six cultural groups (including Roman Catholic seminarians) God was associated more with maternal qualities – particularly that of availability – than with paternal ones of authority and law giving.

## Object–Relations Theories of Religious Belief

The emphasis upon the role of the mother rather than the father in influencing religious belief was in fact stressed by Winnicott (1953), one of the pioneers of what came to be called object–relations theories. In Winnicott's view a devoted mother presents the infant with a range of need-satisfying items such as the breast, and when the child first becomes aware of his/her separate existence he/she starts to "hallucinate" (imagine) these items, with the result that when they appear the child perceives them as his/her own creation. As development progresses, the child goes on to substitute various comforting "transitional objects" such as soft toys and blankets for these items. Winnicott's suggestions is that in due course the concept of God comes to provide a further transitional object, which can only be outgrown when and if the individual is able recognize the realities of an uncontrollable world.

A more comprehensive theory relating religion to relationships is advanced by Guntrip (1969 and 1971), whose orientation toward religion was typically positive. Guntrip, with other object–relationship theorists, held that all human beings share an absolute need to relate fully and positively to an environment that they feel is beneficially related in turn to themselves. This is particularly true in the realm of human relationships. Bad human relationships, particularly in the early years of life, lead the individual either to deny this absolute need (*schizoid denial*) or to feel self-blame and guilt for the failure of these relationships (*depressive reaction*).

For Guntrip, religion represents the saving power of the good object relationship, a refuge for the anxious soul which provides a sense of connectedness to the ultimate, all-embracing reality of the universe. However, the immature neurotic orientations of both the schizoid and the depressive personality inevitably result in some distortions. The schizoid personality (a term which indicates the individual has certain traits in common with the schizophrenic, but does not imply the presence of schizophrenia), with its aloof denial of its own need for love, may vehemently reject religion embedded as it is in emotionality and relationships, and retreat into the cold nonthreatening world of scientific atheism, or may adopt religion only as an intellectualized philosophy of life rather than as what Guntrip calls "a passionate, loving devotion".

By contrast the ambivalent and moody depressive personality, who has directed his/her anger at the failure of early relationships inwards into punitive self-hatred, will bring to religion a conviction of personal sinfulness and a belief in the need to be "saved". Guntrip suggests that many of the religious fanatics and fundamentalist preachers given to such dark warnings of hellfire, are probably depressives who find some relief from self-castigation by attacking the perceived sins of others. Inquisitors, crusaders, and holy warriors who brought torture, fire, and sword to the conversion of others may also have been depressives who found some escape from their own painful awareness of sin by acting with aggressive savagery toward others in the name of God. Experimental support for this aspect of Guntrip's object–relations theory comes from findings by Gallemore, Wilson, and Rhoads (1969) that 52 percent of their emotionally disturbed patients reported conversion experiences as compared to 20 percent of controls. However, full-scale depression, which typically brings with it a sense of hopelessness and apathy, generally leads to a decline in religiosity (Hole, 1977).

Object–relations theories throw further light on how early experiences of relationships can color attitudes toward religion. They differ from Freudian theories, however, in that they do not see religion as necessarily arising directly from the need for a parental substitute. One can either take them to support the idea that religion may be an idealized fantasy of how a perfect object relationship might be, or as arising from a profound need, whose origins lie beyond the reach of current psychological theorizing, for a relationship with the source of one's own being. Further, Guntrip's work, based upon his experience initially as a minister of religion and subsequently as a psychoanalyst, indicates how religion can be distorted by those damaged by deficiencies in early relationships with parents and caregivers. This draws attention to the extent that religion, like politics and much else, can be distorted by those with psychological problems, and to the inappropriateness of judging its truth or otherwise by the behavior of the individuals concerned.

Further evidence that concepts of God appear to be determined more by the nature of the individual's interactions with his or her parents than from the search for fantasy parental substitutes comes from a wide-ranging study designed to study modes of relating to divinity by Spiro and D'Andrade (1958). Findings indicated that individuals who were indulged by parents in early childhood, with signs of need such as crying automatically eliciting nurturing responses, predominantly think of God as someone whose help is contingent upon compulsive rituals. If, however, parental assistance was obtained in childhood only by active solicitation,

God is later conceived as responding to propitiatory rituals, which coax him into giving attention. Finally, if parental nurturing was given without the need for solicitation, the individual comes to see divine help as requiring neither ritual nor obedience. Similar findings, based upon ethnographic reports from 62 widely scattered societies, are detailed by Lambert, Triandis, and Wolf (1959).

Taken together, these various findings suggest that although conceptions of God are in part determined by early relationships with parents, this is very different from accepting that God is nothing but a father or mother substitute. Many of our concepts of people and things, to say nothing of our relationships with them, are determined in large measure by the parenting we receive in early childhood, but the existence or nonexistence of the people and things concerned is independent of these concepts. There are obvious dangers in confusing concepts with the phenomena to which they relate.

There are other dangers if we try to use generalizations from Western psychology to explain the reasons for religious belief in other cultures. The relationships with parents that young Hindus, Jains and Buddhists enjoy with parents in India and the Far East are very different from the relationships experienced by children in the West. Thus Freudian and object–relations explanations for religious belief – if they apply outside the consulting room – may only be relevant to Western cultures. Religious observance in India and in the Far East is far more widespread and far more integrated into daily behavior than it is in the West. To assume that theories based upon Western clinical experience are applicable to these other cultures would be to take up a position based upon surmise and speculation and very little else.

## Ego Defense, Religious Belief, and the Fear of Death

Another Freudian explanation of religious belief is that it is a culturally conditioned ego defense mechanism (Spiro, 1978), adopted like other defense mechanisms in order to cope with psychological conflicts that would otherwise lead to the development of neuroses (Freud, 1923) – such as the conflict between the survival instinct and the knowledge that death is inevitable. Like other defense mechanisms, it proves particularly tenacious because its adherents are typically unconscious of the real reasons for their belief. Such an argument is certainly plausible, but it does not address the reported instances of people who succumb to religious belief only after profound and often sudden and unexpected personal experiences. Some of these experiences may be in response to the persuasive charisma of evangelical preachers, or to the careful arguments of theologians. But others are described as intensely personal, and may involve mystical or semi-mystical occurrences such as an awareness of universal love, of timelessness, of harmony order and unity, of wholeness, even of spiritual presences and of visions of the divine (Zukav, 1991; Grosso, 1997; Deikman, 2000; Wiebe, 2000). Many of the people reporting these experiences even claim to reach religious belief only with the greatest reluctance, prompted by what they take to be insurmountable – and not necessarily welcome – direct evidence (Robinson, 1977).

The nature of ego defense mechanisms, at least in the form in which Freud conceptualized them, is in itself open to debate (Lee and Herbert, 1970), and in their exhaustive and relatively positive study of the scientific evidence for Freudian theory, Fisher and Greenberg (1985) identify nothing to support the argument that ego defense is responsible for belief in an afterlife or indeed for any aspect of religious thinking. Additionally, although Freud considered that the consequence of a breakdown in ego defense is the development of neurosis, there is no compelling evidence that those who lose their religious belief are significantly more subject to neurotic episodes than the rest of the population. Further, it is possible to resolve conflicts such as the fear of death by believing in an afterlife without any of the trappings of organized religion, and it is equally possible to reject the possibility of an afterlife while professing religious affiliation. The national survey conducted by Gallup in the United states revealed that approximately a quarter of those identifying with Catholic and Protestant denominations expressed no belief in an afterlife (Gallup and Proctor, 1983).

There is also some doubt over the extent to which the fear of death (FOD) is a factor in bringing people to religious belief. There have been numerous studies into FOD, some involving scales designed to measure attitudes toward the subject (e.g. Spilka *et al.*, 1977), and others aimed at identifying death denial (such as that of Nelson and Cantrell, 1980). Broadly, the results yielded by such scales in the United States indicate that the majority of the population express little fear of death, at least until it is imminent, rationalizing that death is inevitable and therefore should hold no terrors. On the strength of these results it appears that most people are able to deal with the fact of their mortality in a realistic and nonthreatening way, or by putting it out of their minds, which seems to show they have little need to develop ego defenses against the subject.

Objections can also be offered to the argument that spirituality is a fantasy that compensates for the unsatisfactory nature of real life by offering hopes of another life to come. Many spiritual people have happier personal circumstances than do nonspiritual people, and thus would seem less rather than more likely to seek such compensation. In addition, on the strength of the case studies assembled by Hardy (1979), Bockmeuhl

(1990), Deere (1993 and 1996), and others, belief in an afterlife in many cases appears to *arise from* spiritual insights and practices rather than from a fear of death or a desire to escape from the realities of normal life.

However, FOD may be present as a hidden, unacknowledged fear. In an earlier investigation, Williams and Cole (1968) sought to reveal these hidden fears by monitoring physiological reactions to death-related words, while Feifel (1974) measured delay times on word association tests containing such words. Results of these investigations suggest there may indeed be a significant level of unconscious death anxiety. But we must be careful how we interpret the physiological reactions noted by Williams and Cole, as death-related words may evoke emotions other than fear for oneself. For example they may evoke anxiety if inadequate provision has been made for dependants, or worry over the safety of others, or grief at the memory of a deceased loved one, or even excitement among those for whom death holds a morbid fascination. Similar care must be taken in interpreting the response delay to death-related words noted by Feifel. Individuals may think less often about death than about the neutral words used by him in his investigation, and therefore be unable to supply associations to the former with the same rapidity as to the latter.

More interesting for present purposes is whether or not a brush with death during serious illness prompts people to turn to religion. If it does, then it might be reasonable to assume that religion is indeed a way of coping with death anxiety. However, Croog and Levine (1974), in a study of men with recent experience of heart attack, found no evidence of any effect upon religious belief. Equally pertinent is Feifel's finding during his above study that even terminal illness, during which the prospect and consequent fear of death is likely to be most apparent, does not appear to lead people toward religion (although Feifel did establish that terminally ill people who already possess religious belief report significantly less fear of death than those without such belief). Thus there seems no strong evidence that religion is particularly sought as a defense against FOD, even by those who have been or currently are close to death.

Interesting findings of a different kind are provided by Nelson and Cantrell (1980) and by Levy, Dupras, and Samson (1985) to the effect that groups reporting respectively the most and the least incidence of religious belief show significantly less FOD than do those who are intermediate between these extremes. This suggests that those with strong religious belief have lost their fear of death as a result. Swenson (1961) even found that elderly people with strong religious belief actually express themselves as looking forward to death, which they associate with happiness and reward. Possible explanations for the low incidence of FOD among those with the least incidence of religions belief are firstly that they may be particularly tough-minded in their attitude to life and therefore feel indifferent to losing it, and secondly that they regard all concern with death and an afterlife as associated with the religious belief they have so emphatically rejected.

Whatever the explanations, these various findings suggest that the theory that religious belief is to any major extent an ego defense against the fear of death is at best doubtful. However, Freud considered that God-as-protective-parent is not the only neurotic aspect of religion. He also saw religion as a defense against painful or forbidden impulses such as guilt, aggressive feelings, and sexuality. In particular he regarded religious rituals as analogous in many ways to the ritualistic behavior of obsessional neurotics, for whom ritual is frequently a way of attempting to cope with just such impulses. Some support for this view comes from findings by Dulaney and Fiske (1994) that 13 of the 25 most common symptoms of obsessive-compulsive disorder are associated with the major life-cycle rituals associated in many cultures with birth, initiation, marriage, and death. Of these 13 symptoms, seven feature much more prominently in the practices that form part of these rituals than they do in the daily working life of the communities concerned. The seven comprise fear of misfortune; fear of harming self or others; protection against such misfortune and harm; concern or disgust over bodily functions; concern with the act of passing a threshold or through an entrance; symbolic use of colors; and performance of repetitive actions. But Dulaney and Fiske reach different conclusions from those of Freud, arguing that far from being neurotic, ritual is an inborn psychological propensity, shared by all cultures, to mark life's transitions, to strengthen social relationships, to cope with misfortunes, and to respond to life's mysteries. As such it should not be confused with the ritualistic behavior of the obsessional neurotic, which is an exaggeration or hyperactivation of this propensity. Moreover, it typically proves satisfying for those involved, and is brought to a clear conclusion after which everyday life resumes, whereas the rituals of the obsessional neurotic are all too often embarrassing and perplexing for the sufferer, who is tortured by their unending and compulsive nature.

## Freud's Attitude to Religion

As in so much of his work, Freud's approach to religion reveals his ability to identify the psychological questions that we need to ask, without necessarily coming up with the right answers himself. In the absence of modern large-scale research methods, Freud drew his data from the reported experiences of his clients and the clients of his fellow psychoanalysts, and from his extensive but rather narrow knowledge of anthropology. He was not himself a religious man. In the words of his biographer Earnest Jones

(Jones, 1964), he had grown up "devoid of any belief in a God or immortality and [had apparently never] felt the need for it," and although Jones, as a vehement atheist, may have rather overstated the case, there is little doubt that Freud was unsympathetic to the existence of God or the gods. Wallace (1984) puts this lack of sympathy down to eight factors, namely his: (1) discomfort with certain mystical trends within himself; (2) ambivalence toward the Jewish tradition in which he was raised; (3) conflicts with his father; (4) extensive exposure to neurotic expressions of piety in his clients; (5) disillusionment with the Catholic nanny he had had as a child; (6) ambivalent feelings toward his infant brother Julius, who died when Freud himself was nearly two; (7) aversion to passivity, dependency, and submissiveness; and (8) his adoption of psychoanalysis as a worldview. Vitz (1988) lays particular stress upon two of these factors, namely Freud's conflicts with his father, and his desertion by a nanny who had been like a second mother to him and who had created in him a possible religious neurosis which he dealt with by dismissing religion as an illusion.

To these various points we can add Freud's belief in the superiority of science over religion; his early work with Brucke that initiated him into a belief in causality (the belief that all phenomena have identifiable causes), and his enthusiastic acceptance of Darwinism (Sulloway, 1979), with its implication that religious belief was based in large part upon myth. The combination of these various factors led Freud to ignore both the complexity of religion and its positive influence in many areas of human behavior. Nevertheless, as in many areas of psychology, he did a service to the psychology of religion by drawing attention to the potential importance of childhood influences upon religious belief, in indicating the way in which religion can sometimes be used respectively to feed feelings of guilt, to repress powerful physical and emotional drives such as sex and self-expression, to justify authority and inflexibility, and to command unquestioning obedience. He also highlighted the importance of ritual and of symbolism in religious observance, and the way in which religion can be used as an excuse for the expression of otherwise forbidden impulses such as aggression and sadism. Perhaps above all, he drew attention to the important role that religion can play in the psychological life of individuals and of groups and cultures, and in that sense can be identified as one of the principal founders of the psychology of religion.

## Jung and Religious Belief

While Freud saw religion as essentially a regression to an earlier stage of ego development, Jung (1938) saw it as an expression of aspects of consciousness that have been changed by an experience of the *numinosum* (an invisible quality or presence which Jung thought of as unconscious archetypal material) breaking through from the unconscious. Therefore far from representing regression to an infantile stage of development, religion was for Jung an expression of a natural human instinct, an instinct in fact as powerful as the instincts for sex and for aggression. In his clinical work, he concluded that from mid-life onwards the client's problem was typically religious, that is it represented an inner conflict arising from a failure fully to recognize and come to terms with the religious instinct (Jung, 1932).

> Among all my patients . . . over thirty-five . . . there has not been one whose problem in the last resort was not that of finding a religious outlook to life . . . every one of them fell ill because he had lost what the living religions . . . have given to their followers, and none of them has been really healed who did not regain this religious outlook on life.

Jung considered that for many people throughout history, the *numinosum* takes the form of a God-image which he saw as integrated into what the called the self, the ordering principle of the personality, a principle which reflects the individual's potential wholeness and prompts him or her to seek meaning in life and to undertake experiences – such as work with symbols, dreams, and rituals – that enhance that sense of meaning. Jung made clear that by "religion" he did not mean creed or doctrine, and that by "God-image" he meant the representations men and women make of God, and not the actual reality of God. God, he insisted, remains a mystery; if we knew who or what God is, then we would become God (a notion that compares interestingly with the reported experiences of certain of the mystics referred to later in this chapter).

Unlike Freud, Jung therefore saw religion as an essential aspect of human nature. We are born with a potential to experience the *numinosum* – it might be more correct to say with a need to experience the *numinosum* – within ourselves. Failure to do so leads to a failure fully to achieve individuation, that is fully to realize the self. Such realization demands that we divest ourselves of the "false wrappings of the persona on the one hand, and of the suggestive power of primordial images on the other" (Jung, 1938). Religion, although an "error" in the sense that its representations are human images and concepts rather than the mystery itself, is therefore a positive factor of psychological value. It also gives humans "assurance and strength, so that [they] may not be overwhelmed by the monsters of the universe." However, religion should progress for each individual from a submissive belief which keeps the self in an infantile mental state to a level of mature understanding, moral autonomy, and perfect freedom (Jung, 1952a).

Jung took a particular interest in religious symbols (including ancient symbols such as those that linked God to the sun), and in fact saw the whole complex range of these symbols and of religious phenomena in general as indispensable representations of archetypes that both express human wholeness and draw individuals toward this wholeness. Such symbols are generated by the collective unconscious, that aspect of the unconscious that Jung believed is part of the psychological endowment that we each inherit at birth, much as we inherit the genes for physical development. He saw the carnage and destruction of the First World War as tearing from humankind the certainties associated with centuries-old religious and social systems, and as leaving the Western world in consequence with a civilization increasingly cut off from its archetypes and dominated by materialism and the "demonic" achievements of modern science and technology. The result was the emergence of problems at base spiritual which led the masses, bereft of the old certainties and of the religious symbols associated with them, to project the neglected archetypes previously expressed through inner religious development outwards onto other groups and nations, thus transforming these archetypes into what are in effect dangerous enemies.

If he were alive today, Jung would probably recognize this projection outwards as still at work, for example in some of the so-called New Age cults and superstitions currently so popular, in some of the fanatical adherence of young and old to media, pop, and sports stars, to extreme political groups, and to fanatical religious minorities. He would also see it in the aggressive materialism and amoral professional behavior of many scientists, policy makers, and business people. Essentially, his point was that the religious instinct, like the sex instinct, must be allowed proper expression if individuals and societies are to experience full psychological health. Frustrated from this expression by the dogmas of certain religious teachers on the one hand and by materialistic–reductionist philosophies on the other, the religious instinct expresses itself in a religious or materialistic totalitarianism that prevents individuals from thinking and questioning for themselves and becoming fully conscious of their inner self.

## Jung and Eastern and Western Traditions

Jung was aware of the religious traditions of the East as well as of those of the West. Long before such books became generally known he studied texts from Buddhism and Taoism such as *The Tibetan Book of the Dead* (the *Bardo Thodol*), the *I Ching*, and *The Secret of the Golden Flower*. He also made a study of yoga and of meditation (Jung, 1969). However, he cautioned against the West abandoning its own traditions in order to adopt those of the East, seeing Eastern and Western minds as distinct from each other by virtue of seemingly irreconcilable psychological orientations. The Eastern mind he saw as introverted, with a propensity to sink into the psyche, the source of all existence, while he considered the Western mind to be more extroverted, with an urge to be lifted up into the compelling outer reality of the Wholly Other. Neither mind is fully able to understand the other. To the Westerner, the Eastern mind is antisocial and irresponsible, while to the Eastern mind the Westerner is prey to illusory perceptions and materialistic desires that chain it to the world of suffering (Jung, 1954).

Jung did not mean by this that the Westerner should not take up introverted religious practices such as meditation. Rather he or she should seek these practices within Western traditions such as Gnosticism, a movement within early Christianity based upon the belief in the individual's ability to have a direct relationship with the Divine rather than only through the priesthood, and upon a conception of the world as a battleground between positive forces of good and evil (see e.g. Pagels, 1980; O'Shea, 2000). Jung identified the ascent of the soul through the celestial spheres taught by Gnosticism as analogous to the progressive inner transformations recognized in his own system of analytical psychology. However, hampered by the paucity of Gnostic texts available in his own day, he turned from gnosticism to alchemy, recognizing it not as an immature chemistry that sought to turn base matter into gold, but as a sophisticated symbolic system of inner transformation, a representation of the archetypes of the collective unconscious and of the process of individuation (Jung, 1968).

Like the Gnostics, many alchemists were Christian, and Jung came to see in Christ's virgin birth, his crucifixion death and resurrection, and his consubstantiality with God a supreme archetype of the self. He noted that similar archetypes of gods who die young and are resurrected (e.g. Osiris, Dionysus, Mithras) exist in other Eastern and Near-Eastern traditions, representing the idea that one must die to the limited ego with which we habitually identify in order to be resurrected as the true self. Jung also noted that religious symbols such as the fish and the serpent – creatures that appear suddenly from the depths – are common to many traditions, and represent at a psychological level the emergence of archetypal material from the human unconscious into full awareness. Even the Christian Trinity he saw as psychologically symbolic, in this case of the three-stage process of maturation that is a feature of individuation. The Father symbolizes the first stage, when the psyche is in its original state of undifferentiated wholeness; the Son represents the second stage, the transformation of this original state into the individuated psyche; the Holy Spirit stands for the third, a return to the Father, but now with the reason, reflection, and discrimination gained during the second stage still intact, and supplemented by a self-critical and humble submission to a higher reality.

However, in his own psychological system, Jung saw the three-fold symbolism of the Trinity as in need of supplementation by a fourth element with which the Christian church has never come properly to terms. This element consists of what Jung called the *shadow*, a hidden or "inferior" function that represents the fallen angel, the principle of evil, the dark side of humankind, the energizing oppositional function that provides us with the opportunity for choice and free will, and without which there could be no process leading to actualization and wholeness. By humankind's failure to acknowledge the shadow within each of us it becomes, like all unacknowledged archetypes, projected outwards on to others. It becomes an adversary as in the myth of Satan, and is apparent in the human tendency to demonize other countries, ethnic minorities, other religions, other political parties, business competitors, and even next-door neighbors.

Jung also felt that the Western concept of the Trinity omitted the feminine element (a fact which contributes to the Western identification of religion with power, authority, and even aggression), and welcomed the Papal proclamation in 1950 of the Assumption of the Blessed Virgin, which he regarded as "the most important religious event since the Reformation" (Jung, 1952b). By her Assumption, the Virgin becomes seen in Roman Catholicism as united with the Son in the Heavenly Bridechamber, and this symbolized for Jung the self-achieving wholeness during the stage of self-individuation.

No brief summary can hope to do justice to the extraordinary richness and complexity of Jung's theories of religion, or of his attempt to link religion and religious symbolism with his own psychological system of archetypes and individuation. A fuller picture of his ideas can be gained from the references to his own work given above, and from the excellent biographies by Wehr (1987) and McLynn (1997) and from Jung's auto-biographical sketch (Jung, 1963). Many commentaries exist of Jung's work. That by Jacobi (1968) is regarded as something of a classic, while an illuminating series of papers on his work is edited by Papadopoulos and Saayman (1991). The fullest examination of his ideas on Eastern traditions, with special reference to Buddhism, is edited by Meckel and Moore (1992).

## Criticisms of Jung

The growing popularity of Jung's work with laypeople suggests that his ideas strike a chord with widespread personal experience. As Coward

(1992) puts it, even in his encounters with other religions, Jung frequently "had an intuitive sense of what was spiritually important for the psychological experience" of those concerned. In addition, Jung wrote as a man who claimed personal experience of many of the states of mind about which he wrote. He experienced psychotic states (from 1913 to 1918 he underwent mental disturbances that led him to believe he was on the verge of schizophrenia), visions (for example in October and December 1913 he experienced trance states in which he had visions that he later regarded as prophetic of the First World War), an inner spiritual guide (which he called Philemon and which seemed independent of personal experience in that it expressed thoughts alien to his own consciousness), a near-death experience (in 1944 he had a severe heart attack which left him at death's door for three weeks), and the paranormal (he seemed to have psychic abilities himself as a youth; as a medical student he experienced spiritualistic seances with his cousin Hélène Preiswerk; he reported several examples of poltergeist activity including the famous "exploding bookcase" incident that so alarmed Freud that he is said to have fainted, and he experienced phenomena in a haunted house in Buckinghamshire on a visit to England in 1920).

In addition he spent virtually the whole of his adult life not only working as a doctor with clients but also working on his own inner development. During this time he wrote prodigiously (his collected works run to 21 large volumes), revealing extraordinary scholarship in most of the exoteric and esoteric areas relating to human thought, belief, and behavior. And at the end of his life he showed the tranquil acceptance of approaching death common to those of advanced spiritual development. Ruth Bailey, one of his intimates and who was with him at the end, wrote that "During the last two days he lived in a faraway world and saw wonderful and magnificent things there, of that I am sure. He smiled often and was happy." She further wrote that the last time he sat on the terrace with her he referred to an enchanting dream and said "Now I know the truth down to a very little bit that is still missing. When I know this too, I will have died" (see Wehr, 1987).

Jung was thus uniquely well qualified for exploring and expounding the psychology of religion, and along with Henry James he is arguably the finest intellect to be attracted to the subject. However, he is not without his critics. First and foremost there is the charge that he did not undertake the quantitative research so prized by science. His data came from four sources: his clients, his reading, his interactions with colleagues and with other cultures, and his inner explorations. There are always dangers in generalizing too far from what is essentially individual experience, with all the preconceptions and prejudices to which that experience is subject. Jung would doubtless answer this criticism by insisting that there are common characteristics to the human mind (conscious and unconscious) that if discovered allow such generalizations to be made, and that this discovery depends not upon quantitative investigation but upon qualitative studies with oneself and small groups of others who one comes to know intimately (as with clients in analysis). Further he would point to many of the common characteristics across cultures that are revealed by study and by an acquaintance with the symbol systems and the mythologies of these cultures. These common characteristics again point to universals in human psychology – and the deeper the levels we explore in human psychology, the more these universals reveal themselves – particularly at the level of the collective unconscious.

This does not mean that Jung was anti-scientific. He acknowledged that "science is the tool of the Western mind, and with it one can open more doors than with the bare hands." But he also said that science can obscure our insight when ". . . it claims that the understanding it conveys is the only kind there is" (Jung, 1963). Jung's own understanding can be said to represent a triumph of the introspective method, particularly as he never rested on initial impressions but tested his insights again and again, against his own experience and that of others, and against the esoteric literature of both West and East. The continuing popularity of the psychotherapeutic methods which he developed is some indication of the success he had in understanding the human mind, and many of his ideas have proved of value in the development of humanistic and of transpersonal psychology. However, the absence of full-scale quantitative studies of Jung's work (perhaps due as much as anything to the tendency of university psychology departments still rather to discount Jung) remains a legitimate point of criticism.

After initial apathy, Jung's work has attracted growing interest among Christian theologians and among fringe religions. A recurring point of criticism among theologians, however, is that he refused to clarify the reality of the *numinosum* and the God-image to which it gives rise. However, as mentioned earlier, his reference to the fact that to know God one would have to be "a god himself" comes very close to the sayings of some of the mystics in all the great traditions. In a real sense, the God to whom Jung refers is the Hindu *Brahman* or the Christian Godhead, while the God of whom we can speak is the God-image, the personalization by the human mind of the divine mystery beyond words.

Other criticisms of Jung also deserve mention. Writing of Jung's work on Eastern religions, Coward (1992) makes the point that he tended to take from them those aspects which agreed with and supported his own theories, and ignored those that did not. For example, he tended to ignore the *bhakti* element (the yoga of devotion) in these religions, perhaps because he saw it as evidence of the submissive religious belief which keeps the self in an infantile mental state, and against which he warned. However, in this he may have been mistaken. *Bhakti* (see chapter 6) can be a process in and through which the individual surrenders the persona to the object of devotion, and thus comes to realize the deeper levels of being which lead to individuation. It is possible that in spite of his break with Freud – occasioned in no small measure by their different views on the nature of religion (Wehr, 1987) – Jung was still influenced by Freud's notion that some religious expression can indicate nothing more than a search for a father substitute. Jung was alienated from his own father relatively early in his life, and described him as lapsing "into a sort of sentimental idealism," and as doing "a great deal of good – far too much – and as a result was usually irritable" (Jung, 1968). If he took his own father as a model for this father substitute, it is hardly surprising that he regarded *bhakti* as evidence of a somewhat infantile form of religious observance.

As Ulanov (1992) points out, Jung also does not fully answer where evil, "in both its petty and monstrous manifestations," arises in nature As we saw earlier, Jung provides a convincing explanation for the negative side of the human personality – it allows for the existence of choice and therefore of free will – but does not really address the rationale if any behind negative forces in nature. Sometimes these forces are outside human control and therefore cannot be seen as having relevance to human choice and free will. One assumes nature cannot be said to have a "shadow," yet many people use the hardship created by natural disasters as an argument against the reality of God and against the value of religious belief. However, it is consistent with Jung's ideas to suppose he would argue that man's failure to recognize his own shadow is a main reason for his failure to understand and live in harmony with nature. Failure to recognize the destructive tendencies of his own shadow has led man to destroy and exploit nature for his own selfish ends, thus inadvertently putting himself at the mercy of natural forces to which he could with better sense accommodate himself.

With his insistence on the psychological importance of symbol and myth it is also consistent with Jung's theories to suggest that he would probably argue that prior to humankind's acceptance of a materialist–reductionist philosophy, men and women recognized what they saw as the sacredness of nature, and developed rituals which, even if they had no immediate practical effect upon natural forces, nevertheless demonstrated humankind's feeling of an intimate connection with nature as the sustaining force behind all life. Such a connection would in itself lead to a respect for the environment, and the avoidance of human actions likely to precipitate natural disasters.

Jung's contribution to our understanding of the psychology of religion is likely to become increasingly apparent as we recognize more fully the need to pursue the inner as well as the outer aspects of the subject. To date, no Western psychologist has done more to further this pursuit, or to provide us with the appropriate tools for so doing. Like Freud, Jung did not come up with all the answers to our questions on the origin and purpose of religion, and some of the answers he did provide may now look somewhat suspect. But whereas Freud saw religion as at base an illusion, Jung saw it as arising from a numinous source which he chose to call God, and which he saw us as disregarding at both our individual and our social peril.

## Classification of Belief Systems

An attempt could be made at this point to see if religious beliefs can be classified in any way which makes some kind of coherent sense while recognizing their diversity. However, this task is better attempted at the end of chapter 10 after a discussion of the varieties of religious experience, including perhaps the most significant of all experiences from a religious perspective, namely mysticism.

CHAPTER 9 _____

# Religious Expression in Myth and the Creative Arts

## Religion and the Creative Imagination

The historical association of religion and spirituality with myth and story-telling suggests that there is something about the beliefs and the existential questions associated with religion that act as a powerful stimulus for the creative imagination (Campbell, 1968; Campbell and Moyers, 1988). The sheer volume, the historical consistency, and the sublime quality of much of the fine art, sculpture, music, poetry, and architecture spawned by religious themes is quite remarkable. Beit-Hallahmi and Argyle (1997) consider that the explanation is that art and religion have common psychological processes in that both offer "direct emotional relief and a kind of cognitive meaning." They go on to propose that "Any religious belief is a fantasy, created to serve the needs of both the creative artist and the audience," and quote Kris (1952) to the effect that both religious thinking and artistic thinking reflect a "regression in the service of the ego."

This is a bold statement, and the reductionism of Beit-Hallahmi and Argyle and of Kris is open to challenge, particularly in the absence of evidence in its support. The statement by Kris that both religious and artistic thinking reflect "a regression in the service of the ego" is particularly unscientific, and serves merely to muddy the waters. As with other reductionist attacks upon both religious belief and artistic thinking, one wonders how closely the attacker has actually studied the subjects which he or she (more often he) chooses to attack. Kris is correct in supposing that the expression, through art, of inner religious experience calls upon the creative imagination, just as does the designing and building of religious architecture. And there is little doubt that many of the stories associated with the various religious traditions represent an attempt by the imagination to offer symbolic representations and attempted explanations for natural phenomena. But this hardly warrants the claim that "any religious belief is fantasy." Even if all the stories upon which formal religion is based are mythical, many myths are nevertheless claimed by various authorities (e.g. Jung, 1964 and 1968a; Campbell, 1968) to represent genuine insights into real psychological processes. Similarly, although many of the stories surrounding the founders of the world's religions and their most prominent followers might owe more to the inventiveness of those who set them down than to historical fact, they may nevertheless convey an accurate picture of the states of mind, the moral and ethical teachings, and the insights into spiritual realities of the men and women concerned.

## Religion, Poetry, Story-Making and Music

As we are discussing these issues within the context of the creative arts it is useful to draw an analogy from poetry. Poetry is intended not to provide us with an exact account of happenings, but to convey something of the feelings and emotions that gave rise to these happenings or that were prompted by them (some religious poetry, such as that of the Sufis within Islam, is in fact specifically intended to "elevate mankind to the contemplation of spiritual things, through the medium of their most impressionable feelings" – Palmer, 1984). We identify with the poet because he or she is describing something that resonates with our own states of mind. The message contained in the poem is therefore "true" in a human sense, although it makes no claim to represent documentary truth. Similarly, a painting can capture the "truth" of a landscape, and a portrait the "truth" of a sitter. Both painting and portrait have the power to evoke in us a recognition of the place or person concerned, and to arouse the emotions associated with the place or person more powerfully than photographs, despite the ability of a photograph to reproduce detail more accurately.

If we take an example from religious teaching itself, the parables of the New Testament are stories in the sense that they are not claimed to be literally true, and yet they represent perceptive observations on human motivation and behavior. Sufi literature is also full of teaching stories (see e.g. the collections by Shah, 1967, 1968, 1972), some of them concerning the Mullah Nasrudin, a species of holy fool whose wisdom is carefully concealed in apparent stupidity. Zen Buddhism is equally fond of using teachings stories, most of them attributed to the various Zen patriarchs and Zen masters down the centuries, and all of which seek to convey accurate insights into the human condition (Watts, 1957; Reps, 1957; Griffiths, 1977). Religious art, architecture, and sculpture are intended less to convey factual information about the religious life, than to arouse in the onlooker the emotions associated with religion (which, as noted earlier, McDougal lists as admiration, awe, and reverence), and thus to facilitate the state of mind that leads to spiritual insight.

Music provides us with an equally telling example. Music by itself cannot present us with factual information. The purpose of the musician is rather to express his or her own feelings through musical composition, and in doing so to convey these feelings to others and arouse in them similar sentiments. Music is thus a direct language of the feelings and the emotions. Great church music, such as Handel's Messiah, the requiems of Mozart and of Verdi, Bach's St. Matthew Passion, Christmas Oratorio, and B Minor Mass are not only monuments to the deep religious convictions of the composers concerned, but also leave many listeners with the exalted states of mind often described as spiritual. Critics sometimes argue that these great works were simply composed in response to requests from patrons, but one cannot produce great music to order. The inspiration to do so must be driven in part at least by the composer's own religious feelings and convictions. Gammond (1997) says of Bach that "Although [he] wrote music without a pause all his life, he did it with no wish for fame, his one desire being to serve the Church." He published only a handful of his prodigious output during his life, and it is illuminating that his great B Minor Mass was not even written for performance. It was primarily the expression of a man's fervent religious feelings.

## Revelation and Fantasy

Whatever we make of the extraordinarily rich and creative outpourings that have gone into religious art and music and of the sentiments they arouse in many people, it is clear that for centuries men and women have been moved by religion in a way that is not paralleled by reactions to known forms of fantasy in other areas of creative expression. Thus attempts to equate religious belief with fantasies or with regressions in the service of the ego remain statements of opinion rather than of demonstrable fact. And there is a further consideration. Religion is said by its adherents not only to tell us truths about human nature and human behavior, but also to base these truths upon the claims of religious leaders to obtain direct knowledge of ultimate truths through revelation that are outside the reach of normal processes of thought. Islam tells us that Mohammed received the Qu'ran through revelation prompted initially by the Angel Gabriel who informed him that he was "Allah's messenger." Hinduism regards the Vedas (particularly the Upanishads) as having superhuman origins and divine authority. Judaism believes that the Torah (the first five books of the Old Testament) were revealed word for word by God to Moses, and that many of the subsequent books of the Old Testament contain divine revelations entrusted to prophets such as Ezekial, Isaiah, Samuel, Nathan, Elijah, and Elisha. Christianity takes the view that the New Testament is a further example of revelation, this time through the life and works of Christ and subsequently through those of the apostles and of St. Paul, St. John the Divine, and many others. The Buddhist Sutras, although not written down until some 400 years after the death of the historical Buddha, are said by Buddhists to contain accurate accounts of the profound insights which he obtained during his final enlightenment under the Bo tree at Bodh Gaya in India, and which revealed to him the truth behind existence and the reasons for human suffering.

Science has no way of testing whether these and other revelations are what they are claimed to be rather than the productions of the human mind. But it can examine the consequences of these revelations upon the beliefs and behavior of the individuals concerned and of subsequent generations. The Bible, the Qu'ran and the Vedas have for more than 2,000 years been among the most influential sets of writings in human history, exercising a profound formative impact upon moral, ethical, and legal codes, upon education, upon beliefs as to the meaning and purpose of life and in the existence of an afterlife, upon cultures and the texture of their social fabric, and upon the making of war and peace. No works of known fantasy have had anything approaching this effect. The psychologist is bound to seek the reasons for this. Why should texts written centuries ago (3,000 years ago in the case of the Vedas) have had, and continue to have, such a hold over the human mind? Even when we take into account their usefulness to religious and secular authorities in maintaining power over the lay population, we are still left with much that requires explanation.

It is clear that there is something in these scriptures that rings true for vast numbers of people in a way not achieved by even the greatest works of fiction. Those with religious belief typically claim that scriptural truth is also confirmed and justified by direct experience, and it is to this experience that we turn in the next chapter. Works of fiction may inspire temporary suspension of disbelief and may influence subsequent ideas and behaviors, but few people confuse the fantasies which they contain with actual events or with binding teachings. It is of course fair to concede that whereas scriptures claim to convey actual truth, works of fiction do not. However, this fact in itself is unlikely to account for the difference in impact between the two. If nothing else, it seems that the founders of the great traditions were very effective psychologists.

# Varieties of Religious and Spiritual Experience

## Religious Experience

Whitehead (1974) tells us that "the dogmas of religion are the attempt to formulate in precise terms the truth disclosed in the religious experience of mankind. In exactly the same way [that] the dogmas of physical science are the attempts to formulate in precise terms the truth disclosed in the sense-perception of mankind." In Whitehead's terms, religion is therefore experiential in origin, rather than simply an effort after meaning and explanation. The human race became religious less through its need to concoct stories to account for its own existence than through intimations that this existence depended upon something greater than itself. Johnson (1963) makes a similar point when he tells us that this direct – or mystical – experience "is the core of all the great religions . . . it is from this that all true religion has sprung." Such mystical experience brings with it "knowledge rather than belief, certainty rather than faith, and life is henceforward viewed in the perspective given to it by that glimpse of underlying Reality."

The close link between mystical religious experience and religious doctrine seems clear. Thus religion does not depend for its survival solely upon attempts to explain the cosmos and our place within it. Research by Hay and Heald (1987), summarized in Table 10.1, shows that a sizeable percentage of the people sampled by them in the UK confess to having mystical experiences which come under the heading of religious.

Many of the people in Table 10.1 may have had more than one of the experiences listed. If in addition we include forms of religious experience that do not appear in the table, such as Wordsworth's nature mysticism (e.g. *Intimations of Immortality Recollected from Early Childhood*), the ecstatic experiences that are a feature of some religious communities

**Table 10.1**  Percentages of people in the UK reporting various religious experiences (adapted from Hay and Heald, 1987)

| Type of experience | Percentage reporting experience |
| --- | --- |
| Awareness of: | |
|   God's presence | 27 |
|   help received in response to prayer | 25 |
|   a guiding presence not called God | 22 |
|   the presence of someone who has died | 18 |
|   a sacred presence in nature | 16 |
|   an evil presence | 12 |
|   the unity of all things | 5 |

(Christie-Murray, 1978), and reported visions of angels, saints, and of the Virgin Mary (McClure, 1983), the overall percentage would doubtless be increased. It may also be appropriate to include in this percentage sudden insights into the real meaning of religious teachings and their relevance to oneself, such as those experienced by John Bunyan during his readings of the Bible and that inspired many of his writings. It may also be appropriate to include near-death experiences (NDEs), those episodes reported by a percentage of men, women, and children when resuscitated from brief episodes of clinical death or when narrowly escaping death from accident or trauma, and which seem to contain religious or spiritual content (chapter 11).

A notable feature of Table 10.1 is that the percentages reporting positive religious experiences greatly outweigh the percentages reporting negative or evil experiences. There could be several reasons for this. People may be more reluctant to admit to negative than to positive experiences, or may reinterpret negative experiences in positive terms with the passing of time, perhaps because they consider the latter form of interpretation shows themselves in a better light. It is also possible that people may remember positive experiences and forget negative ones; or may be liable to imagine benevolent rather than malevolent contacts with spiritual beings. Nevertheless, the finding provides some support for the argument that religious experience involves more than just fantasy-driven altered states of consciousness, particularly as research indicates that in other altered states such as dreaming, people report more unpleasant than pleasant fantasy episodes (Hall and Nordby, 1972).

Some accounts of religious experiences maintain that should negative episodes occur they can be remedied by calling for spiritual help. Sometimes these experiences appear to take on a tangible nature, as in one of the cases collected by The Religious Experience Research Center (Hardy, 1979).

> Suddenly I became aware of a sense of the uttermost evil . . . I could feel
> this sense of evil enveloping me. I had the terrifying impression that this
> evil force or presence was bent upon taking possession of me . . . I could
> almost taste the evil. I was in terror, so much so I could not call out or
> move. A part of my mind told me I must at all costs act or I would be
> lost . . . I managed by a great effort to stretch out my right hand and with
> my index finger I traced the sign of the Cross in the air. Immediately . . . the
> evil presence . . . fell away completely, and I felt a wonderful sense of peace
> and safety.

At other times the sense of evil is less tangible, but the effect of calling
upon religious belief is the same, as another of the cases reported by
Hardy illustrates.

> I was very nervous of being left alone. Fear gripped me in a great grip; I
> think I never had such fear. Then I came to remember the story of Elisha
> revealing to his servants the Host of Angels, and I accepted this as being
> true now. The fear left me and I was "still.". But directly I let my thoughts
> fall from that Vision, that awful fear returned – so I would quickly renew
> my "vision."

One difficulty for the psychologist is that none of the various experiences that appear in Table 10.1 is susceptible to objective test (although
there is evidence from NDEs that suggests that at least some part of the
experiences concerned may be verifiable), and much must therefore be
taken on trust. However, the psychologist can both look for similarities
between the reports of these experiences and carry out some form of
classification, and can also, as with research into all aspects of religious
belief, look for the influence of the experiences upon the subsequent
behavior of the individuals who claim to have had them.

## Mysticism

It is clear from the above that mystical religious experience is not the
preserve of saints and initiates. It seems indeed to be the essence of
religious experience for many lay people as well as for visionaries. By its
nature mysticism is hard to define and appears to operate at different
levels, from the ecstatic experiences of various of the saints to the quiet
moments experienced by ordinary men and women, some of which arise
suddenly and unexpectedly, and yet have life-changing power. Grant
(1985) defines mysticism as the "poetry" and the "creative spirit" of
religion, and sees it as an experience of the Divine "beyond the boundaries

of culture and language." Cox (1983), in exploring a wide range of definitions of Western mysticism, considers that all contain the concept of a direct experience of God, the "unitive acquisition of knowledge that is inaccessible to rational understanding." Eastern mystics – Buddhist in particular – would replace the term "God" with phrases such as "absolute reality," "emptiness," or "essential nature," but whatever terms are used, the concepts remain the same. In a moment of sudden insight, the mystic sees into the real nature of things, the essential reality behind the world of appearances, and typically is fundamentally changed as a result.

Various attempts have in fact been made to classify mystical experience. Hood (1975, 1995) proposes a division into transcendent mystical experience (the sense of being in contact with divine and/or creative energies outside oneself), and immanent mystical experience (the sense of the divine presence pervading and unifying all things). Further support for the existence of these two forms of mysticism comes from the work of Hood (1975, 1995) who used Stace's criteria (given below) to construct a 32-item scale designed to measure the incidence of this form of religious experience. Factor analysis of his results revealed two factors, one of general mysticism on which most of the items in his scale loaded (and which represented immanence), and the other of what he called religious, noetic, and positive affect items (which shared some similarities with transcendence). Stace's criteria and Hood's derived 32-item scale are both biased towards immanence rather than transcendence. Were this not the case it seems probable that this second factor would emerge more strongly. Hood found that his two factors showed a .47 correlation, which suggests that the two forms of mysticism show considerable overlap, and may in fact derive from a single common factor, with the divergence in reports owing more to cultural variables, religious teachings, and semantics than to actual experience.

The two forms of mysticism are frequently reported in accounts of mystical experience, and are apparent in what Gupta (1978) and other Hindu writers refer to respectively as the *savikalpa* and *nirvikalpa* states of *samadhi* sometimes experienced in deep meditation. In *savikalpa samadhi* or *transcendent samadhi* the meditator is said to retain consciousness of the self contemplating the divine, while in *nirvikalpa* or *imminent samadhi* the experience is of becoming one with the divine. Zaehner (1957) regards these two distinct forms of *samadhi* as consistent with the two different conceptions of the divine found in all the major religions, namely monism (the divine is one and indivisible, and is the object of contemplation and worship by his creation), and pantheism (everything is an expression of the divine, and there is nothing that is not the divine). Smart (1996) makes a similar observation.

## Varieties of Mystical Experience

This distinction between transcendence and immanence is a vital one in any understanding of the psychology of mysticism, and has been noted by many other writers over the years using a variety of terms – for example Schjelderup and Schjelderup (1932) referred to it as *union mysticism* and *self-mysticism* respectively, while Hinduism as we saw recognizes it as *savikalpa samadhi* and *nirvikalpa samadhi*. Using these Hindu terms, Wilber (1993) argues that *savikalpa samadhi* is the blissful experience which allows an understanding of *saguna Brahman*, the mythological or personified image of the divine, while *nirvikalpa samadhi* is direct experience of *nirguna Brahman*, the ground of all being. In *nirvikalpa samadhi* "One no longer contemplates reality, one becomes reality! All dualities and images are totally and clearly removed. So [*savikalpa samadhi*] is the truest image of reality, while [*nirvikalpa samadhi*] is reality itself." Wilber in fact considers the distinction between the two forms of *samadhi* represents the major difference between the various forms of mystical experience, with *savikalpa* the "lesser" of the two (though Hindu sages such as Ramakrishna – see Gupta, 1978 – consider that both states should be experienced at various times if one is to obtain full mystical realization), as it still indicates in some measure the action of one's own mind rather than a full experience of the One Mind of undifferentiated reality. In other words, it indicates the filtering of the ineffable experience of this reality through the limited conceptual abilities of the finite human mind.

Table 10.1 shows that the percentage of people in the UK reporting experiences of immanence is much smaller than the percentages reporting either transcendent experiences or experiences of a helpful presence not specifically thought of as God. Although the percentage reporting immanence appears to be higher in the United States, where from a large and representative sample Gallup and Proctor (1983) found some 10 percent report experiencing at some time "an otherworldly feeling of union with a divine being," the religious experience in the West seems more likely to take a transcendent, personalized form than an immanent, impersonalized one. Personalized experiences of another kind are also listed in Table 10.1, with 18 percent of those with religious experiences reporting an awareness of the presence of a deceased person. Classifying such experiences as religious suggests a link in the mind of the experiencer between religion and an afterlife. (The relative frequency with which people report sensing the presence of the deceased is documented by a number of other investigators – e.g. Lagrand, 1997, 1999.)

This preponderance of transcendent over immanent mystical experiences might of course have been reversed if the research had been conducted not in the West but among followers of Eastern religions, in particular of the Theravadin School of Eastern Buddhism or of the Vedantic School of Hinduism, both of which agree with Wilber that the limited finite mind has still not been overcome in *savikalpa samadhi* and in all transcendent beliefs and experiences. The question that remains to be answered is the extent to which the greater prevalence of transcendental mysticism in the West and of immanence mysticism in the East arises from cultural differences (the West places more emphasis upon individuality – upon defining, developing, and defending individuality – than does the East, which recognizes more commonality between human beings and between human beings and the rest of creation.), and the extent to which these two forms of mysticism, as experienced and taught by the founders of the respective religious traditions, are responsible in part at least for these cultural differences.

## Immanent Mystical Experience

Wilber and others (e.g. Stace, 1960; Cohen and Phipps, 1979) indicate that advanced mystical states are attainable on a regular basis only after lengthy mind-training, but there are many accounts by individuals of brief, spontaneous glimpses of them, even if only once in a lifetime. One of the best known is by Richard Bucke, a leading nineteenth-century Canadian psychiatrist, which William James considered brought "this kind of consciousness . . . to the attention of students of human nature in a way so definite and inescapable that it will be impossible henceforth to ignore it . . ." (quoted by Acklom in his foreword to Bucke, 1969). Bucke, James considered, was "a benefactor of us all." Bucke's account, writing of himself in the third person, tells us that:

> All at once, without warning . . . he found himself wrapped around . . . by a flame-coloured cloud . . . Directly afterwards came upon him a sense of exultation, of immense joyousness, accompanied or immediately followed by an intellectual illumination quite impossible to describe . . . one momentary lightning-flash of Brahmic Splendour which has ever lightened his life . . . leaving thenceforward for always an after taste of heaven.

Bucke goes on to tell us that as a result of this experience he "did not come to believe, he saw and knew that the Cosmos is not dead matter, but a living Presence, that the soul of man is immortal, that the universe is also built and ordered. . . ." The similarities between this experience and those reported by many others is worth noting. One typical example from the many cases collected by the Religious Experience Research Center and quoted by Hardy (1979) tells us that there was:

. . . a perception of oneness, all was a manifestation of Being. Through all the objects in the room glowed a radiance. All problems dissolved or rather, there were no problems, there was no death and no "I-ness"; it was a feeling of absolute bliss . . . It is . . . becoming aware of the Universal Self, the Absolute. Perhaps one could interpret this as God.

Something of the unchanging nature of this form of mystical experience becomes apparent when we read the accounts given over 1,300 years earlier by Buddhist sage Han Shan (translated and summarized by Lu K'uan Yu, 1971, and again given in the third person):

. . . His body and mind disappeared and were replaced by a great brightness, spheric and full, clear and still, like a huge round mirror containing all the mountains, rivers and great earth. Thereafter he noticed a still serenity inside and outside his body . . . the resultant bliss was without compare.

The reference in the above extracts to the blissful nature of mystical experiences of this kind is repeated time and again in the various accounts given to us, as is the fact that no words can adequately describe either the true nature of these experiences or of the feelings which they induce. Seventeenth-century Zen Master Hakuin tells us, in Suzuki's translation (Suzuki, 1953) that the experiences are:

. . . beyond description and can never be transmitted to others. It is those who have actually drunk water that know whether it is cold or warm . . . the past, present, and future are concentrated in this moment of your consciousness . . . no joy is ever comparable to this.

In the mystical experience of the oneness or unity of all things it is not implied that worldly things are unreal, simply that they are not real in the form in which we usually experience them. We see them habitually as separate, each with its own individual existence, whereas the mystic somehow directly experiences them as a moving, dynamic, everflowing unified manifestation of the one life force from which they arise.

Much is written in various books of popular science (e.g. Capra, 1975, 1996; Zukav, 1979) about the similarities between this mystical vision, the teaching of the ancient Hindu and other sages, and the theories of subatomic physics (in particular quantum mechanics). The point is further urged in more academic works (e.g. Bohm, 1980; Goswami, 1993). It is unclear how far these similarities can usefully be sustained, but the common emphasis upon the interconnectedness of all animate and inanimate systems is certainly of interest, and prompts some writers to wonder whether mystical experience gave sages living many centuries ago some of the insights into the reality underlying the world of appearances now revealed by modern science.

## Transcendent Mystical Experience

In contrast to mystical experiences of the unity of all things, transcendent mysticism speaks of an awareness of a divinity separate from the mystic him or herself, although this divinity is sometimes described more in terms of its power, wisdom, and love than as a physical presence. Johnson (1989) quotes the words of the thirteenth-century mystic The Blessed Angelico of Foligno:

> I beheld the ineffable fullness of God . . . I beheld the plenitude of God, by which I understood the whole world both here and beyond the sea, the abyss, and all other things . . . And in this I beheld nothing save the Divine Power, in a way that is utterly indescribable . . . Wherefore I understood that the world is but a little thing; and I saw that the power of God was above all things and the whole world was filled with it.

Sometimes, however, the transcendent mystical experience includes the presence of other beings. The sixteenth-century Abbess St. Theresa of Avila for example wrote of seeing her deceased parents during one of her mystical episodes (St. Theresa of Avila, 1960):

> I thought I was being carried up to Heaven; the first persons I saw were my mother and father . . . such great things happened in so short a time . . . while the light we see here and the light [we see there] are both light, there is no comparison between the two, and the brightness of the sun seems quite dull if compared with the other. Afterwards I was . . . left with very little fear of death of which previously I had been very much afraid.

Cox (1983) gives many examples of the writings of Christian mystics who feel they have experienced the presence of the Virgin Mary, while there are also accounts of experiences of Christ. Mother Julian of Norwich, in a mystical treatise written in the fourteenth-century (Julian of Norwich, 1966), writes:

> Our Lord showed himself, in glory . . . By this I was taught that our soul can never rest until it comes to him, and knows him to be fullness of joy, friendly and considerate, blessed and life indeed. And he said again and again "It is I; it is I; . . . it is I who am all . . . it is I who showed myself to you here."

## Similarities between Transcendent and Immanent Mysticism

In spite of the differences between these transcendent experiences and the immanent experiences quoted earlier, there are certain similarities, in particular the presence of light or brightness, the assurance of immortality, the enduring influence of the experience, and of course the sense of bliss.

Smart (1996) considers that there are cultural factors that help determine which of the two kinds of mystical experience is likely to occur. He recognizes an intermingling of the two experiences in the accounts given by those who have encountered transcendent mysticism, but for individuals from cultures where there is no concept of the Other beforehand, the experience appears to be exclusively of immanence. Thus those reared in a theistic culture such as Christianity or Islam (where the emphasis is upon salvation by the grace and power of the Other) will experience transcendence or a mingling of transcendence and immanence, while those reared in non-theistic cultures such as Theravadin Buddhism (prevalent in South East Asia, which places the emphasis upon enlightenment through self-power) will experience exclusively immanence. However, Buddhist mysticism among the Mahayana sects (prevalent in Tibet, China, Japan, and India) contains many accounts of visions of the Buddhas (the historical Buddha, *Buddha Sakyamuni,* and the various transcendent Buddhas such as *Amoghasiddhi, Samantabhadra,* and *Vairochana*) and transcendent Bodhisattvas such as *Kuan Yin, Manjushri,* and *Tara.* Pure Land Buddhism, popular in Japan and China, which reveres *Amida Buddha,* the Buddha of Boundless Light and Boundless Life, goes further, and is indistinguishable for many practical purposes from theistic religions in that it teaches that faith in *Amida* leads to a rebirth in his Pure Land, where the process of final enlightenment is, with his help and that of various transcendent Bodhisattvas, rendered easier than it is on Earth.

Orthodox Buddhists explain away these transcendent experiences on the grounds that even the transcendent Buddhas represent the action of one's own mind which seeks to personalize the absolute, undifferentiated energy which is the ground of all being. Thus the visions of the Buddhas are true, but yet do not represent ultimate truth. The Absolute, when channeled through the human mind, can appear in these personalized forms, but ultimately enlightenment consists of seeing beyond these forms to the source from which they arise. The claim that the mind has a tendency to personalize what is in reality beyond personalization has certain echoes in the suggestion by William James (James, 1960) that:

> It is as if there were in the human consciousness a *sense of reality, a feeling of objective presence, a perception* of what we may call "something there,"

more deep and more general than any of the special and particular "senses" by which the current psychology supposes existent realities to be originally revealed.

## The Relationship Between Immanence and Transcendence

The difference between the two viewpoints is that James refrains from speculating upon whether this "something there" possesses a reality other than that personalized by the action of the mind. If James is correct, and there is an innate sense (possibly connected to the "God Spot" in the brain discussed in chapter 7) within the human consciousness *of objective presence* we would expect it to be common to human consciousness irrespective of culture, and to be expressed in a similar form. This expectation appears to be realized. In all the great traditions we find what Smart (1996) calls the "double-decker Divine – the impersonal ultimate and manifesting from it the personal Lord." In mystical Christianity we have on the one hand what Eckhart (Blakney, 1941) refers to as the Godhead, the ground of our being, the Infinite, the One, the undifferentiated unity beyond adequate description and only known through direct mystical experience, and on the other the manifest God, who arises like man from the Godhead ("God's ground is my ground and my ground is God's ground").

As discussed in chapter 6, in the Jewish mysticism of the Kabbalah we have *Ain Soph*, the unmanifest absolute, and *Kether*, the crown, the first emanation from this Absolute. In Hinduism we have Brahman, the eternal, imperishable, nondual reality, and Brahma the creator god; in Mahayana Buddhism we have transcendental reality, infinite potential (the *Dhamakaya*) from which arises the *Sambhogakaya* (the embodiment of this infinite potential, personalized in the form of the transcendental Buddhas). In Sufi mysticism within Islam we have, if not a "double-decker Divine," at least the concept of a God with whom one can have mystical union as well as a God who remains the separate object of devotion. And in the Orthodox Christian tradition of Greece, Russia, and Eastern Europe we have the concept of God as essence (described as the nature or inner being of God) and God as energy (described as the operations or acts of creative power), and it is with the latter rather than with the former aspect of the divine that union is possible through mystical experience (Ware, 1979).

Although attempts have been made in Freudian theory (chapter 8) to explain the transcendent God as a fantasy arising from the human need for a protective father-substitute, it is more difficult to advance a similar explanation for the experience of immanence. It might be argued that immanence is linked to a human self-destructive urge; individuals who find their lives intolerable for one reason or another take comfort from the fantasy that all existence is nothing more than a single, all-embracing unity empty of individual phenomena, which means that the self is an illusion that can be symbolically banished by merging it with this "emptiness". Such an argument might obtain some theoretical support from the Freudian notion of the *thanatos*, the supposed death instinct which is taken to explain aspects of violence and of self-destruction. However, there is no evidence that the cultures of South East Asia, Tibet, China, and Japan, which are partly or wholly Buddhist, suffer any more from the psychological ill-health that would prompt individuals to wish for annihilation than do the cultures of the West. Rather to the contrary. In addition, properly understood, the mystical experience of immanence does not imply annihilation of the self but an infinite expansion of the self until it embraces all things. These two interpretations – annihilation or infinite expansion – of the experience of immanence may appear to the Western logician to be two versions of the same thing, but this is not how they appear to the Buddhist (the Buddha in fact specifically warned against the former interpretation). A further point is that we have repeated references in the literature to the blissful nature of the experience of immanence, which hardly makes this experience sound like a depressive seeking an imaginary escape from the intolerable prison of the self.

## Stages in Mystical Experience

The ubiquitous nature of mystical experience strengthens the notion that it is in some sense an endemic property of mind. Underwood, in her classic work on the subject first published nearly a century ago (Underwood, 1995), tells us that "The most highly developed branches of the human family have in common one peculiar characteristic. They tend to produce . . . a curious and definite type of personality . . . which refuses to be satisfied with that which other men call experience" and is inclined to "deny the world in order to find reality." She goes on to say that "Their experience . . . forms a body of evidence, curiously self-consistent and often mutually explanatory. . . ." This body of evidence suggests to her that the advanced mystic – i.e. the individual who devotes his or her life to this attempt to "find reality" – typically goes through five stages, each with a number of defining characteristics:

1. *The Stage of Awakening.* The individual becomes conscious, either through a religious experience of some kind or through acquaintance with appropriate teachings, of the existence of a "Divine Reality"

(usually an abrupt experience characterized by great joy), followed by a desire to experience it more fully.

2.  *The Stage of Purgation.* Awakening is followed by a recognition of one's own inadequacies and of the immense distance between oneself and this Reality, which is followed by intense anguish leading to a profound commitment to eliminate this distance by self-discipline study and effort.

3.  *The Stage of Illumination.* Through this self-discipline the mystic becomes increasingly detached from material pleasures; an awareness of the proximity of the Divine Reality returns, bringing with it once more the sense of bliss.

4.  *The Dark Night.* The mystic now proceeds to suffer once more the sense of separation from Divine Reality, a sense of separation which can only be resolved if the *personal satisfaction* that has come from mystical experience is, like other things that strengthen the sense of self or personal ego, relinquished. The purification process must now be extended to the very center of personal identity itself. The human craving for happiness must be abandoned, and the small personal self surrendered by desiring nothing for oneself. Sometimes described by Christian mystics as a "spiritual crucifixion," it seems that the Dark Night arises from a realization that by regarding the mystical experience as something given to *oneself*, it is now *oneself* that is the obstacle preventing full realization.

5.  *The Stage of Union.* Once this self is surrendered, the goal of mysticism is reached. The self becomes one with Divine Reality – or perhaps it would be more accurate to say it realizes that it *is* that Reality. A state of great equilibrium arises. Life becomes purely spiritual, and is characterized by an intense and enduring certitude rather than by the transitory ecstasies experienced during the stage of illumination.

Some of Underwood's language (e.g. "The Dark Night of the Soul") reveals her Christian background, but these five stages do appear to represent important features of the accounts of mystical development given by members of all the great traditions. It is notable that Underwood's fifth stage appears to indicate that the experience of immanence rather than that of transcendence is the culmination of the mystical life, but mystics within the theistic traditions might describe the final stage as total surrender to the Divine ("Verily not I live, but Christ lives within me" in the words of St. Paul) rather than absolute union.

## Mysticism and Psychosis

One explanation for these stages is that they represent a series of violent mood swings during which (in stages two and four) the individual experiences feelings of guilt, inadequacy, and self-rejection, from which (stage five) there is release into a state of equilibrium between the opposite poles of the personality, a state which produces feelings of unity and of release from the old, divided self. Such an explanation views mysticism as essentially an affective disorder. In addition, some commentators (e.g. Taylor, 1979) refer to the similarities between mystical experiences, whether transcendent or immanent, and certain of the accounts given by those suffering from cognitive disorders.

However, although some such similarities exist, many of the accounts of mystical experience collected and published by the Religious Experience Research Centre and extensively discussed and analyzed by a number of authorities (Robinson, 1977; Hardy, 1979; Hay and Morisey, 1978; Hay, 1982, 1990) are from people with no record of cognitive disorders previous or subsequent to their moments of illumination. In addition, there is a coherence about their accounts of the experiences themselves and of their long-term influence upon beliefs and behavior that is not a common feature of the histories of those who have manifested such disorders. It is true that the experiences reported by laypeople are usually more fleeting than those of the more famous mystics with whom Underwood was concerned. It is also true that the accounts given by laypeople are often too brief to tell us whether or not they involved Underwood's five stages (it is probable that they only glimpsed stage three and rarely stage five), but if mystical experiences are indeed psychotic we would expect substantial evidence to this effect to have emerged from the many thousands of reported cases.

A particularly strong argument against the equation of mysticism with psychosis is that only just over 4 percent of the respondents reported by the Centre speak of feelings of fear or horror connected with their experiences. The overwhelming emotions are those of exaltation, awe, harmony, timelessness, optimism, love, joy, security, and peace (Hardy, 1979). The same absence of the negative emotions and cognitions typically experienced during psychotic episodes is also apparent in the accounts of mysticism across centuries and traditions assembled from the literature by Abhayananda (1996) and by Eliade (1977). Further, Robinson (1977) and Hoffmann (1992) present a wide range of accounts of mystical experiences recollected by respondents from childhood. Assuming the memories concerned are accurate, this also argues against the notion that such experiences can be equated with psychotic episodes. Not only are these episodes a very rare feature of childhood, there is no evidence that the individuals reporting them showed any particular incidence of mental ill-health in later life. (The possible relationship between mysticism and psychosis is returned to in chapter 12 in the context of religion and psychological health.)

## Features of the Mystical Experience

Hardy (1979) presents a long list of the various features of the mystical experiences collected by the Religious Experience Research Centre. Many of these appear to be very much more frequent than others. Among them are:

- visions – of a transcendental nature or of deceased relatives and friends;
- a sense of spiritual presence;
- a bright light or lights;
- a voice or voices, typically guiding or calming;
- transformation and beatification of the surroundings;
- feelings of unity with the surroundings and/or with other people;
- feelings of warmth and/or of being touched;
- a sense of security, protection, and peace;
- a sense of joy, bliss, and well-being;
- feelings of awe, reverence, and wonder;
- release from the fear of death;
- a sense of certainty, clarity, and enlightenment;
- a sense of conversion and of heightened awareness.

Looking back at Hay and Heald's list given in Table 10.1 and comparing it with that of Hardy, it is clear that even though Hay's work was closely linked to that of Hardy, researchers (and respondents) appear to define what is meant by religious experience in a number of different ways. This means that all the various lists which emerge from research show interesting differences as well as similarities. Stace (1960) comes up with the following experiences:

- unifying visions in which all things are experienced as one;
- a sense of timelessness and spacelessness;
- a sense of access to real knowledge;
- feelings of blessedness, peace, joy, and happiness;
- feelings of contact with the holy/sacred/divine;
- experiences beyond logic;
- experiences beyond words;
- a loss of the sense of self.

Greeley (1975), from a sample of 1,467 men and women in the United States, produces a longer list, with attendant percentages (summarized in Table 10.2).

Several differences are apparent between Geeley's list and those of the other authors just quoted. There is no mention in Table 10.2 of help received from prayer, of a guiding presence, of the presence of someone known to have died, of nature, or of an evil presence, all of which appear in Hay and Heald (Table 10.1). A sense of unity (mentioned more often by Geeley's respondents than by those of Hay and Heald) is the major

**Table 10.2**   Percentage incidence of various forms of religious experience among those reporting one or more experiences (adapted from Greeley, 1975)

| Form of experience | Percentage reporting |
| --- | --- |
| Profound peace | 56 |
| Certainty that all will be well | 48 |
| Conviction of need to contribute to others | 43 |
| Conviction that love is the center of all things | 43 |
| Joy and laughter | 43 |
| Increase in understanding | 32 |
| Sense of unity | 29 |
| Confidence in personal survival | 27 |
| Sense that the universe is alive | 25 |
| Sense of being taken over by something more powerful | 24 |
| Sense of being bathed in light | 14 |

common feature. Geeley's respondents also make no mention of many of the things referred to by Hardy's respondents such as a sense of spiritual presence, a sense of awe, transcendent visions, a voice or voices, and transformation of the surroundings. And there is no reference to Stace's sense of timelessness, to feelings of contact with the holy/sacred/divine, or to a loss of the sense of self. However, a bright light or lights, a sense of peace, loss of the fear of death, a sense of understanding/knowledge/enlightenment, feelings of joy and warmth, and feelings of unity with the surroundings and/or with other people all appear in one sense or other.

Other items listed by Greely are less readily connected with religion and are consequently omitted from Table 10.2. These include "an experience of emotional intensity," "a sense of a new life and a new world," "a feeling I could not describe," "a sensation of warmth/fire," "a sense of being alone," "a loss of concern about worldly problems," and "a sense of desolation". The most interesting thing about these items is that they show us how broadly some people classify the religious experience. This may indicate the difficulty they have of putting such experience into words that carry religious meaning, and/or that it is less the experience itself than what is felt to be the source of the experience that prompts them to see it as religious. For example "emotional intensity," "a sense of desolation," and "a sense of warmth/fire" may all be prompted by many different things. We need to know why they are seen as arising from a religious impulse. Possibly indepth interviews might tell us, and there is clearly a need for more research along these lines.

Without such interviews, researchers face obvious difficulties when attempting to sample religious experience. This is particularly evident when we compare the high incidence of this experience found by researchers who ask only a single question with that revealed in response to multiple criteria questionnaires. Hardy for example disapproved of questionnaires on the grounds that religious experiences are "so precious and personal to the people who have them that many are likely to be put off by being asked to fill in such a form about them." Even more importantly in his view "the very manner of asking the questions would be apt, I believe, to give a slant to the content of the replies." Hardy thus used a single general question, asking people in effect whether they had at any time been conscious of, and perhaps been influenced by, a power and purpose outside themselves – whether they called it God or not – as a result of which they achieved a religious interpretation of the universe. (Somewhat curiously Hardy initially sought to discourage people from reporting ecstatic or mystical states, but soon discovered that experiences of such states were contributed in fair numbers from the very outset of his research.) By contrast, Thomas and Cooper (1978) consider that the more lengthy criteria listed by Stace for rating religious experience is the most suitable starting point.

Something of the difference between results yielded by the single question method and by the multiple question method is suggested by the fact that whereas Hardy and those using his methods report religious experiences as occurring among around one-third of the population, Thomas and Cooper (defining religious experiences more narrowly in terms of mystical episodes) found them present in only 2 percent. The former figure would appear closer to the truth if findings by Gallup Polls, in one of the most extensive surveys available to us, are to be believed. Extrapolating from their results, Gallup calculated that some 47 million Americans have had religious experiences (Gallup and Proctor, 1982).

In addition to variations in the kind of questions asked by the researchers, cultural factors (and therefore expectations) in the respondents may play some part in explaining response differences. Poloma (1995) draws particular attention to the role played by social factors and social settings in the type of religious experience reported, and Beit-Hallahmi and Argyle (1997) suggest that the content and character of religious experience is in part the product of historical development, though this suggestion must not be pushed too far as consistency in reported experiences across the centuries among the Eastern traditions is one of their most striking features. Even across traditions, there are sufficient similarities to suggest that reference is being made to a core experience.

## Mysticism and the Sense of Unity

A sense of unity is the most striking feature of this core experience, followed in any order by an awareness of light, a sense of access to some ound knowledge, feelings of bliss, loss of fear of death, and some se of a divine presence. Zaehner thus appears justified in his claim that widely authenticated fact" of the central mystical experience is this sense of unity, a sense "of Nature in all things or of all things being one" (Zaehner, 1971). He goes on to argue that "In all cases the person who has the experience seems to be convinced that what he experiences, so far from being illusory, is . . . something far more real than what he experiences normally through his five senses or thinks with his finite mind." Zaehner adds that the experience, at its highest, appears to transcend time and space, and constitutes "an infinite mode of existence."

Zaehner is describing what has been referred to in the present chapter as immanent mysticism. For the description to be complete, we would have to add the experience of visions, of a sense of presence, and of the holy/sacred/divine referred to by both Hardy and Stace – in other words transcendent mysticism. Spencer (1963), in an extensive study of the subject across the various great traditions, shows clearly the ubiquitous nature of both forms of mysticism, with immanence, as we mentioned earlier, more apparent among those who follow non-theistic teachings, and transcendence more common among those who adhere to theistic beliefs. However, Spencer emphasizes a quality that he regards as a defining characteristic of both immanence and transcendence, namely universal love. Among non-theistic traditions, this love is often expressed as providing emancipation from the fetters which chain us to the ego and a limited conception of self which sees it as individual and separate from the rest of creation. In theistic traditions, universal love is regarded as the manifestation of God's divine nature, and the experience of this love is thus God-realization. In both traditions, love is expressed through an outpouring of compassion to all sentient beings – in effect what Spencer describes as a taking "to ourselves of the sorrows and sufferings of others." In the case of non-theistic traditions the process is enhanced by the realization that all living creatures are essentially part of ourselves, part of the unity which is the real nature of being. In the theistic traditions it is enhanced by the recognition that God's love is limitless and intended for all creation; thus by channeling this love through ourselves to others, we are fulfilling God's purpose on earth.

To summarize, the evidence largely supports the view that mystical experience takes two forms, one a realization of the unity of all things, the other of the divine presence. Both forms of experience can be accompanied by an awareness of light, which can have the effect of appearing to transform the surroundings. Both forms can lead to feelings of bliss, of knowledge/enlightenment, and of a release from the fear of death. Both forms of experience bring with them a conviction of the importance of universal love.

## What Prompts Mystical Experiences?

Hardy (1979) records the various events said by respondents to have triggered their mystical experiences. The most frequent of these, reported in nearly 25 percent of cases, is – somewhat unexpectedly – depression and despair. This finding has certain affinities with the statement by the Hindu saint, Sri Ramakrishna (see Gupta, 1978) that when the individual has need of the Divine as desperately as a drowning person needs air, then the Divine will be found. Despair, suffering, feelings of loss or of hopelessness seem to help create the particular state of mind that leads to religious experience, and to the transforming effect of this experience.

The second most frequent trigger reported by Hardy (13.5 percent of cases) is prayer and/or meditation. The act of stilling and focussing the mind by means of meditation has traditionally been regarded by all the great traditions as a way of opening the awareness to spiritual dimensions. The theory is that when the mental chatter which typically dominates the mind becomes quiet, new insights, perhaps from the personal unconscious, perhaps from some spiritual source, are allowed to enter into awareness. The trigger in third place is natural beauty (12.2 percent of cases). This is perhaps not surprising. Poets with a particular feeling for nature such as William Blake, Alfred Lord Tennyson, William Wordsworth, Ralph Waldo Emerson, Gerald Manley Hopkins, and William Butler Yeats all write of finding through nature a contact with either the divinity of transcendental mysticism, or with the sense of unity experienced in moments of immanence. All the poets mentioned, together with many others, are well represented in the *Oxford Book of Mystical Verse*, which is an extensive collection of poetry inspired by such themes.

The importance of nature for mystical experience is noted and stressed by a number of other authorities. Walsh (1999) points out that the Christian Desert Fathers (practitioners within the Christian Orthodox tradition who chose the solitude of the desert for their prayer and meditation), shamans, yogis, Taoists, and Native Americans all report that nature sensitizes us to the sacred, "and is a superb setting for self-discovery and the birth of wisdom." He quotes Saint Bernard to the effect that:

> What I know of the divine sciences and of Holy Scriptures I learnt in woods and fields. I have had no other masters than the beeches and the oaks. Listen to a man of experience: thou wilt learn more in the woods than in books.

Why should this be so? The Koran tells us that the largely superficial demands of society serve as distractions from the spiritual life and act, like internal mental chatter, to divert the mind from its own true being, which all religions tell us is spiritual. So nature, by offering the possibility of peace, stillness, and – if we wish for it – solitude, makes it easier to experience this true being. The Christian Bible admonishes us to "Be still and know that I am God." Walsh (1999) remarks that modern psychological research confirms ancient claims that periods of solitude foster "reflection and refreshment . . . (and) enhanced creativity and physical health." Certainly many writers on stress management point to the demonstrable benefits of periods of tranquillity (Fontana, 1989).

The earthy, grounded philosophy that is an essential aspect of Taoism and of Zen Buddhism serves as a constant reminder to practitioners that humans are part of nature, come from nature, are sustained throughout their lives by nature, and have bodies that after physical death are returned to nature. The feeling reported by mystics of union with nature further emphasizes this interconnectedness between ourselves and the natural environment. Although such speculations lie beyond the bounds of scientific proof, it may also be that an innate aesthetic sense prompts us to respond to the beauties of nature in a way that not only delights the senses and calms the mind, but also enhances self-understanding.

The fourth most frequent trigger of mystical experience identified by Hardy from his sample was participation in religious worship (11.8 percent). In view of the emphasis placed upon church attendance and the act of communal worship by the Christian religion it is surprising that this trigger is not more frequently reported. Some authorities might argue that the purpose of worship is not mystical experience but a rendering to God of those things – devotion, gratitude, awe, service, homage – which are rightly his. Nevertheless, aspects of the formal act of worship in Roman Catholicism and other Christian denominations such as plainsong, chanting, and the scent of incense – to say nothing of the soaring splendor of church and temple architecture with its murals, stained glass, icons, and statuary (or in the case of Islam, of its abstract and geometrical decorations) were and are intended to help induce altered states of consciousness in worshippers. Even in the more austere environment of Christian nonconformist chapels it might be assumed that the intensity of public and private prayer and the uplift of corporate hymn singing may similarly be intended to induce religious experience.

It may of course be that the percentage in Hardy's sample gaining religious experience from corporate acts of worship represents more than 11.8 percent of those who actually attend church regularly. Nevertheless, the fact that nearly 90 percent of religious experiences are reported as arising outside the context of corporate worship does pose certain questions as to the role of such worship in facilitating this experience. These questions are further emphasized by Hardy's discovery elsewhere in his analysis that when reporting the development of religious experience arising from contact with the thoughts and ideas of others, nearly four times as many people refer to contact with literature and the arts as refer to church or institutionalized religion. Although these figures can be interpreted in a number of ways, they certainly suggest that churchgoing does not feature particularly prominently as an instigator of religious experience.

Other triggers mentioned by Hardy include sacred places (2.6 percent), music, visual art, literature, drama, and film (which if taken together are mentioned by 16.4 percent, putting the arts as triggers second only to depression and despair), the prospect of death (1.5 percent – an interestingly low figure in the light of our earlier discussion on the part that fear of death may play in religious belief and experience), the death of others (2.8 percent), creative work (2 percent), crises in personal relationships (3.7 per =cent), and happiness (0.07 percent – which low figure, when compared with the percentage of experiences triggered by depression and despair, is particularly revealing).

## Mystical Experiences and Sport

A significant omission from Hardy's list is participation in sport (although physical activities are mentioned by 1 percent of respondents). By contrast, Murphy and White (1995) consider that the many reports they have collected (from over 6,000 books, articles, letters, and dissertations) of transcendent experiences "show us that sport has enormous power to sweep us beyond our ordinary sense of self, to evoke capacities that have generally been regarded as mystical, occult, or religious." They concede that people do not (or only rarely) take part in sport in order to have transcendent experiences – they do so in order to seek enjoyment. But in their view the "*mystical moment occurs as often as it does in sport in part because you don't have to have one*" (original italics). Further, their findings suggest to them that "spiritual experience seems to depend to some extent on the distance a person has come from his or her ordinary habits and on a willingness to give up set responses. Stepping into *terra incognito* by deed seems to trigger openings into the *terra incognito* of metanormal experience."

We can question whether all the mystical experiences reported by sports people really are transcendent, and thus suitable for inclusion in any account of religious experience. They may indeed vary in relevance (just as some of those reported to Hardy vary), but at their clearest they bear comparison with many of those found in the mystical literature. For example, Murphy and White quote from the account provided by George Sheehan, a medical doctor and regular runner. Sheehan reports that 30 minutes into his run a change takes place in his consciousness with the result that:

. . . I see myself not as an individual but as part of the universe. In it, I can happen upon anything I ever read or saw or experienced. Every fact and instinct and emotion is unlocked and made available to me through some mysterious operation in my brain.

When reported by sports people, experiences such as this are sometimes put down to the chemical changes that occur at certain points during feats of physical endurance like long-distance running, but Murphy and White observe that proficiency in sport requires "concentration, freedom from distraction, and sustained alertness" – all qualities they consider necessary in meditation practices. The authors further point out that, "a wandering mind diminishes athletic ability . . . The greatest athletes are legendary for their powers of concentration," and that other features necessary for success in some sports – such as living fully in the present while taking part, blocking out everything except the immediate task in hand, directing an unbroken flow of awareness toward the object of attention, self-discipline, the coordination of mind and body so that they function as one, and an effortless absorption in the experience to the extent of full identification with it – are all similarly emphasized in manuals of meditative and spiritual training going back over 2,000 years to Patanjali's *Yoga Sutras*, a seminal text in Eastern religious thought.

It would be wrong to suppose that the majority of those who engage in sport encounter the mystical experiences of which Murphy and White speak. In fact, judging by the behavior of many leading sportsmen and women, it is abundantly clear that they do not. Physical activity, unaccompanied by the right attitude of mind, is manifestly insufficient. However, the reports furnished by those who have developed this attitude reveal particular similarities with the experiences of leading martial arts experts for whom the practice of their discipline is intended above all else as a way toward spiritual enlightenment. An even more remarkable example of the way in which physical activity and attitude of mind can produce religious experience is provided by the Tendai Buddhist monks of Mount Hiei in Western Japan who, at certain points in their training, complete what is effectively a marathon every day for 100 consecutive days (1,000 days for a few exceptional beings at the culmination of their noviciate), always following the same route – a superhuman feat of endurance far beyond either the duplication or the comprehension even of the most highly trained Western athletes. Sleeping and eating little between each day, negotiating rocky paths and steep mountain slopes during their marathon, and stopping at numerous designated stations of worship en route to carry out prostrations and other devotions, the monks are sustained, we are told, not by physical energies but by spiritual strength – a strength derived from an all-consuming desire to realize Buddhahood (full enlightenment) during their present lifetimes for the sake of all sentient beings.

Stevens (1988) reports that by way of helping them gather this spiritual strength, the monks undertake another practice beyond the capacity of most men and women, namely a period of 700 days in solitary meditation in remote mountain retreats. At the end of their various feats of psychological and physical endurance, the monks, we are told, have become "one with the mountain, flying along a path that is free from obstruction. The joy of practice has been discovered, and all things are made new each day." In addition to these experiences of what can be described as immanent mysticism, the monks are reported as describing their state of mind as gratitude – gratitude to their teachers, gratitude to the mountain and to nature, gratitude to the charity of their fellow men and women whose offerings sustain them in the monastic life, and gratitude for the opportunity to carry out their arduous practice. Gratitude, rather than any sense of pride, of ego-driven achievement or even of ascetic accomplishment, is therefore a major part of the legacy of their experiences. But the monks are also said to have entered states of transcendental as well as of immanent mysticism, apparently perceiving during their daily marathons the dynamic image of an incarnation of the cosmic Buddha *Mahavairocana* (Japanese *Dainichi*), believed by members of the Tendai sect of Japanese Buddhism to be the active element in enlightenment, an element which burns up evil passions and reveals the deepest levels of wisdom.

## Motivation for Mysticism

The feats of the monks of Mount Hiei raise important questions concerning the psychology of human motivation. For the monks, neither fame nor fortune feature in their rewards. And there are many other examples of extreme acts of physical endurance and hardship in the name of religion where fame and fortune are not involved, from Hindu yogis who spend years of their lives without respite in a standing posture in order to subdue the wandering mind and the physical appetites of the body, to members of monastic communities in both East and West who subject themselves to life-long regimes of early rising, of lengthy sessions of daily meditation interspersed with frequent acts of corporate prayers and ritual, of monotonous and meager meals, of a paucity of personal possessions, and of a total absence of even the most basic of creature comforts. The Freudian argument that they do so in the belief that they are pleasing a heavenly father supposedly substituting for an earthly one hardly holds good – particularly so in the case of the monks of Mount

Hiei and of other Buddhist practitioners, since Buddhism does not preach the existence of such a heavenly being who desires to be worshipped by his followers. Even the primordial Buddhas and the various other gods and demons whose existence is acknowledged in certain Buddhist sects are said ultimately to be simply universal energies personified by the actions of one's own mind. One venerates them solely in order to arouse and develop these energies in oneself.

Which brings us back to the stated motivation of the monks of Mount Hiei, namely to achieve enlightenment for the sake of all sentient beings. Put another way, their aim is to produce a profound and permanent alteration in their consciousness, and in so doing to benefit the consciousness of all their fellow men and women, since they regard all consciousness as ultimately one. Such an alteration is not regarded as providing access to some celestial paradise, there to spend an eternity enjoying the rewards of their long years of self-sacrifice, but to the state of mind that underlies all states, a state which – since it is said to lie beyond normal conceptualization – can only be fully known through experience. Thus it seems that their motivation either stems from a profound trust in their teachers, who are thought to have attained that state and who therefore speak from it, or by some intuitive, innate sense that the state exists. A Buddhist would emphasize the importance of both these forms of motivation, and would add that as this state is in fact our own true nature, it is not surprising that we are able to become aware of its existence through intuition if we undertake the necessary practices required to still the activity of our normal consciousness.

To judge by the many reports of the mystical experiences of sportsmen and women collected by Murphy and White (1995), this intuitive knowledge does indeed arise spontaneously once the body and mind satisfy certain conditions. Prior belief systems appear to play little part. A useful, although incomplete analogy, might be a child's first experience that water is wet. No prior knowledge or belief system is required, simply the satisfaction of certain conditions, such as being placed in a bath. The child's nervous system is programmed by nature to respond to the water in a particular way, a way which, to the best of our understanding, is common to everyone with a fully functioning nervous system. Similar examples could be drawn from all tactile, auditory, visual, and physiological responses, which arise not as a consequence of instruction, but from the simple fact of exposure to the appropriate stimuli.

Future research into the so-called God Spot (chapter 7) may help us to understand better the mechanism involved in this innately determined religious response. For the present we have to be content with a behavioral analysis which notes the extraordinary experiences reported alike by some athletes and some dedicated religious practitioners, and the equally extraordinary lengths to which both groups are prepared to go while these experiences are being induced. As for the purpose and the value of such experiences, we must each make our own choice. Some will see them as linked to an inborn sense of ourselves as spiritual beings, others will see them as a form of superfluous behavior which tells us nothing other than the extent to which humans can delude themselves and needlessly squander both time and energy.

There are certain aspects of scientific exploration, in particular quantum physics, which also seem to prompt if not mystical experiences then at least mystical views. Einstein, Planck, Heisenberg, Pauli, Schrödinger, Jeans, Eddington, Bohm, Eccles all held such well-documented views (Wilber, 1985). It seems that each of them recognized that science, for all its ability to take them into the mystery of existence, reached a point where it could go no further. And yet the mystery remained, a mystery which it seemed could be penetrated only by a sense of the mystical. In the words of Schrödinger (1967) "The overall number of minds is just one. I venture to call it indestructible . . . I am now talking religion not science – a religion, however, not opposed to science, but supported by what disinterested scientific research has brought to the fore." Whitehead, a towering figure in both mathematics and philosophy, put it that materialistic science has been remarkably effective at abstracting facts from the circumstances in which they occur, but that when we pass beyond these abstractions "either by more subtle employment of our senses, or by the request for meanings and for coherence of thoughts, the scheme breaks down at once" (Whitehead, 1933). The implications of this are twofold, firstly that materialistic science is not competent to answer questions on the existence or otherwise of God, of the soul, and of life after death, and secondly that these answers can arise only from "more subtle employment of our senses" as in mystical experience, prayer, intuition, and introspection, all of which academic psychology has tended largely to ignore over the last decades.

## Religious Conversion

Religious conversion can be associated with mystical experience, but may occur independently of it, and is best discussed separately. Conversion is taken to mean the transition – often abrupt – from disbelief or indifference in spiritual matters to the certainty of faith. In some respects it is akin to so-called enlightenment in that the individuals concerned believe that, through what seems like an act of grace over which they have no direct control, they are suddenly put in possession of fundamental spiritual truths. What do we know of the psychology behind conversion? Are individuals converted as a result of meeting a charismatic teacher (in the Eastern traditions sitting with such a teacher is known as *darshan*, a practice said potentially to have profound effects even upon skeptics, though no words are exchanged)? Is conversion a byproduct of joining a social group one admires and adopting their ways of being? Does it arise from reading the scriptures and allied literature? Or is it a consequence of internal processes, such as a form of direct religious experience? Or, more importantly, does conversion owe most to the state of mind of the individual prior to the conversion experience?

Is this state of mind a recognition that life is currently unsatisfactory, the *dukka* ("suffering" – or better still "sourness") of which the Buddha made so much? Is it a compelling need to search for some form of meaning to counteract *dukka*? Is it a response to traumatic life events such as a bereavement or a broken relationship? Does it owe anything to temperament? And once converted, what prompts people to stay converted? Is conversion a form of compensation for unhappiness, and if so does it achieve results?

There are many attempted answers to some of these questions. Freud (1928) considered that conversion is the resolution of an unconscious conflict, a resolution which allows the ego to become revitalized by an intense emotional attachment to an internalized fantasy love object. This revitalization is of far greater importance to the individual concerned than the actual content of the religious teachings and beliefs involved in the conversion. Once again, he saw the father–child relationship as of great importance. A good relationship tends to prompt the search for a fantasy figure who can fulfil the role of the protective, loving father, while a bad relationship prompts rebellion and the need for an alternative authority figure as a way of resolving the fear and anxiety this bad relationship engenders.

The trouble with these theories, as with so much of Freud, is that it is difficult to falsify them. He explains the conversion experience as arising from the father–child relationship, whether this relationship is a good one or a bad one. Whichever way the results of an investigation into the association between the parent–child relationship works out, Freudian theory is thus said to explain it. Heads he wins and tails his critics lose. This is hardly the stuff of science, which looks for more clear-cut results. If Freud is right, we would have to conclude that only when the relationship between parent and child is a neutral one – whatever that would mean – is a conversion experience unlikely. Such a conclusion hardly seems compelling.

In fact the various studies that have some bearing upon Freud's theory suggest that it is bad rather than any other form of parenting that seems most likely to precede the conversion experience. For example Ullman

(1989) found that converts' perceptions of their parents are more negative than are those of individuals with a stable religious identity, while Kirkpatrick and Hood (1990) also found those experiencing sudden conversion have more distant relationships with their parents. Other authorities support Freud's link between many instances of conversion and pre-existing psychological disturbance. In his classic work, William James (1902) suggested that dramatic conversion and the profound personality change that follows it are often preceded by a serious personal crisis such as deep depression. In support he cites famous cases such as Tolstoy, Bunyan, and St. Augustine, all of whom showed signs of disturbing levels of melancholia. Low self-esteem, lack of social support, frustration of deep-seated aspirations, stress and tension, insecurity, low social status, and the search for identity are all cited as other precipitating conditions (e.g. Lofland, 1978; Weimann, 1987). Conversion is thus seen as a way of experiencing a "new" self, perhaps avoiding in the process a total psychological breakdown. In a major meta-analysis of 25 studies covering a total of 4,513 converts, Oksanen (1994) concluded that conversion indeed appears to be a fantasy compensation for an attachment deficit. Other studies link conversion to high levels of the emotional reactivity found in those with manic depressive psychosis (Gallemore, Wilson, and Rhoads, 1969), to anxiety and denial (Spellman, Baskett, and Byrne, 1971), and to psychosis generally (Stone, 1992).

These various findings (and there are many other similar) suggest that at times conversion can be an escape from a perceived reality that has proved insupportable (an escape which incidentally seems to have significant psychological value, a point to which we return in chapter 12). What is unclear, however, is why some people, faced with this need to escape, turn to religion while others turn to drugs, others to therapy, and others manage to get on with life as it is. Underlying their neurotic or psychotic symptoms is there among those who choose religion a genuine desire to find an answer to life's existential questions? Which brings us to another query, namely whether or not there is at times something more positive to conversion than a form of emotional escape. This query is particularly relevant to those who experience conversion without any of the overt signs of psychological disturbance to which we have just made reference. The answer to it is that indeed there seems not infrequently to be a burning desire to *know*, to find answers, to embark on the kind of search sometimes associated with the quest orientation detailed by Edwards (2001) and others, and mentioned earlier in the chapter.

Zen Buddhism refers to this desire to know as "great doubt" (or "great spirit of inquiry"), and if it is not already present the Zen practitioner is taught to arouse it in him or herself (Sheng Yen, 1982). Certainly Buddhism and other Eastern traditions are replete with accounts of men and women who spent years in intensive spiritual quests, abandoning normal life and journeying from teacher to teacher, and sometimes spending long periods in solitude before achieving conversion or enlightenment experiences (see e.g. Luk, 1970, for examples). Such a way of life is held in high esteem in these traditions. In India, there is a convention still followed by many that the householder, on reaching the age of 60 and with his responsibilities to family and to profession left behind him, gives away his possessions and sets out to devote the rest of his life to the spiritual quest. Western literature also contains numerous relevant examples, particularly in the Christian Orthodox Church (French, 1972 and 1973, provides one of the most illuminating of these), of the devoted intensity with which some men and women seek spiritual illumination. Sustained, single-minded, and effective determination of this kind, often in the face of extreme physical and psychological hardship, is hardly compatible with the presence of significant levels of neurosis or psychosis.

Does this burning desire to know arise from the creative imagination, which is able to fantasize a better world? Does it come from curiosity, the same curiosity that motivates scientists to find out more about the material world? Does it come from an innate sense (whether associated with the so-called "God Spot" in the brain or not), more developed in some people than in others, that there is a spiritual dimension to life? Is it a recognition of the *dukka* to which we referred earlier, the unsatisfactory nature of material life? Does it come from sudden, unexpected experiences which the individual concerned attributes to God, or from some supposedly miraculous or paranormal experiences, such as spontaneous healing or supposed communication with the deceased? These are all questions requiring answers if we are to understand more about the phenomenon of conversion. Probably conversion arises from all of these precipitating factors, but we need to know the relative frequency of each of them, and the extent to which each leads to long-lasting changes in beliefs and behavior.

## Personality Factors and Religiosity

Psychiatric data (aided by some extrapolations from conditioning studies) led Sargant (1974) to conclude that although "weak inhibitory characters" (i.e. melancholics and unstable introverts) are most susceptible to stress and most likely to undergo dramatic religious conversion, those with "strong characters" (stable extraverts and introverts) are more likely to retain new beliefs and attitudes once conversion has taken place. This suggests that while the former may turn temporarily to religion in an attempt to deal with their psychological problems, the latter may be motivated more by the desire to know which we have just been discussing. However, work with the Personal Orientation Inventory (POI), one of the standardized personality tests most frequently used in the exploration of personality and religion, seems to confirm Maslow's conviction that self-actualization (the full realization of oneself and one's potential) is actively hindered by involvement in traditional religious beliefs and practices, and correlates more with intense personal experience and an ecumenical outlook. Designed to measure self-actualization tendencies (though there is some doubt as to its accuracy in this respect), the POI assesses such variables as the ability to like oneself despite recognizing personal weaknesses, the flexibility to follow one's own principles, the ability to recognize and express feelings and needs, the readiness to live in the present rather than in anxieties about the past or future, the capacity for intimacy with others without becoming subservient, and the belief in the essential goodness of human nature and in a certain commonality between life's opposites. In a number of studies among those preparing for or in the ministry, those who are assessed on measures such as clinical interviews to show greater sociopsychological development score significantly higher on the POI than those who show lesser development (e.g. Kennedy *et al.*, 1977), although among general student samples and laypeople regular church attendees tend to score *lower* than non-attendees (e.g. Hjelle, 1975).

These various findings seem to indicate that among those with spiritual beliefs, maturity of personality goes with an attitude to religion which is undogmatic and nonrestrictive, and which is more interested in seeking the truth behind religious teachings than with strict adherence to any one set of doctrines. This lends support to the view expressed earlier that maturity of personality goes with a desire to answer fundamental existential questions rather than with the need to use religion as some form of psychological crutch. However, results on other personality inventories suggest it would be wrong to lay too much emphasis upon the connection between the neurotic tendencies mentioned in this chapter and religion. In another widely used personality test, Eysenck's EPQ, there is no overall correlation between religiosity and the Neuroticism dimension in the general population. Nor is there any correlation between religiosity and either end of the Extraversion-Introversion Scale (Francis and Pearson, 1985). However, there is a significant *negative* correlation between religiosity and the third of Eysenck's dimensions, Psychoticism – a trait indicating tough-mindedness and lack of empathy (Francis, 1993), which suggests religious people are more compassionate and forgiving than the norm. Religious people do score higher on the Lie Scale in the EPQ than the average, which perhaps indicates denial – that is a reluctance to accept the negative personal characteristics which we all share and to which the EPQ expects us to own up if we are being truthful.

Currently, personality traits are generally seen by psychologists to reduce to the so-called "Big Five" (Norman, 1963), which in addition to Extraversion and Emotional Stability (equivalent to Eysenck's Neuroticism-Stability Scale) include Agreeableness, Conscientiousness, and Culture – which some commentators think should more properly be labeled "Openness". As with the EPQ, neither Extraversion–Introversion nor Emotional Stability–Instability have been found to correlate significantly with religiosity. Only Culture – or Openness – shows any link (Hampson, 1988), and the suggestion is that this scale covers the same qualities as the negative end of Eysenck's Psychoticism dimension. In other words, religious people emerge once again as more empathic and compassionate than the norm.

The relationship between religiosity and authoritarianism (measured most frequently by the F Scale first developed by Adorno and colleagues in 1950 and more recently by the Right-Wing Authoritarian Scale constructed by Altemeyer in 1988) is a complex one. The authoritarian personality is characterized by conformity, fondness for authority, distrust of other human beings, inflexible patterns of thinking, and exaggerated nationalism and ethnocentricity. Certain religious sects actively encourage these traits by their claims to being the sole possessors of spiritual truths, and a number of studies in the United States and elsewhere indicate that those with orthodox religious beliefs do in fact tend to be higher than the norm on some aspects of authoritarianism (see Altemeyer, 1994). But "authoritarianism" covers a number of variables, and scores on these individual variables show a rather confusing picture. For example, although Roman Catholics on average appear to have higher overall authoritarian scores than other religious groups, they have significantly lower ethnocentrism scores (e.g. Stark, 1971). Another anomaly is that there appears to be a curvilinear relationship between church attendance and another of the variables of authoritarianism, namely prejudice, in that churchgoers who attend less frequently score higher than those who attend regularly (e.g. Hoge and Carroll, 1973). The same curvilinear relationship appears to exist between religious belief and laboratory measures of authoritarian behavior (Bock and Warren, 1972).

Links between overall authoritarianism and religiosity may be partly explained by the fact that religion, whether theistic or non-theistic, involves accepting that life is ruled by levels of consciousness superior in many ways to our own, to which supplication may be made. Thus religion by its very nature cannot be democratic in the generally accepted sense of the term. In addition, there is the belief common to most traditions that a hierarchy necessarily exists among worshippers, with a priestly caste at the apex who have access to spiritual wisdom and authority in advance of that of the rank and file. The emphasis in both Eastern and Western traditions upon sacrificing the self (or in the case of Buddhism recognizing its illusory nature) to the divine may further strengthen the tendency toward submission, as may the emphasis upon service to others and upon humbling rather than exalting individuality. One could argue that there is in fact an element of depersonalization in this process that bears some similarities to that used in military training and in some political parties.

What is unclear is whether those who are drawn to religion tend to be authoritarian in the first place, or whether in becoming religious they learn to submit themselves to the suzerainty of a higher power. Probably there is truth in both. Of particular interest in this context is the curvilinear relationship that appears to exist between prejudice and religious observance. This relationship suggests that as people become more knowledgeable about religion, and apply its teaching more closely to their own lives, so they move beyond mere tribalism and sectarianism, and become more compassionate and more conscious of our shared humanity. Higher levels of intelligence may also help this process, as authoritarianism is stronger among those who score less well on intelligence tests. It seems that the more one is able to analyze situations, to think independently and to identify the need for flexibility, the less authoritarian one is likely to be. In a particularly relevant study, Hoge (1974) found that social and religious liberalism is indeed positively correlated with verbal intelligence, and that religious skeptics score more highly than believers on both verbal and quantitative intelligence.

It is an open question whether or not religion must of necessity be authoritarian. Behind this authoritarianism lies the belief that the founders of major religions have not only handed down teachings which are necessary for the spiritual life, but that they have in some way ordained successors who in turn ordain others, thus carrying on a direct line of transmission from the founder to the present day. The Roman Catholic Church, with its belief that this line of ordinands represents an apostolic succession back to St. Peter and through St. Peter to Christ is an obvious example of this, but even Zen Buddhism, in spite of its original iconoclasm, has its line of patriarchs. And Islam, which has no priestly caste, nevertheless accords the Iman a special status in that he has a particular responsibility for maintaining and transmitting the purity of the teachings. The emphasis upon finding a teacher runs through virtually all traditions, and in the East in particular the belief is often expressed that one cannot make real progress unless one is successful in doing so. Further, there is sometimes a warning that without a teacher there is the risk of falling into error, particularly in the practice of the various yogas.

One is entitled to inquire why, if the priest and the teacher are so essential, religions have such a tendency to fall away from the principles of their founders. Authoritarianism should not be condemned out of hand. It may help produce stability, order, and peace, and the sacrifice of short-term goals for long-term. Without some measure of authoritarianism it is difficult to see how social groups can deal responsibly with the world. But beyond a certain point authoritarianism can stifle individual thought and initiative. Much creativity arises from nonconformity, and in religion as elsewhere, the opposite of creativity can be stagnation and unthinking obedience. If spiritual development is an intrinsic process, there must always be a measure of individuality and personal questing. The extent to which religious orthodoxy held up the progress of science and philosophy in the West is too well known to require elaboration – as is the extent to which in some areas scientific orthodoxy has also hindered the advance of knowledge. The dangers of too great an emphasis upon orthodoxy are as apparent as are the dangers of too great a degree of unstructured thinking.

## Religion and Magical Thinking

Historically religion has always been linked to the supernatural, and the question arises, are religious people even in these times more likely to believe that supernatural events – events that appear to break the known laws of science – are possible? Freud saw such belief as related to what he called omnipotence thinking, the early conviction that parents, and later God or the gods can, bring things about through the power of thought. Currently such thinking is more often referred to as magical, and is seen as finding expression for example in superstition, in the belief that by making light of possible disaster one is "tempting fate" and, by skeptics, in the belief in a nonphysical, spiritual dimension. In a pioneering study into religious belief in children aged 6 to 10 years, Thun (1959) identified five characteristics, one of which was *magical thinking* (the others were a *readiness* for religion, a capacity for *religious experiences*, a *dependence* for religious ideas upon influential others, and *changeableness* a strain of *magical thinking*. Anthromorphism, egocentricity and a tendency to concretize even abstract ideas were also present. It seemed that these characteristics were a stage on the road either to religious maturity or to neurotic self-defense or indifference. Work of this kind suggests that magical thinking is a childish way of misinterpreting the world, particularly as later work by Thun with adolescents (Thun, 1963) revealed that for most individuals this form of thinking is quickly left behind.

However, Thun draws attention to the fact that the majority of his adolescents had also left behind the capacity for religious experience, and in his view this indicates "the spiritual destruction of modern, uprooted man," who with the development of abstract conceptual thinking loses contact with the language of inner images and with the inner world of wholeness. He goes further and suggests that the disappearance of these images is reflected in the modern intensified need for visual stimulation from the outer world, and indeed for the insatiable craving for experience in the adolescent and young adult. If Thun is correct, this implies that it may be the loss of the capacity for magical thinking that is a sign of immaturity, rather than its retention. Such a capacity may play some part in psychological health, or at least in the exploration of the full resources of one's own mind.

Many would disagree with this implication. Claridge (1985) has put forward the idea of the personality dimension labeled *schizotypy*, characterized by a tendency to hallucinate and have other anomalous perceptual or cognitive experiences, and which may reveal a disposition toward schizophrenia itself. This would support the argument that magical thinking, which is linked to schizotypy, is indeed a sign of disordered psychological development. But to complicate matters, schizotypy appears to be an enabling factor in artistic, religious, and literary creativity, so it seems inappropriate to label it as a disorder. In addition, McCreery (1993) found that subjects who reported out-of-body experiences (OBEs – the feeling that one's consciousness is temporarily located outside one's body), though high on the part of the schizotypy scale dealing with dreams, hallucinations, and delusions, were low on anxiety. Thus there may be more to the link between religiosity and schizotypy – and magical thinking – than meets the eye. Even if religion is regarded, along with the arts, as emanating only from the creative imagination, it would nevertheless seem potentially to have a significant role to play in expressing the fullness of the human personality, and perhaps in the maintenance of psychological health, a point to which we will return when discussing religion and well-being in chapter 12.

## Religious Experience in Dreams

Many religious experiences are reported in dreams, perhaps because the dreaming mind duplicates one of the important conditions which serves to facilitate these experiences in waking life, namely the stilling of the internal chatter which dominates much of normal consciousness. Once this stilling is achieved, information from the unconscious appears better able to bring itself to the attention. Judging by the evidence of scripts such as the *Chester Beatty Papyrus*, the ancient Egyptians took the messages contained in dreams very seriously, regarding them as revelations from the gods to the Pharaohs. The ancient Babylonian epic *Gilgamesh*, although fictional, is replete with accounts of dreams which convey religious messages of one kind and another. The ancient Greeks, who borrowed extensively from both Egyptian and Babylonian methods of dream interpretation, also regarded dream messages as coming from the gods. The methods for inducing significant dreams developed by both Egyptians and Greeks consisted essentially of spending the night in the temple after ingesting a sleep-inducing potion, and submitting the resulting dreams to interpretation by the priests the following morning.

Aristotle rather dismissively considered that if God really did speak to men and women in dreams he would only do so to the wise, but the early Christian Church also regarded dreams as a context for religious experience. St. John Chrysostum, St. Augustine, and St. Jerome all taught that God reveals himself in dreams, and despite growing opposition from Church authorities, who saw their own power threatened by any suggestion that men and women could obtain knowledge of God other than through the scriptures and the priesthood, belief in the potential spiritual purpose of dreaming persisted, surviving even the scientific rationalism of the eighteenth century (Fontana, 1995). Even noted philosophers such as Fichte and Herbart adhered to the view that dream content could be psychologically revealing.

The belief that dreams and divine revelations are associated in some way was buoyed up across the centuries by the fact that the Bible contains many references to religious experiences arising in dreams. For example we are told that when God descended to Earth in a pillar of cloud and stood at the door of the tabernacle (a religious experience which in itself was presumably not without note for those present) he informed Aaron and Miriam that "If there be a prophet among you, I the Lord will make myself known unto him in a vision, and will speak unto him in a dream" (Numbers 12: 6). Other Biblical examples abound. King Saul laments that God has forsaken him, and communicates with him no more "neither by prophets nor by dreams" (Samuel 28: 15). Elihu assures Job that "God speaketh in a dream, in a vision of the night, when deep sleep falleth upon men . . . Then he openeth the ears of men, and sealeth their instructions" (Job 33: 15–16). Joseph assures Pharoh's officers that God interprets dreams (Genesis 40: 8). Daniel learns from God in a "night vision" not only the content of King Nebuchadnezzar's prophetic dream but its interpretation, thus saving the wise men of Babylon from the sentence of death imposed upon them by the King for their failure over dream interpretation (Daniel 2: 19 ff.). Jacob dreams of the celebrated ladder ascending to heaven and of God informing him of the future fecundity and prosperity of the tribes of Israel (Genesis 28: 12–15). Solomon is told by God in a dream that his wish for a wise and understanding heart will be granted because he has not asked for long life or riches for himself, or for victory over his enemies (I Kings 3: 5–14). Gideon is emboldened to attack and defeat the Midianites when he hears that the dream of one of his followers has predicted success (Judges 7: 13–15).

Divine warnings also abound in Biblical dreams. King Abimelech is warned by God in a dream that Sarah, abducted by him, is in fact Abraham's wife and must be returned to Abraham on pain of death (Genesis 20: 3–7). Laban the Syrian is similarly warned not to harm Jacob (Genesis 31: 24). The three Wise Men are warned by God in a dream not to return to Herod and to disclose the birthplace of Jesus (Matthew 2: 12). Joseph is warned in a dream to take the infant Jesus and to flee into Egypt (Matthew 2: 13), and later given in another dream the message that it is safe to return home (Matthew 2: 19–20). Pilate's wife tells her husband that she has been warned in a dream that he should not harm Jesus, who is a "just man" (Matthew 27: 19).

Walsh (1987) considers that "The role of dreams . . . can be essential to the process [of religious conversion]," and there are numerous examples of such conversions and various other religious experiences arising from dreams in all the great traditions. Mohammed received the prophetic call that led to his rising from obscurity and founding Islam in a dream, and in the Koran he relates how the Angel Gabriel led him on a silvery mare to heaven where he met Christ, Adam, and the four apostles and then entered the Garden of Delights where he received the words of God himself. From early times, Hindu rishis or seers interpreted dream content in terms of the symbolic attributes of gods and demons, a practice made explicit in the *Atharda Veda*, one of the earliest Hindu scriptures dating from c.1,500–1,000 BCE. Tibetan Buddhists consider spiritual revelations are conveyed in trance and in dreams to monks who serve as oracles. Such dreams, which are thought to foretell the future and to provide guidance and answers both to spiritual and practical questions, are believed to be communications from the tutelary deities who undertake the task of protecting and instructing the monastery to which the oracle belongs.

## Dream Yoga and Grand Dreams

The *Nyingma*, the oldest sect of Tibetan Buddhism, place particular emphasis upon dreams, regarding them in effect as a dress rehearsal for afterlife experiences. In the practice known as dream yoga, the adept is taught to remain conscious during dreams, and thus to control dream content. By learning dream yoga, he or she is said not only to be able to have much greater command over waking consciousness, but also to remain fully conscious during the process of dying, and thus to assert greater control over the afterdeath experiences and ultimately over the conditions of rebirth, whether rebirth takes place in this world or in other worlds (Powers, 1995). Indigenous American peoples and shamanic cultures in Africa and Asia manifest somewhat similar beliefs (Bulkeley, 1995; Gillette, 1997). The soul is thought to leave the body during sleep, and the shaman learns to direct this process in order to journey to the spirit worlds, where the soul is said not only to meet with the souls of the deceased but also to receive guidance and healing from spiritual helpers. We are also told that the shaman can be given his or her "power song" while dreaming, which is then used to summon spirit guardians and other helpers to assist with healing and divining. Shamanic cultures recognize in fact that there are two types of dreams, ordinary dreams which come from the dreamer's own mind, and big dreams which involve spirit journeys and communications from spirit guardians. Big dreams are described as so vivid that they resemble the experiences of waking consciousness, and are usually repeated several times on different nights. Typically they contain spiritual guidance or warnings, and the shaman is taught to take them literally, not to regard their meaning as presented in the symbolic form found in ordinary dreams (Harner, 1990).

There are some similarities here with Carl Jung's theories of dreaming. Jung also accepted the existence of "grand" or "big" dreams (Jung, 1964, 1966, 1968b, 1984), which stay undiminished in the memory for many years afterwards, and that appear to originate from outside oneself and to contain material of an apparently spiritual nature. He noted that such dreams are reported in "primitive" cultures as well as in more sophisticated ones, which he took to indicate that they arise from deep levels of what he termed the collective unconscious (that part of the unconscious mind genetically determined and in his view common to all humans). Jung differed, however, from the shamanic interpretation in that he considered even big dreams were symbolic in content. In his view all dreams are compensatory, and their symbolic meaning must be unraveled before we can know what part of psychological life is actually seeking compensation. His clinical experience led him to believe that if the spiritual side of a person's nature is repressed or unacknowledged, it will seek expression in big dreams. And even where the spiritual side is acknowledged there will still be unrealized aspects that emerge in such dreams.

## Creative Artists and Mystical Dream Experiences

Many writers and poets detail what appear to be accounts of religious – particularly mystical – experiences in dreams. One of the best-known such accounts is by the seventeenth-century English poet Henry Vaughan, who in his poem *The World* wrote the well-known lines:

> I saw Eternity the other night,
> Like a great ring of pure and endless light,
> All pure as it was bright;
> And round beneath it, Time in hours, days, years,
> Driv'n by the spheres
> Like a vast shadow mov'd; in which the world
> And all her train were hurl'd.

William Blake, one of the most prolific poets of mysticism, reported that he was even given the secret of a process of copper engraving in one of his dreams. Desperately short of money, he had been searching for some time without success for an inexpensive way to carry out the engravings with which he illustrated his poems. One night, his dead brother Robert appeared to him in a dream and "revealed the wished-for secret." Blake was in no doubt that it was indeed his dead brother who appeared to him, and next day sent out his wife with their last half crown to buy the simple materials "necessary for setting in practice the new revelation." As a direct result of the dream he developed the technique of engraving which was to provide his principal means of support for the rest of his life.

Blake's experience is of particular note because it appears not only to have involved one of the experiences listed by Hay and Heald in Table 10.1 as religious (an apparent visitation from the deceased) but also because it produced practical results which provided Blake with the means to continue with his creative work. Many other poets and creative writers – for example Robert Louis Stevenson, John Keats, Walter Scott, Charlotte Bronte, H. G. Wells, Edgar Alan Poe, and Mark Twain – have claimed to receive inspiration in dreams. Not all of these inspirational experiences can be regarded as religious, but that of the eighteenth-century Italian musician, Giuseppe Tartini, is, in the light of Hay and Heald's inclusion of evil presences in their definition of religious experiences (Table 10.1), certainly intriguing. In Tartini's account the devil appeared to him during sleep while he was – somewhat paradoxically – staying at the monastery of Assissi, and played on Tartini's own fiddle a sonata whose beauty "surpassed the wildest flights of my imagination." On waking, Tartini struggled unsuccessfully to recall the exact details, but he succeeded in remembering enough to write his *Trillo del Diavola* (*The Devil's Trill*), which is the best known of his many works for violin, and which he considered the best thing he had ever done (see e.g. Brook, 1987; Fontana, 1995).

## Dream Mysticism and Spiritual Guidance

Accounts of religious experiences through the centuries and up to modern times show that dreams have consistently provided an appropriate
setting for these experiences. Starting with the work of Guerney, Myers,
and Podmore (1886) and Myers (1906) there have been many systematic
attempts to collect relevant dream accounts, together with reports of
other anomalous and possibly spiritually related experiences. Hardy (1979)
includes a number of such accounts, but among the most recent collections are those of Lagrand (1997, 2000). Many of these accounts, like
that of William Blake, relate to the appearance of someone known to be
deceased. One of Lagrand's respondents (Lagrand, 1997) writes that
after the death of her father she dreamt of his appearing to her, hugging
her ("I felt this – it was very real") and asking if she wished to come with
him. She feared that this might mean she was about to die, but he
reassured her that "next time . . . you can come with me." She reports
that the dream "helped me so much . . . I saw him strong and happy and
vital again . . . I could let go of the pain and fear. . . ." Another of Lagrand's
respondents dreamt of seeing her recently deceased infant daughter
"bathed in a kind of light that was more than the light we know of. This
light was a presence of a universal kind of knowledge . . . of peace, of
wisdom, of love . . . I felt it in my soul." She goes on to say that such
dreams are "not from my psychology or my trauma or my memory or
anything else from my life . . . They are an externally placed experience,
conscious and generated by something outside, instilling in me a kind of
joy and peace that is infinite."

Sometimes such dreams impart guidance or, as with Biblical dreams,
apparent information about the future. Another of Lagrand's respondents
provides examples of both these occurrences. In each dream she dreamt
of her deceased father-in-law. On the first occasion he gave her "clear
instructions" about her daughter, whose behavior was causing a great
deal of concern at the time, and assured her that all would be well (as it
proved to be). In the second he warned her that her father, who was
unwell, "would be leaving. He left me with an impression that he would
be coming to greet my Dad . . . at the time of death . . . I was given in a
sense some preparation time." When her father died she was "not
surprised . . . I was totally at peace with Dad moving on. I knew he was
safe."

Dreams of the deceased can be recurring. A final example from Lagrand
concerns a high school teacher whose 17-year-old son had been lost in
an automobile accident. Each time, the dream involved her walking down
the school corridor that passed the door of the cafeteria, and seeing her
son sitting at one of the tables in the company of several other boys.

Each time she chided him for scaring everyone that he was dead, and each time he looked up and assured her "Ma, you knew I was all right." After experiencing the dream some five or six times, the dreamer at last accepted that her son was indeed assuring her of his continued existence and well-being. After this acceptance, as if satisfied that the message had at last been fully conveyed, the recurring dream ceased.

## Can We Explain Mystical Dreams?

Judging by the reports of people who have religious experiences of this kind in their dreams, the effects upon subsequent behavior and belief systems are considerable and enduring. This in itself is significant. In some cases we are even assured that the dream details relate accurately to future events. The problem is how to subject dreams to scientific scrutiny in order to establish whether any apparent religious experiences they contain are more than attempts by the dreamer on waking to read significance into the characteristically illogical mass of dream material. All shades of opinion within psychology accept that the *process* of dreaming performs a useful function, but the importance of the *content* of dreaming still remains something of a contentious issue (Empson, 1989). If dreams are simply the brain ridding itself of unwanted cognitive material during sleep, then their actual content is no more than a confused jumble of images unlikely to warrant serious attention or to contain religious experiences. Efforts to remember dreams may even be as wasteful and as likely to lead to confusion as attempts to retain unwanted material when a computer goes off-line at the end of the working day. If on the other hand dreams give insights into deeper levels of the mind usually inaccessible during waking life, then their content is of importance for self-understanding, and may be highly relevant to any investigation of religious experience. Efforts to remember dreams may therefore facilitate psychological development and even psychological well-being.

Although the evidence that the above dreams may give insights into deeper levels of the mind and perhaps reflect genuine spiritual experiences can be contested, research data nevertheless exists which suggests that dreams may be able to make use of certain as yet unexplained mental abilities which could also be implicated in these experience. In view of the controversy over the very existence of these abilities we have to remain cautious about this evidence, but it derives from work at the Dream Research Unit at the Maimonides Hospital in New York (Van de Castle, 1977; Ullman, Krippner, and Vaughan, 1989 – see also Ullman and Limmer, 1989). The protocol involved an agent in a soundproof room gazing at a picture (chosen by random numbers from a large pool of several hundred) each time a signal from a monitor signified that a subject connected to an EEG and asleep in another soundproof room had entered REM sleep, when most dream episodes occur. Some 15 minutes into each REM episode, the subject was aroused by the monitor via an intercom, and invited to record any dream impressions into a tape recorder.

The object of the exercise was to establish whether or not the dream impressions bore any relationship to the target picture (the identity of which was unknown to the subject) at which the agent had been gazing. To this end the subject was subsequently shown a set of randomly chosen pictures (usually eight in number), one of which was the target picture, and asked to rank each of them for its similarity to the dream material. In addition, the subject was asked to rate each of them for similarity to this material on a scale from one to 100, using the tape record of the previous night's mentations as a guide if required. The experiment was repeated with a number of subjects over many nights, and on its termination copies of all the material arising from each nightly trial were sent to a panel of two or more independent judges (blind to the actual target pictures and to the ratings) who were asked to compare transcripts of the tapes with each of the sets of pictures, and also to rank and rate the pictures for closeness of fit with the transcripts. The results of the subjects' and of the judges' evaluations were then statistically analyzed to establish their deviation, if any, from chance expectancy.

Thirteen major studies of this kind were carried out using the above protocol or variations of it at the Maimonides Dream Research Unit between 1964 and 1972. Findings from nine of the 13 sets of results reached statistical significance, and three of the subjects (one of whom was Robert Van de Castle, subsequently Director of the Sleep and Dream Laboratory at the University of Virginia), each of whom had completed at least one series of eight nights in the Maimonides Laboratory, achieved particularly impressive scores. A thorough and scholarly review of the Maimonides research program by no less than the chair of the psychology department at Yale University (Child, 1985) concluded that the outcome was clear. "Several segments of the data, considered separately, yield significant evidence that dreams (and associations to them) tended to resemble the picture chosen randomly . . . more than they resembled other pictures in the pool." On Child's analysis, the odds against these resemblances occurring by chance were of the order of 100 million to one.

A number of criticisms have been leveled at the Maimonides research (e.g. Hansel, 1980; Grant, 1984), but Child berated critical fellow psychologists either for ignoring the experiments altogether or for engaging "in nearly incredible falsification of the facts. . . ." He goes on to say that in his view none of the criticisms concerned "has correctly identified any defects in the Maimonides experiments other than ones relevant only to the hypothesis of fraud or of inappropriate statistical reasoning (easily remedied by new calculations from the published data)." Van de Castle (1994) also identifies failings in the arguments advanced by critics, including a number of factual errors relating to the protocols in Hansel (1980), and also considers that where subsequent attempts at replication by Foulkes, with himself once more as subject, failed to produce significant results, the reason lay in the variations in experimental conditions, a point which Foulkes himself seems inclined to accept (as quoted by Ullman, Krippner, and Vaughan, 1989). Rechtschaffen (1970), who obtained some positive results using the Maimonides methods, concluded that success is more likely when the pictures used feature emotional topics with which physical sensations are associated.

There the matter rests, for the present at least. These results, taken at face value, appear to show some evidence for direct communication between the agent and the dreaming mind of the subject. And if dream content can indeed be directly influenced by the mind of someone other than the dreamer, then believers in religious experience may well suggest that it can be influenced by spiritual sources external to the dreamer, and also perhaps by those who have survived physical death. A counter-argument from those who accept the possibility of direct influence from other minds might be that, in the case of claimed communications from the deceased, the information concerned may come from the minds of those still living – possibly from relatives or friends who are themselves still grieving for the deceased, and unwittingly conveying images of him or her to the dreamer. However, this counter-argument fails to account for the cases where the information apparently conveyed by the deceased is not known to anyone alive at the time, as occurred for example in the case of the copper engraving technique communicated to William Blake by his dead brother.

A more skeptical counter-argument would be that the individuals who report experiencing contact with the deceased may be unwittingly embellishing their dreams – given the difficulty of dream recall. Alternatively they may already have arrived at the information concerned for themselves at an unconscious level, and the dream may simply serve to bring it to their attention. Thus William Blake may have hit upon the idea of copper engraving, but failed to formalize the idea at a conscious level. Another possibility is that dreamers who report religious experience may be deliberately falsifying the evidence. William Blake may have already discovered the method of copper engraving for himself, and attributed it to his dead brother in an attempt to convince others of the reality of survival after physical death.

Before leaving the subject of dreams, it is relevant to point out that research has now firmly established that it is indeed possible to remain conscious in dreams, as claimed by the *Nyingma* sect of Tibetan Buddhism and by Islamic, Hindu, shamanic, and other spiritual traditions (including what has come to be known as the Western mystery or occult traditions, see e.g. Regardie, 1972). One of the earliest accounts in the Western literature is reported by St. Augustine CE 415, and there have been many similar accounts throughout the succeeding centuries. The term for dreams in which consciousness remains continuous, and in which the dreamer therefore knows that he or she is dreaming and can to some extent take control of dream content, is *lucid dreams*, a term first proposed by the Dutch psychiatrist, Frederik Van Eaden, who published a full account of no fewer than 352 lucid dreams of his own collected between 1898 and 1912 (Van Eeden, 1913). But it was not until researchers at the Stanford University Sleep Laboratory in the United States (LaBerge, 1985; LaBerge and Rheingold, 1990) and at the Hull University Sleep Laboratory in Great Britain (Hearne, 1990) developed the idea of requesting subjects (while EEG tracings confirmed sleep) during REM sleep to signal by certain prearranged eye movements that they were conscious in their dreams, that the existence of lucid dreaming was demonstrated to the satisfaction of the scientific community.

The fact that the dreamer can remain conscious during dreams does not guarantee that the religious experiences reported by individuals as occurring in the course of these dreams are anything other than creations of the dreamer's own mind. However, it does lend some support to the long-standing claim by Eastern spiritual traditions that the ability to lucid dream is a sign of enhanced mind control (and thus, in their submission, of spiritual development), and that lucid dreams can be a way of actively seeking religious experience, from insights into the conditions prevailing in the claimed post-mortem world to dream-meetings with apparent spiritual guides and helpers.

LaBerge gives full details of the techniques which have proved successful in helping some subjects to develop the ability to lucid dream (LaBerge and Rheingold, 1990). A number of mechanical devices also now exist, such as the *Dreamlight* developed by LaBerge himself, which are claimed to assist in this development by alerting the subject through a weak electrical signal such as a pulse at the wrist each time REM sleep commences. Once aware that dreaming is taking place, the individual is then theoretically able to become fully conscious within the dream, and take partial control of its content. The existence of such techniques and devices raises the intriguing possibility that people other than those practicing Tibetan dream yoga or with the requisite natural ability, can induce a form of dreaming which may facilitate religious experiences. This could provide us with new ways of investigating these experiences. Currently, however, reports of the extent to which these techniques and devices are successful in facilitating lucid dreams are mixed. It seems that in this area, as in so many others, nature does not give away her secrets to science very readily.

## Psychodynamic Explanations for Mystical Experience

Not surprisingly, various attempts, based primarily upon psychodynamic theories, have been advanced to explain mystical experience by normal psychological means. Schjelderup and Schjelderup (1932) considered that union mysticism (transcendental mysticism), in which the longing is for the divine, corresponds to a regression to the infant's desire for union with the mother, while self-mysticism (immanent mysticism), which seeks oneness with all creation, expresses a regression to the narcissistic grandiosity of an even earlier infantile state.

Narcissism is seen in fact by many psychoanalysts writing on the subject of religion to be inextricably bound up with mysticism. One of the architects of psychoanalytic theory, Franz Alexander (1931), illustrates the point by reference to certain Buddhist meditation practices based upon the *Satipatthanasutta* ("Sutra on the Applications of Mindfulness"), a meditation sutras of prime importance in the Buddhist canon. The *Satipatthanasutta* stresses the importance of recognizing the repulsiveness of the human body. Thus the meditator focuses in turn upon each of the "impurities" in the body (which seemingly include virtually everything), and is then instructed to "draw along his own body for comparison" with that of a decomposing corpse in order to realize that his own body "is going to be like that." Alexander considers this practice reanimates the meditator's libidinous attention, previously suppressed by the general asceticism of monastic life, but turns it inwards toward his or her own body in a purely sadistic way. The result is a state of melancholia over the loss of the body as a pleasurable object.

However, subsequent meditation practices lead to emancipation from grosser feelings such as disgust and melancholia, which allows full narcissistic regression and the pleasurable flooding of the whole body with libido, a "narcissistic orgasm of the whole body" which is experienced as mystical ecstasy. Finally, the meditator achieves the full state of mystical union with all creation, an utter mental emptiness which takes him/her to the threshold of Nirvana, but which is in fact simply a recovery at last of the experience of the mother's womb. Alexander likens the state of mystical ecstasy to the catatonic ecstasy of the schizophrenic, and the subsequent nirvanic state to the final stage of schizophrenia. Through these states the Buddhist goal of triumph over old age, sickness, and death (the three manifestations of suffering which the Buddha set out to understand and conquer) is achieved by "nullifying" the fact of one's own birth. The Buddha's reported recall of countless previous lives is interpreted by Alexander as an even deeper regression, to the state in fact of the very beginnings of embryonic development.

This looks suspiciously like manipulating the facts to fit the theory. It is also somewhat surprising that, if psychodynamic explanations such as that of Alexander are true, a scholarly tradition like Buddhism has so signally failed to recognize exactly what is happening to the mind during the various stages of a meditative journey that it has been teaching for over 2,000 years. Similarly it is odd that those who have experienced mystical states have never possessed sufficient self-insight to recognize what might be happening. Nevertheless, attempts to explain mystical experience as narcissistic regression to early infancy, when at least at times the child experienced (we assume) a blissful state of total peaceful unity with loving parents and with various comfort objects associated with them, must be seriously considered. Ultimately, however, as with attempts to link mysticism to psychosis, the evidence points in a different direction. Although attempts have been made, many years after their death, to diagnose schizophrenia in various of the Christian saints, mystical experiences, as we have seen, are not confined to saints and other advanced practitioners. And as we saw earlier in the chapter when discussing mysticism and psychosis, there is nothing to support the notion that the people who have these experiences are any less stable than the rest of the population. Further, as we discuss in due course in chapter 12, research suggests that religiosity is associated in various ways with above average physical and mental health and general well-being.

## Naturalistic Explanations for Mystical Experience

More extensive attempts have been made to provide naturalistic explanations for transcendental than for immanent mystical experiences, as the former sometimes involve auditory and visionary experiences which allow comparisons to be drawn with both auditory and visual hallucinations. Thus West (1975) draws attention to arguments in favor of the *perceptual release theory* – i.e. that information received through the normal senses becomes distorted while stored as unconscious memories, and is then abruptly released (often during a period of relative sensory deprivation) into consciousness at a later date and experienced as an hallucination. Horowitz's *information processing model* (Horowitz, 1975) proposes that hallucinations may also arise when information from both internal and external sources is blended incongruously, and consequent upon stimulation of the neural connections between both eyes and ears and cerebral cortex. Similar effects may be produced through stimulation of the temporal lobes. Developments in brain-scanning techniques such as MRI (magnetic resonance imaging) and CT (computerized tomography) have allowed researchers to identify other brain functions that correlate with some hallucinatory experiences. For example, working with diagnosed schizophrenics, Silbersweig *et al.* (1995) have found these functions include activity in the subcortical nuclei, in limbic structures such as the hippocampus, and in paralimbic regions. Certain drugs, both legal and illegal, can also prompt hallucinations, as can certain types of dementia (see e.g. Brasic, 1998; Brabbins, 1992).

Neural models of religious experience based upon research with epileptics, who sometimes report experiencing seemingly mystical states during seizures, have also been advanced by Persinger and others (DeSano and Persinger, 1987; Persinger, 1987), leading Persinger to propose, as we saw in chapter 7, that religious experience is "an artifact of transient changes in the temporal lobe" (i.e. in the so-called "God Spot"), and serves as an adaptive mechanism that compensates for the human capacity to anticipate aversive stimuli, in particular death. Persinger does not, however, make clear why a mechanism that compensates for the aversive realization of death would have survival value. The contrary would seem to suggest itself in that individuals would fight harder to secure physical survival if their belief was that this life is all that there is.

Nevertheless research by Dewhurst and Beard (1970) reveal a significant increase in religiosity in subjects consequent upon the onset of epilepsy, while Bear and Fedio (1977), using their *Temporal Lobe Personality Inventory*, found epileptics to be significantly higher on a measure of religiosity (feelings that events are under divine guidance) than control groups. Geschwind (1983) also reports from clinical experience an incidence of a particular configuration of personality traits among epileptics, one of which is an increased concern with philosophical and religious issues. On the strength of these various findings, it would thus seem as if some association between epilepsy and what appear to be mystical experiences and religious concerns has been demonstrated.

A particularly interesting theory linking transcendent mystical experience to brain states is advanced by Jaynes (1976) and Witelson and Kristofferson (1986). Their proposal is that self-reflective consciousness only arose around 1000 BCE, and that prior to that humans possessed a *bicameral mind* with a hallucinatory right brain whose processes were interpreted by the left hemisphere as messages or visions from the gods. With the advent of writing and in the face of pressures such as migrations and geological catastrophes the temporal lobe areas of the right hemisphere became increasingly inhibited, and the bicameral mind became replaced by subjective consciousness. To replace the now silent voices of the gods, men and women resorted to a variety of strategies such as the use of ritual, of omens, and of divination. Experimental evidence such as that reported by Persinger supports Jayne's localization of religious experience to the right temporal lobe, but although his theory undoubtedly carries considerable explanatory power, much of it is speculative and based upon an interpretation of historical evidence.

The weakness in all these attempts to attribute transcendental mystical experience to specific areas of the brain is, as we saw in chapter 7, that correlation does not imply causality. Because two things – in this case hallucinations and brain states – happen in concert with each other does not mean that one necessarily causes the other. During hurricanes, damage to shipping and damage to housing are correlated, but neither causes the other; both sets of damage are due to an extraneous factor in the shape of the hurricane. Pointing this out is anathema to those who wish to reduce all mental events, mystical and otherwise to brain states, yet failure to do so is a failure of scientific logic.

A further weakness is that it may be wrong to see similarities between the hallucinations of those experiencing psychotic episodes and those experiencing transcendental mysticism. The data summarized in Table 10.1 and elsewhere in the present chapter indicates that the percentages of people reporting the latter experiences as positive far outweigh the percentage reporting them as negative. In addition, in many cases the effect of the experiences concerned appears to be positive and in some cases life-changing. This is in contrast to the high percentage of psychotics (as much as 54 percent in some studies) who are reported as experiencing religious delusions and preoccupations of a bizarre kind (Koenigh, McCullough, and Larson, 2001). Thus there seems little warrant for attempting fully to explain these positive experiences by findings arising from work with psychotics.

Objections can also be advanced to direct comparisons between epileptic incidents and the transcendent mystical experience of non-epileptics. Quite apart from the fact that there are always certain dangers in attempting to derive generalizations for normal behavior from the behavior of those suffering from disabilities, over 60 percent of epileptics in Beard's sample did not show increased interest in religion after the onset of their seizures. In addition, we do not know the extent to which his sample had already learnt that there is a posited connection between epilepsy and religious experience, and had in consequence started to take an interest in the latter in the hope of finding some meaning in their condition. The same can be said for the sample studied by Bear and Fedio. And even if we do choose to accept that the experiences of some epileptics during seizure are analogous to the religious experiences of non-epileptics this may simply indicate that seizures temporarily inhibit the mechanisms that usually prevent mystical experiences from emerging into consciousness.

For these various reasons, Wiebe (2000) would seem on balance to be justified in concluding, after a review of the relevant literature, that the visions associated with transcendental mysticism "elude adequate naturalistic explanation at present . . . and continue to provide a profound sense that a reality that does not belong to our world has been manifested." Although identifying the need for further research, he considers in addition that the current attempts by those who propose physical explanations for mystical visions and thus seek "the elimination of persons in favor of . . . brain states . . . can be seen as part of the profaning of the universe," a profaning which he argues "ranks with the most ambitious [research programs] undertaken in the history of human thought."

As already mentioned, there have been fewer attempts to advance psychodynamic or naturalistic explanations for immanent mystical experiences than for transcendent experiences. It will be recalled that Freud proposed that immanent mysticism is an *oceanic* state that indicates a regression to an earlier phase of ego-feeling, a phase associated with experiences at the breast before the conscious mind learns to distinguish the ego from the rest of the world (Freud, 1930). When feeding, the infant feels a sense of oneness with his or her mother, and occasionally in adult life may recapture the memory of this feeling and misinterpret it as a state of oneness with all creation. The theory, like much of Freud's work, is interesting and imaginative, but again like much of his work, is not supported by any large-scale research evidence, and certainly by no research evidence based upon those who have actually had experiences of immanent mysticism (see chapter 10).

## Drugs and Mystical Experience

Studies with psychedelic substances have shown that they can induce a state of depersonalization which involves feelings of union with the surrounding world and even the cosmos (Weil, Metzner, and Leary, 1965). Although the way in which psychedelic drugs affect the nervous system still remains something of a mystery, it is tempting to suppose that their action upon the brain is analogous to what happens in spontaneous mystical experiences. However, a higher percentage of those with religious beliefs report these experiences after ingesting psychedelics than do those in psychotherapy (Weil *et al.* report the frequencies of mystical experience under LSD range from 83 percent to 24 percent), which suggests that prior beliefs and experiences rather than simply chemical changes in the brain are implicated in the experiences concerned. In addition, as with epileptic seizures, it can be argued that the drugs concerned temporarily inhibit the mechanisms that usually *prevent* mystical experiences from emerging into consciousness.

The mystical or quasi-mystical experiences associated with the taking of psychedelics are in any case not always blissful. Grof (e.g. 1988, 1998) presents evidence to show that some involve agonizing encounters with loneliness, guilt, and death, followed by a kind of shamanic rebirth. In some cases individuals report being present at scenes of violence, torture, and cruelty, or being engulfed in putrefaction and subsequently receiving ritual purification. Grof suggests that the psychedelics concerned may be giving subjects access to the archetypal layers of the unconscious postulated by Jung – or, we could say, may be removing the censorial mechanisms that normally prevent these levels from breaking through into consciousness.

The effect of existing belief systems upon the experiences that enter consciousness after the ingestion of psychedelic drugs is illustrated by research reported by Pahnke (1963, 1966) which involved dividing a group of 20 male graduate theology students into 10 pairs matched for religious background, religious experience, and general psychological make-up. One member of each pair was randomly assigned to the experimental group and the other to the control group, and all then participated in a total of five hours of discussions on the design of the experiment intended to maximize trust. Ninety minutes before watching a broadcast of a Good Friday service, the experimental member of each pair was given 30 milligrams of the psychedelic drug psilocybin, while the control members were given a placebo of 200 milligrams of a B vitamin which at that level produces mild physical symptoms that can be mistaken for the early sensations produced by psychedelics. Neither Pahnke nor the students knew who received the psilocybin and who received the placebo.

After the service each subject wrote down his experiences, and a week later filled in a questionnaire designed to measure experience of the nine elements identified by Stace (1960) as common to all mystical experience, irrespective of tradition, namely:

1.  experience of unity;
2.  transcendence of time and space;
3.  positive mood (joy, blessedness, peace);
4.  sense of the sacred;
5.  objectivity and reality (of finite self and of ultimate reality);
6.  paradoxicality (i.e. a sense of emptiness in the unity which is nevertheless full and complete);
7.  ineffability (i.e. beyond words);
8.  transiency (i.e. perceived brevity of the experience when compared to the normal passage of time);
9.  persisting positive changes in attitude and behavior.

Results showed that although the experimental group did not experience the full range of mystical experiences, on all comparisons with the control group their experiences resembled those of mystics far more than did those of the control group. However, results were somewhat contaminated by the fact that the control group generally became aware quite early in the experiment that they had not been given the psychedelic. Thus their levels of expectation became depressed before those of the experimental group. In addition, the one member of the experimental group who was convinced beforehand that drugs do not produce religious experience reported no evidence of mystical states.

Nevertheless, the enduring effects of the experiences of the other members of the experimental group was demonstrated in a follow-up study by Doblin (1991), which revealed that the seven members of the experimental group and the nine controls who he was able to contact still showed the same significant between-group differences in the rated intensities of their experiences during the experiment. The experimental subjects were unanimous in their view that they had all had genuine mystical experiences.

Psychedelics do seem to facilitate mystical experiences even in less overtly religious individuals than Pahnke's theology students, though the incidence of such experiences may be significantly lower. These two points are both illustrated by a later, unpublished study by Pahnke in which he again used psilocybin and found that seven out of 20 subjects in his experimental group of professional people reported mystical experiences as compared to one in his control group. However, any suggestion that mystical experience is linked just to brain chemistry is somewhat negated by the fact that hypnotic suggestions appear able to induce some quasi-mystical states (Aaronson, 1970), as apparently can some specially designed mind games (Masters and Houston, 1972) and even a period spent blindfolded on a trance-inducing platform that sways, rocks, or twirls in response to the subject's slightest movement. Certain sound and light shows may have similar trance-like effects, as can shamanic drumming.

The best that can be deduced from these various studies is that mystical experience cannot be said to arise solely from drugs or hypnosis or any other form of intervention. The experience itself arises from the individual mind rather than from the intervention, and its arisal and the form that it takes are dependent in large measure upon the subject's previous experience and expectation. Two important questions remain. Firstly, how does the mind construct the experiences concerned, and why should there be commonalties between them even across different traditions? And secondly, what is the actual role of the intervention? Does it remove brain mechanisms that prevent these experiences from being commonplace (with the difficulties that this might cause for relating to and surviving in the physical world)? Or do they excite certain areas of the brain into manufacturing quasi-mystical experiences (in which case what role do these areas play in survival and why have they evolved?). It may be that further research on the so-called "God Spot" in the frontal lobes of the brain may help to throw some light on these questions.

## Classification of Religious Belief

In view of its role in spiritual experience, mysticism perforce features in many classifications of religious belief systems, particularly in those that attempt to cut across the various traditions. Such classifications accept that in the nature of their beliefs (though not in the content) and in the effects of these beliefs upon behavior, fundamentalists in one tradition have more in common with fundamentalists in other traditions than they do with liberals in their own and vice versa. Nevertheless these classifications cannot be regarded as anything other than somewhat crude. It is difficult to separate the nature of a belief in something from the content of that belief, and indeed from the grounds upon which that belief is held.

Of existing classifications, that by Wulff (1997) is one of the most persuasive and accessible. Wulff recognizes two dimensions of belief, namely *inclusion of transcendence–exclusion of transcendence*, and *literal–symbolic*. My own preference is for *transendence–immanense*, and *tough–tender*, with the latter referring to the rigidity with which beliefs are held and the consequent attitudes and behavior of the believer toward other traditions. However, there remain difficulties in any classification of this kind. Even within the same religious groups individuals may differ significantly from each other in their beliefs (and may themselves vary in the nature and strengths of these beliefs, even in the short term). Members of some Eastern traditions, who dislike our Western tendency to dichotomize things into *either–or*, and insist instead that things can be *both–and*, would argue for example that the divine is *both* transcendent *and* immanent, and that it is meaningless to try to separate the two. In addition it must be re-emphasized that the fact certain faiths fall into the same category does not imply similarity between the content of their beliefs. It refers only to psychological orientation. Furthermore, psychological classification does not in any sense imply judgments as to the relative value of the beliefs concerned. Thus it would be incorrect to see *tender* as being in any sense better than *tough*, or *transcendence* as in any way better or at a more advanced level than *immanence*.

With these reservations very much in mind, categorization along the two dimensions is nevertheless a useful, if imprecise, way of thinking about the various psychological orientations taken by religious and

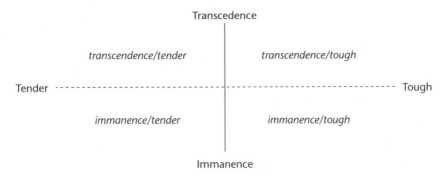

**Figure 10.1** Classification of religious and spiritual belief systems

spiritual beliefs. As the two dimensions of *transcendence–immanence* and *tough–tender* are not correlated with each other, we can place them on orthogonal axes, thus yielding four separate quadrants of belief as shown in Figure 10.1.

Members of the Roman Catholic and Eastern Orthodox Christian Churches would then fall within the *transcendence/tough* quadrant, along with orthodox Islam and Judaism. Buddhism would generally fall within the *immanence/tender* quadrant (*tender* in the sense of tolerance toward other faiths in the belief that there are many doors into the monastery), along with Taoism, Advaita Hinduism, and certain Protestant Christian sects such as Quakers and some Unitarians, while Jainism might be more properly placed in the *immanence/tough* quadrant (*tough* in the sense of extreme insistence upon nonviolence to any living creature, rather than tough in any confrontational sense). Vaita Hinduism would fall within the *transcendence/tender* quadrant, while militant Hinduism (to use a contradictory term, yet one which has recently become familiar in the West) would come within the *transcendence/tough* quadrant.

Some belief systems are almost impossible to classify in this or any other way, partly perhaps because we in the West have neglected or lost the concepts upon which they are based. This is certainly true of shamanism, which is intensely linked to immanence within the natural world, yet at the same time speaks of a transcendent Spirit which refers variously to the consciousness of the Earth itself and to something outside the material world. Pure Land Buddhism is also difficult to place, because its practices (along with some of those of Tibetan Buddhism) appear to be addressed to a power outside oneself, but which doctrinally we are told refer to a potential actually present within. This makes perfect sense to Pure Land Buddhists, though to the Western scientific mind it poses obvious difficulties. However, the more one studies the Pure Land and other Eastern traditions, the more it becomes clear that our Western desire for classification, valuable as it is in so many ways, can be an active hindrance to a fuller understanding of the psychology of religion and spirituality.

Our categorization of the major traditions into the four quadrants demonstrates the fact that theistic religions, at least in their most orthodox form, tend toward the *transcendent/tough* quadrant, while non-theistic religions incline more toward the *immanence/tender* quadrant. This is explicable in that theistic religions place emphasis upon direct revelations from God, and therefore upon the absolute authority of these revelations, while non-theistic religions place more emphasis upon finding the truth already present within oneself (though there is no reason why theists should not argue that this truth is also God-given). Wilber, whose system of classification is discussed in chapter 11 and who addresses different issues, speaks of transcendence beliefs as characterized by the desire to *ascend* to the spiritual dimension, while immanence beliefs are characterized by a sense of the spiritual as *descending* into the human dimension (Wilber, 1998). The use of these terms is of particular value in illustrating why theistic religions, with their belief in transcendence, tend toward the tough end of the *tough–tender* dimension while non-theistic religions, with their emphasis upon immanence, group toward the tender end.

# CHAPTER 11 ────────────────────

# Concepts of Self, Soul, and Brain

## The Nature of the Self

The nature of the self has proved as much of a concern (and for much longer) of religion as it has for Western psychology. The Oracle of Apollo at Delphi in Greece, dating back to the sixth-century BCE, presented the supplicant with the written injunction to "Know Thyself," the implication being that in self-discovery lies the key to all wisdom. As emphasized in chapter 2 and elsewhere, from its inception 500 years before the birth of Christ, Buddhism has placed great emphasis upon seeing through the illusory, conditioned self and thus realizing one's true nature. Adherents of the *Rinzai* (Chinese *Lin-Chi*) sect of Zen Buddhism attempt to do this by, among other practices, meditating upon *koans*, enigmatic and apparently nonsensical questions or statements that help the meditator to go beyond the linear thinking that intrudes between the mind and direct experience, and which all to some degree reduce to the fundamental conundrum "Who am I?". Again as we saw in chapter 2, Hinduism traditionally talks in terms of the "self" in small letters and the "Self" with an initial capital, the latter referring to one's own true nature which is said to be identified with the Absolute, and the former to the small, conditioned self which arises from learnt experiences and reactions to experiences and which we mistakenly take to be who we really are. Theistic religions such as Christianity and Islam, although they conceptualize the individual's relationship with the Absolute rather differently, nevertheless stress the importance of surrendering the self to God, and that by so doing one's true relationship with the Divine is realized.

The idea that we must see through the conditioned self we think we are if our true being is to be revealed naturally perplexes many Western psychologists, who regard true being as nothing more than this limited self. Can there be any meeting points between these two opposed views? Western science is handicapped by the fact that, owing to its relative neglect of inner states, its advocates cannot call upon personal experience to verify or otherwise the notion of a higher level of being beyond that of the conventional self. On the other hand the traditions are handicapped by their inability to demonstrate this higher level in any objective way (even the changes in physiological measurements that accompany its claimed experience in profound levels of meditation tell us nothing about the nature and meaning of the inner experience itself).

## The Role of Thinking

The difficulties of finding common ground therefore look intractable. However, one approach is to look at what the great traditions on the one hand and Western psychology on the other have to say about thinking. In both schools, thinking is seen as inextricably linked to the self. In both schools, what we understand as ourselves is sustained by the concepts we have about ourselves and about our relationships with others and with the world of phenomena in general. Since thoughts are constantly changing – in response to life experience, to moods, to levels of arousal, etc. – it would seem that the self sustained by thought cannot be other than impermanent, even granted that there are certain core constructs associated with it which are relatively durable. Buddhism formalizes this view when it talks of the five *skandhas*, the aggregates which constitute the person, namely form (*rupa*), sensation (*vedana*), perception (*samjna*), mental formations (*samskara*), and consciousness (*vijnana*). The self is bound up particularly with the last two, and strongly influenced by the other three.

Although Western psychology would want to be more specific than the rather general term "mental formations," and in some cases might even have trouble with "consciousness," the five *skandhas*, as omnibus terms, would seem reasonably acceptable as ways of defining what it is that underpins the sense of self. We are each of us, essentially, our particular human form, the sensations we receive through the various receptor mechanisms that are part of that form, our perceptions of the outer world, our cognitive processes, and our consciousness (which for present purposes we need think of only as our consciousness of self, of our individual sentient existence). The theory of the *skandhas* is also similar to the view of the self proposed by the eighteenth-century Scottish philosopher David Hume which has been so influential in Western thought (Hume, 1965, 1980). Hume, who as far as I know had no contact with Buddhist ideas, also speaks of the self as no more than a bundle of sensations and perceptions, thus rejecting the previously currently popular

Cartesian notion of a consciousness distinct from the body (yet located in it), a unifying principle, an "I" which lies behind the thoughts, feelings, sense impressions, etc. of the mind. Hume claimed to have looked within himself in vain for this unifying principle, and have concluded that it is therefore fictitious and on the level of the identity which we assign to vegetables and physical bodies. In his view, the two prominent factors in human nature are change and complexity, neither of which appears conducive to belief in the self as an abiding entity or as an immutable, simple substance (nevertheless, he did admit that such doubts departed each time he left his study).

Ludwig Wittgenstein, whose philosophy also has had a profound influence upon modern Western thought, joined Hume in rejecting the Cartesian model. Although deeply influenced by religion (on at least three occasions in his life he contemplated becoming a monk), Wittgenstein's final position seems to have been that it is the use of the word "I" to refer to oneself as subject that creates the notion that there is something nonphysical inhabiting the body (Wittgenstein, 1958, 1963). However, he goes on to argue (if I understand him correctly, which is by no means certain) that this does not in any sense mean that such a nonphysical element does not exist, simply that discourse concerning it, along with all moral, religious, aesthetic, and even philosophical ideas, lies in reality beyond the limits of language. Nevertheless, he conceded that all these ideas play an important role in our lives, and our failure to articulate them in any logically consistent way must not therefore be seen as failed attempts at factuality.

Gilbert Ryle, another highly influential philosopher of the mysteries of mind, was more directly dismissive of any concept of a nonphysical element in the body, referring to it as the myth of "the ghost in the machine," the myth of an enduring, unifying self. For Ryle (1949, 1979), mental terms can only be verified by physical terms used in statements about behavior and behavioral dispositions. If such verification is not possible, then these terms are meaningless. This philosophical behaviorism accorded well with behavioristic theories in psychology and up to a point with the Buddhist theory of the skandhas, but there is an objection to it. If there is no more to the self than a bundle of *skandhas*, how does this self *know itself* as no more than this bundle? How does it even recognize that such a question exists and needs to be asked? What organizing principle is there to carry out this recognition and to do the asking? At the very least, we have to invoke Mead's notion of a multiplicity of selves. Put simply, this acknowledges that when we reflect upon the self there must be another self to do the reflecting, and for us to be aware of this second self carrying out the act of reflection there must be a third self which contains this awareness. And the fact that we are aware of this third self means there must be a fourth self containing *this* awareness, and so on *ad infinitum*. The fact that we can only be conscious of three or four of these selves at any one moment makes no difference. Each time we are aware of one of our selves there must be another self in order for this awareness to take place (Mead, 1934). Though not directly related to Mead's thinking, the useful model sometimes used in psychotherapy which speaks of the client's "I" as victimizing his or her "me," like an internalized and censorious parent constantly looking over one's shoulder and passing judgment on every thought and action, also assumes the existence of more than one level of self (e.g. Austin, 2000).

## The Higher Self as Organizing Principle

Western psychology has tended to ignore the question of whether or not there is an organizing principle to the self, in spite of the fact that we recognize there is a need to find the organizing principle that coordinates the many different aspects of brain function. However, religion has always concerned itself with this question, and attempts to answer it with the concept of the soul, a nonmaterial Higher Self, which is seen as our essence or true nature and outside the constraints of the physical body but interactive with it.

By its nature the existence of this Higher Self cannot be demonstrated by physical measurement. However, Buddhism insists that once we fully realize the illusory nature of our relative and socially constructed self (which we do through intensive meditative practices) there comes an awareness that in its place there is an expansive state of being which is an integral part of the unified whole that is ultimate reality. This state of being – rather misleadingly labeled "no-self" (*anatta*) in Buddhism – is one's true nature, and in becoming aware of it one is said to become aware of the true nature of everything else (Abe, 1995). Thus although it cannot indeed be subjected to physical measurement, our true nature is supposedly accessible by direct experience if we are prepared to do the necessary psychological work on ourselves. Moreover, by comparing the accounts of "true nature" given by people who have done this work we can observe the degree of uniformity that exists among them, and come to an informed conclusion as to its reality (Wilber, 1998).

If Western psychology is prepared to accept this as a working hypothesis, its next questions are bound to be how does this awareness of "true nature" or Higher Self translate back into everyday life? Does this awareness contain and recognize both itself and the relative self? And how does the limited, relative self arise in the first place? If unity is all that there is, how can unity give rise to illusory ideas on self-identity? And what in any case is the purpose behind our creation of the limited self, with all the challenges that it experiences, if ultimately this self and along with it individuality, is no more than an illusion? Theistic religions would probably reply (thereby disagreeing in particular with Buddhism) that individuality is no more an illusion than unity. God by his nature is infinite and all-powerful, and thus the creator of an infinite multiplicity of phenomena which contains all possibilities, including both unity and diversity. Western psychology might reply that this is purely a statement of faith. Theistic religions cannot use the multiplicity of phenomena as evidence of God's existence, and then use God as the explanation for the multiplicity of phenomena. The reply to this would be that religion is based not just upon faith but upon revelation. And so the argument would go on.

There is however, another area of Western psychology, namely psychotherapy, which may help throw some light on the matter. Experimental psychologists are somewhat suspicious of inferences drawn from the findings of psychotherapy and psychological counseling, dependent as they are primarily upon case material and thus lacking the rigor of laboratory work. However, good case study material is based not only upon self-reports of inner cognitive and affective states, but also upon observed changes in client behavior, and thus cannot be lightly dismissed. One of the psychotherapists most concerned with levels of the self, Robert Assagioli (the founder of *psychosynthesis*), considered that work with clients does indeed suggest the existence of two levels of the self, termed by him the *personal self* and the *higher self*. In his view the former is always present, while the latter is a potential to be realized during psychotherapy (Assagioli, 1965 – see also Ferrucci, 1982; Hardy, 1987).

Assagioli's starting point is that for most people self-identity is a hazy construct, due to its many diffuse identifications. Accordingly in psychotherapy the client is helped to relinquish some of these identifications by progressively disidentifying from form, from emotions, and from intellect. Form, emotions, and intellect are what we *have*, and not what we *are*. (The similarity here with the Hindu meditation technique in which the practitioner repeats as a mantra "I have a body but I am not my body, I have emotions but I am not my emotions, I have thoughts but I am not my thoughts" is obvious.) Once disidentification has taken place, Assagioli maintains that the self can be realized as a center of pure consciousness, simple, unchanging, constant, and aware of itself. In other words, the higher self is what remains once the confused and fluctuating physical, emotional, and mental contents of the personal self have been discarded.

Like Freud and Jung and many other prominent psychotherapists, Assagioli was a psychiatrist rather than a trained psychologist, but this allowed him perhaps to be less circumspect in his approach to issues such as the possible existence of a higher self. He also demonstrated the value of what Lehman and Shriver (1968) called a *scholarly distance from religion*, a concept which they successfully used to study religiosity among academics. Their conclusion was that academic disciplines such as psychology, which have a low distance from religion (i.e. disciplines for which the study of religion is a relevant undertaking), prescribe an analytical stance toward the subject, and thus make it less likely for their practitioners to be (or to admit to being) religious themselves, or to take the psychological models proposed by religion seriously. All scientists are supposed, in theory, to approach their subject matter with skepticism and doubt, and psychologists seem – again in theory – to adhere particularly strongly to this supposition, perhaps because their subject matter is notoriously slippery, and mistakes in inference are therefore an ever-present problem. Malony (1977) in fact pointed out that at the time he was writing, many of the psychologists identified with religiosity or with the psychology of religion (from Calvin Hall to Carl Rogers) are untypical of the profession in that they have had – or aspired to have had – theological training at some point in their professional careers.

Psychiatry has no particular brief to carry out in-depth research into religion, and consequently has a higher distance from the subject than has psychology, which may be why practitioners of the standing of Assagioli have no qualms about taking a concept such as the higher self (which he also refers to as "the spiritual self") seriously, and about reporting not only the positive way in which such a concept can be used in psychotherapy, but also its demonstrable validity as part of psychological life. In his view "the little [personal] self is acutely aware of itself as a distinct separate individual, with a sense of solitude or of separation." By contrast, the higher self experiences "a sense of freedom, of expansion, of communication with other Selves (sic) and with reality, and there is a sense of Universality. It feels itself at the same time individual and universal." The success of psychosynthesis (and of transpersonal psychotherapy, which is closely allied to it – see e.g. Wellings and McCormick, 2000) in helping clients come to terms with inner conflict and to find meaning and purpose in individual and social life, provides some evidence for the value of Assagioli's personal self/higher self model, even if skeptics consider it to be no more than a theoretical artifact.

The claimed experience of the higher self also has many parallels with the so-called "peak experiences" of people termed by Maslow as "self-actualized" (e.g. Maslow, 1970, 1971). Maslow used the term "self-actualized" for those in his samples who were found to have achieved "the full use and exploitation of talents, capacities [and] potentialities" and thus to have fulfilled "themselves and to be doing the best that they are capable of doing" and to have satisfied the basic needs (in his hier-archy of needs) for safety, belongingness, love, respect, and self-respect. On the basis of his research he described such people as:

> perceptive, emotionally open, natural and spontaneous, problem-centered rather than self-centered, happy with their own company, autonomous, self-accepting and other-accepting rather than over-critical and judgmental, appreciative of life, capable of deep and loving relationships, humorous, creative, ethical, democratic and consistent.

Peak experiences, in which they felt themselves to be outside time and space and to be experiencing awe, wonder, and ecstasy and the subsequent certainty that something extraordinary had happened which strengthened everyday life, were a common feature among his self-actualized group. There are certain similarities between these experiences and those of the mystic, and between Maslow's self-actualization and the realization of Assagioli's higher self. Jung's theory of the self as man's fullest potential and the unifying principle behind psychological life also seems related. For Jung, the self is not only the center of this life "but also the circum-ference which embraces both conscious and unconscious; it is the center of this totality, just as the ego is the center of the conscious mind" (Jung, 1968).

Which brings us back to the great traditions, with their similar em-phasis upon a soul or higher level of self which in a sense "possesses" the temporary qualities of the lower self, and which must be discovered if we are to realize who we really are. There seems agreement too between the great traditions and Assagioli, Maslow, and Jung that this discovery takes place when the small self falls silent. Typically this small self is so noisy and demanding that the attention of the higher self (which is by nature unselfish) is focussed upon it rather than upon itself, much as a kind parent's attention is taken up by a difficult child.

## Stilling the Small Self

But how can the small self be persuaded to fall silent, to become still? Interestingly – and this is one of the strongest arguments in favor of their psychological authenticity – there is much agreement among the tradi-tions on the way this can be done (e.g. Fontana, 1992). In particular, all place major emphasis not only upon practicing unselfish behavior (along the lines of the *karma yoga* practices discussed in chapter 6) but also upon gaining some control over the processes of thought. There are various ways in which it is said that this control can be exercised, but common to them all is the idea that the mind, preferably through formal meditation practice, must find a point of focus and stay with it, refusing to attend to or become distracted by the constant stream of thoughts and emotions that normally occupy the attention. With practice, a stage is reached where not only do fewer and fewer moments of distraction occur, but also thoughts and emotions (apart from serenity) cease to arise.

The point of focus can be the breathing, a mantra, or a visual image such as a mandala, a sacred icon, or even a candle flame. In theistic religions the mind can also be turned toward God and the small self and thus "surrendered" to God. Whatever the method used, thought is seen not as an enemy, but as typically out of control. The Christian admonition to "Be still and know that I am God" is one way of summing this up. Thought, instead of being an efficient servant, has become for most people a highly inefficient and willful master, spilling over into each moment of waking life and dominating consciousness. It has been allowed to become the mouthpiece of the small self with all the demands, self-centeredness, and erratic behavior that are such features of the small self. (A few minutes spent observing one's own mental processes are enough to demonstrate the accuracy of this.)

Furthermore, when extolling the virtues of meditation, the traditions remind us that typically the thoughts that habitually dominate our attention take the form of words. And it is argued that the problem with words is that they are always *about* experience and are not direct experience itself. They can thus get in the way of this experience. We have verbal labels and descriptions and concepts for the material world and for our inner psychological lives, but these various descriptors are separate and distinct from the phenomena to which they refer. They can thus distance us from a real relationship with these phenomena, and take away not only our sense of connection with them, but also our awe and wonder at their very existence. Again a few minutes of reflection are sufficient to demonstrate the accuracy of this. For example, nature and the creative arts are best appreciated in a wordless state in which ideas about what we are experiencing are put aside, and the phenomena allowed to communicate themselves directly to us through the senses. This sounds suspiciously like the language of mysticism, but this wordless state is also one in which creative insights can arise – sometimes coming unexpectedly and unbidden, and from a source which no amount of analytical thinking can identify. Jung (1963), the scope of whose creativity is not in doubt even if some of his inferences are, referred to this state when he wrote "In the end, the only events in my life worth telling are those when the imperishable world irrupted into this transitory one. That is why I speak chiefly of inner experience. . . ." The great traditions would equate this imperishable world with the higher self.

It is claimed in addition by meditators that by gaining control over the processes of thought, one not only stills the small self and realizes the higher self, but also ensures that thinking itself can operate more efficiently. When thinking is appropriate, the mind is able to concentrate and direct the flow of thought in a way difficult if not impossible if thinking is untrained and disorganized. Unfortunately, in spite of the extensive range of research into meditation, little work has yet been done to test this claim. If found to be justified it will not in any sense demonstrate the existence of the higher self, but it will help indicate some of the loss of cognitive potential consequent upon the disorganized, often seemingly compulsive, selfpreoccupied thought processes of the small, habitual self.

As an adjunct to formal meditation practice, the Eastern traditions lay particular emphasis upon *mindfulness*, an emphasis which finds echoes in some Western literature (see e.g. Tart, 1988). Mindfulness refers to the ability to focus clearly and consistently upon whatever it is one is doing. The stereotype of the absent-minded professor would find no sympathy in these traditions. The argument is that by attending to the inner dialogue instead of to the events of real life, one again places a barrier between the self and direct experience. The more this happens, the less one is able to experience the direct connection between the self and the rest of creation. One has in a sense unplugged this connection, and by doing so an unhelpful distance is allowed to develop not only between the self and the world but also between the small self and the higher self. For just as the process of self-discovery leads to an experience of the real nature of the rest of existence, so the experience of the real nature of the rest of existence leads to the process of self-discovery.

The problem for the psychologist is once again how to put beliefs such as this to the test. It is true that the experiences associated with these beliefs have been reported from many cultures and for many centuries, but by itself this is insufficient to a Western science which seeks to subject things to experimental test. And here the problem is not only how one can go about testing these states, but that the states themselves seem so alien to the experience of most Western scientists. Meditation and the cultivation of mindfulness require long periods of intense and sustained commitment from the practitioner. In the West, we are used to knowing in advance exactly what will be achieved by such commitment – what exam-ination will be passed, what qualification achieved, what career advancement, what new skills and techniques, what financial rewards. The uncertainties that appear to surround practices such as meditation and mindfulness hardly conspire to make them attractive areas for the researcher. There is good evidence for the physical and psychological benefits of meditation (e.g. Benson, 1996), but large-scale investigations into their role as aids to self-understanding are conspicuous by their absence.

Before leaving the subject, mention must be made of an argument against the importance of stilling the thought processes in meditation, namely that the mind, including the consciousness of self, *is* these processes. By stilling them one is in effect switching off the mind and together with the mind any sense of self-awareness. The consequence is a kind of vegetative state in which mental life is restricted to experiencing the physical sensations of the body. There are two objections to this argument. The first is that the reported experience of dedicated meditators is of anything but a vegetative state. Instead it is one of heightened alertness in which a much deeper awareness of the supposed higher, unlimited self becomes apparent. The second is that it would seem to be a mistake to equate the mind with thinking. Thinking is an activity *of* the mind rather than necessarily the mind itself. To equate the mind with its activity is not unlike equating the legs with walking. Or, if one prefers a purely physicalist interpretation of mental life, to equate the brain with thinking. The distinction between an object and its activity is generally accepted in all other areas of Western scientific thinking as well in the great traditions.

## The Freedom of the Will

Central to ideas on the self in all the great traditions is that it possesses the power of choice. Without such power, the concept of morality becomes meaningless, as does the concept of self-improvement through choosing certain forms of action over others, and as does the teaching common to all the traditions that this life is a form of trial ground in which our behavior determines what happens to us in lifetimes to come. For the traditions, humans therefore possess freewill and are in the last analysis autonomous beings. The alternative to the theory of freewill, namely determinism, argues that all our actions are determined for us by our genetic predisposition modified and developed by the environment in which we live. Humans are therefore in the last analysis highly effective biological robots. The compelling objection to determinism was pointed out many years ago by Streeter (1926). If determinism is correct in denying the existence of spontaneous initiative, this denial applies not just to behavior but also to wishes and thoughts and theories. In that case, it is determined for each of us which theories we will accept and which we will not. Thus a preference for the theory of determinism over that of freewill, or for the theory of freewill over determinism, stems not from the fact that the arguments of the one are superior over the arguments for the other, but because heredity and environment have determined that that is the way we will think. Reasoning therefore can prove nothing. It is merely a clever way of providing us with apparently rational reasons for believing that which in fact we cannot help believing. And – to go one step further – if all reasoning is thus ineffectual, and we have no powers of discrimination, there is no criterion of truth and falsehood. All knowledge collapses, one hypothesis is as good (or as bad) as another, and even science itself is no more than an ingenious fable.

Davidson (1980) concedes the point, and concludes that "there are no strict deterministic laws on the basis of which mental events can be predicted and explained." Mental events such as perceiving, remembering, deciding, and acting appear to be insulated "from the strict laws that can in principle be called upon to explain and predict physical phenomena." Davidson is clearly correct, and although we cannot, through this or any other form of reasoning, prove that we have freewill, the important thing, as pointed out by Immanuel Kant over 200 years ago, is that we believe and act *as if we have* (Kant, 1787). Our discussion of freewill is thus no mere sparing with words. It illuminates the importance of another way of knowing in addition to that of reason, that is intuition, an area ripe for further investigation by scientific psychology. If we did not intuit that we have freewill, and live our lives in accordance with this intuition, humanity could not exist in its present form. Not only would there be no theories of value and morality, there would be no aesthetics, and of course no science. And if intuition is so vital to us in the critically important area of freewill, it is reasonable to suppose that it may be of value to us in other areas as well. The great traditions would argue that one of these areas is our intuition that we have a higher self, and our intuition of the existence of spiritual realities and of our own immortality.

It is true that the presence of value does not guarantee truth, yet value, usefulness, lies behind all the laws of science. In fact usefulness is the prime test of truth in science. Scientific laws are not held to be inviolable. If a law is found to be no longer useful in predicting and explaining physical events, then it is discarded and replaced with something that proves more successful in doing both these things. The great traditions insist that our intuition of a law of spiritual realities is of value to us psychologically, and this is something that can be tested by research designed to draw comparisons between those who follow religious teachings and practices and those who do not, just as in psychological research we compare groups of people on other measures. We shall return to such research when we discuss religion and psychological and physical health in chapter 12.

## The Problem of Evil

If there are indeed spiritual realities, the great traditions are faced with the problem why such realities allow the existence of evil and suffering.

The question why a loving and merciful God should allow unfairness, injustice, cruelty, and even physical and mental illness to exist has been of particular concern to followers of the Christian religion, and attempts to provide answers to this question and explain away an anomaly which has been extensively used as an argument against God's very existence have powerfully concentrated the minds of theologians and many philosophers across the centuries. The psychologist might plead that the matter, involving as it does issues of value and metaphysical speculation, lies outside his or her professional concern. There is no way in which answers to the problems of evil and suffering can be put to scientific test. However, this does not excuse psychology from a professional interest in the area. Psychologists engaged in psychotherapy and in counseling, and in clinical and educational practice find that suffering and attempts to find a meaning in suffering, are frequent and major preoccupations for many of those with whom they work. The strategies that people adopt to help them accommodate to suffering, and the relative success of these strategies are not only psychologically revealing, they can be subjected both to analysis and to measurement.

For the materialist of course the problem of good and evil does not exist. The Universe is the product of blind chance, and it cannot be expected to function ethically. Good and evil are purely man-made value judgments placed upon events, and morality is no more than a man-made invention designed to protect property and to enable people to live together in social groups as harmoniously as possible, since this is what most people seem to want. For very different reasons the problem also does not exist for those who, like a majority of the followers of Eastern traditions, believe in the "law" of *karma*, first formalized by Hindu sages more than 600 years before the Common Era. *Karma* expresses the belief that all beings incarnate over many lifetimes before finding enlightenment and with it release from the cycle of births and deaths. The good that comes to a person in the present life is a consequence of virtuous actions in previous incarnations, while the bad is the result of actions that are unvirtuous.

Neither of these explanations is particularly satisfying. Although the former may appeal to those who stoically reject any explanation for human existence that seems to smack of superstition and wishful thinking, it fails to take account of the fact that human beings are undeniably capable of selfless and altruistic actions, actions which appear inexplicable in a universe driven by chance, and in a species whose evolution has depended upon natural selection. It also fails to explain why members of this species should search so assiduously for meaning in life, a search that appears to carry no particular survival value. Thus, whether true in essence or not, as an explanation it hardly proves sufficient for those faced with suffering and the consequences of evil. At the very least, there can emerge in such individuals the need to blame some higher power for present predicaments, even if only by professing to withdraw belief in such a power.

The latter argument, that *karma* is responsible – again whether true in essence or not – can be subjected to equal criticism. How, assuming that individuals all spring from the same source, did inequalities first arise among them, with some choosing meretricious behavior and others the opposite? The answer sometimes given, that every human has existed since beginningless time, with no starting point, again may be true, but opens up even more questions (particularly in light of the fact that even the universe appears to have had a beginning in the Big Bang – or the "outbreath of Brahma" as Hindus have traditionally and rather more poetically termed it). And how (and by whom) is the colossal logistical exercise of ensuring that everyone receives exactly and only the just rewards and deserts in this life for actions in previous existences carried out? And if someone has to treat me badly so that I can pay for my negative *karma* from a previous life, am I not then responsible for his or her bad treatment of me, and therefore am I not creating more negative *karma* for myself? And how, in a constantly changing world, can I receive back the equivalent of bad actions I committed many lifetimes ago in a cultural context and against a background of education and moral instruction that have now changed out of all recognition? The law of *karma* may have seemed to make good sense centuries ago in small, settled, relatively unchanging communities, but it is more difficult for it to appear credible these days.

Leaving *karma* aside, however, it is clear that, given the existence of free will and the notion of this life as a developmental opportunity, the traditions can reasonably argue that the choices we make between good and bad play an important role in this development. Just as we develop physical muscles by resisting and pushing against an opposing force, so the traditions maintain that we gain spiritual muscles by resisting and pushing against suffering and against the temptation to engage in behaviors likely to prove harmful and hurtful to others. This doesn't answer the question why things should be arranged by a benevolent providence in this way, but within the compass of human understanding, the existence of opposites such as good and evil not only gives definition to experience, but also provides challenge and opportunities for refining personal behavior in what appear to be spiritually desirable ways.

Christian doctrine has it that by becoming man through Christ, God demonstrated that pain and suffering, even the pain and suffering of the crucifixion, can be spiritually curative and redemptive. Although arguing from rather different beliefs, Eastern traditions place similar emphasis upon the positive role that suffering can play, maintaining in addition that if suffering – and the apparent evil that leads to suffering – exists in order to help us make spiritual progress, then it cannot ultimately be regarded as bad. At a relative level certainly suffering causes deep and abiding misery and consequently must be recognized for what it is and resisted or transcended, but it is these very acts of resistance and transcendence that bring ultimate benefit. Thus for these traditions the hard and fast distinction between good and evil disappears. If the world contained only goodness we would certainly find this congenial, but no progress would be possible. As we saw earlier, in Buddhism it is said that the heavenly realms (in which rebirth can take place as a result of meretricious lives, but which are still not the highest, Nirvanic level of being) are an example of this all-pervading goodness, and that those who find themselves there must, after they have used up the benefits gained by their meretricious previous life, eventually return to this Earth in order to continue their progress toward final enlightenment and thus toward release from birth and death and rebirth.

It is for the individual to decide between these various explanations for the presence of evil. But in addition to looking at the effect that belief in any one of them has upon human behavior, there are other points of interest to psychology. Why do people choose one explanation instead of another? How do they test these explanations, if at all? How consistent is their belief in them, and how firmly is this belief held? What kind and what degree of comfort do the explanations bring? So far, little extensive and consistent attempt has been made to find answers to these questions, and there is clearly much scope for future research.

## The Potential for Evil and Jung's Shadow

A further important question relating to evil and suffering is the extent to which people recognize the potential for evil in themselves, and the nature of the strategies they adopt for dealing with this recognition. Jung in particular placed great stress upon these questions (particularly Jung, 1943, 1951, 1954). As already explained, for Jung, the potential for evil resides in what he termed the *shadow*, which is the negative or inferior side of the personality. Often unrecognized and unacknowledged, the shadow is made up in part of the reprehensible qualities that we prefer to deny in ourselves (including primitive animalistic tendencies), but which also contains qualities that, properly used, may be highly desirable – for example anger and fear can respectively be expressed as determination to right injustices and as caution in the face of avoidable danger.

For Jung, self-development depends crucially not only upon achieving this recognition and acknowledging the shadow, but also upon fully integrating it into consciousness. The more unaware of the shadow we happen to be, the more we are likely to project it outwards onto other persons and groups – which we then claim embody all the negative qualities unacknowledged within ourselves. In this way we may even gain clandestine gratification for our repressed shadow tendencies. Although there is no clear research to this effect, it is possible that religious people particularly inflexible in their beliefs may be particularly prone to engage in this projection. For example it seems reasonable to suggest that the inhuman tortures and executions initiated by the medieval churchmen, mostly Dominican friars, who comprised the Inquisition may have gratified sadistic inclinations from within the shadow. Equally the barbaric behavior of the representatives of the Church, mostly Franciscan friars, toward the native Indians of South America after the Spanish conquest – which decimated the population and destroyed their culture – may have owed something to the same inclinations. In more recent times, the zeal of some anti-pornography campaigners may arise from similarly unacknow-ledged shadow tendencies, in this case an interest in the very material and behaviors that they appear so anxious to condemn and suppress in others. The justification for the hatred and persecution shown toward religious and cultural minority groups, and in times of war the misleading attribu-tions to the enemy of barbaric behaviors, may also in their various ways provide evidence of further unacknowledged shadow inclinations.

An even more obvious example of what may be the work of the unacknowledged shadow is the treatment that so many religious sects have meted out to women. Dominated by masculine power, such sects have projected onto women the blame for almost every imaginable sin – in particular for the sins associated with sexuality. From Adam blaming Eve for his action in eating forbidden fruit (God the Father was naturally not taken in by Adam's protestations, and sent him packing along with Eve from Eden) to the modern tendency to keep women out of all positions of real authority in many of the most powerful branches of the great traditions, women have been made the scapegoats for male failings. (Yet in spite of this women as a group have more religious sympathies than men, which one might argue shows their greater intuitive under-standing of the real message of the religious life.)

If these examples of the shadow at work are correct, religion has at times been used, among many other things, as a neurotic defense against self-recognition, and thus as a justification for all manner of crimes toward one's fellows. This emphasizes the particular importance of Walsh's in-sistence (Walsh, 1999) that "The underlying motive is crucial in spiritual life and ethical action" (he goes on to quote Mohammed who made clear that "all actions are judged by the motives prompting them"). Thus little of spiritual or ethical benefit is likely to arise if the motive for one's actions is neurotic self-defense, however strongly one may seek to justify this action by appeals to religious authority.

## The Study of Consciousness

Everything that has been said in this chapter about the self, the higher self, and the mind includes the notion of consciousness. Neglected for much of the second half of the twentieth-century by psychologists (with a few notable exceptions such as Ornstein (1972) and Wilber (1977)), the study of consciousness is once more attracting scientific attention. This study merits some specific attention in this chapter, not because in the context of the psychology of religion there is any need to separate consciousness from what has just been said about the self and the mind, but because some at least of the ideas discussed currently and in the past in relation to consciousness throw further light upon what we have been saying. (This should not be taken to mean that consciousness and mind have the same meaning in psychology; "consciousness" is specific to direct experience, while "mind" refers not only to consciousness but also to psychological processes which may not have conscious content, such as those that take place in the unconscious.)

Consciousness is still something of a mystery to science, because there is no apparent reason why it should have evolved. As a species we would have survived well enough without it. Sir John Eccles put it that "We can in principle explain all our input–output performances in terms of the activity of the neuronal circuits; and consequently consciousness seems to be absolutely unnecessary" in evolutionary terms (Eccles, 1976), and if consciousness is thus "causally impotent, its development cannot be accounted for by evolutionary theory" (Eccles, 1980). So its very existence is a challenge, a challenge which has led not only to its relative neglect within psychology, but also to a denial that it is of any consequence. Thus it is explained away as an epiphenomenon of brain activity, something that happens as an unimportant byproduct of something else, rather as noise is simply the unimportant byproduct of the workings of the internal combustion engine. By this reckoning, the brain has no need for consciousness, and does not "intend" to give rise to it.

Such an idea is of course quite contrary to the intuitive sense that we have that consciousness – as an activity of mind – helps makes us what we are. There is no agreed definition of consciousness, but we can think of it as a special form of awareness, special in the sense that it reflects upon experience and upon the experiencer him or herself (i.e. shows self-consciousness). Jung (1954) saw human consciousness as the momentous achievement of nature becoming conscious of itself. In the West it is generally assumed (even taught in schools) that humans are the only species with this special form of awareness, but there is no real warrant for such an assumption. The central nervous systems of even the more highly evolved animals are indeed different from our own, but this does not allow us to decide with any certainty that such animals do not, in some cases at least, have a consciousness of self (and also perhaps a degree of free will and of conscious decision making). The assumption that animals do not have self-consciousness seems to be based more upon our wish to justify our exploitation of them, much as the medieval church and the colonial powers sought to dehumanize as heathen savages the indigenous people they exploited and often ended up destroying.

## Models of Consciousness

The existence of consciousness is demonstrated for each one of us by direct experience. The question is not whether it exists or not, but what form does it take. In many ways the most useful Western approach is that proposed by Freud (e.g. 1937) and amplified by Jung (e.g. 1954), namely that consciousness is best studied in the context of a four-level model that also embraces the unconscious. Level one is normal waking consciousness, that is whatever is currently going through the mind. Level two is the preconscious, everything that is not currently in the mind but that can be recalled at will. Level three is the personal unconscious, everything that is not readily available, but which intrudes in dreams and can sometimes be accessed in psychotherapy. And level four is the collective unconscious, an inherited psychological component common to us all, rather as we inherit the common physical characteristics of the human race.

Jung's shadow features in both the collective and the personal unconscious, and in his view it is in the latter that our religious sense has its genesis. The concept of the collective unconscious came from his clinical experience that clients frequently brought up common or very similar mythical ideas during analysis that could not be accounted for by their previous learning and experience. In his view the collective unconscious contains the *archetypes* – "the gods and images of the dominant laws and principles, and of typical, regularly occurring events in the soul's cycle of experience" (Jung, 1943). These are responsible for our human qualities, and serve as the active agents that cause the repetition of the same psychological experiences from person to person and from generation to generation. We can never encounter the archetypes directly in our inner life – they remain a formless psychological and spiritual potential. We experience them only in symbolic and mythical form, often influenced not only by our personal unconscious but also by the experiences of our ancestors over the centuries (which suggests the existence of inherited racial memories – a concept unacceptable to Darwinians).

Thus we have for example the archetype of the *mother* (symbolizing our innate sense of motherhood as compassionate, sympathy, magical authority, wisdom, fertility, rebirth, and a spiritual exaltation that transcends reason), the *anima* (symbolizing man's idea of womanhood), the *animus* (symbolizing woman's idea of man), the *child* (symbolizing the potentiality for the development of wholeness), the *wise old man* (symbolizing meaning and spirit) and the *self* (the most important archetype of all, symbolizing individual wholeness and harmony and balance between the various opposing qualities within psychological life). For Jung, religion is inextricably linked to archetypal energies. Our concepts of God may be influenced by our personal unconscious, but they arise from a dynamic energy which is part of the collective unconscious.

The persistence of religious ideas and religious beliefs across cultures and across the centuries lends some support to this notion of religion as an innate feature of the human consciousness. In fact the first known studies of consciousness were carried out within the context of religion. Analyses of levels of consciousness are referred to in the *Upanishads*, some of the most sacred of Hindu writings, and are greatly enlarged upon in other Hindu texts such as the *Brahma-Sutras* and the *Bhagavad Gita*. They also feature largely in the writings of the *Yogacara* school in Buddhism which reached its intellectual peak in the sixth-century CE, and in the work of Plato, Plotinus, and other notables spawned by the civilizations that flourished around the Mediterranean Basin before and after the coming of the Common Era (Nielsen *et al.*, 1988).

Together with the perspectives on consciousness to be found in other major Eastern traditions such as *Taoism* and *Jainism*, and in the Hebrew *Kabbalah* and other Western esoteric traditions, there is apparent in all these writings a number of common features which strengthen the impression that they are based upon direct experience. Most obvious of these is the insistence – many centuries before the existence of the unconscious as anything more than a repository of largely unwanted memories was taken seriously by Western science – that normal consciousness is only a very small part of our potential for rich and meaningful inner experience. Allied to this insistence is the conviction that the purpose of human life is to realize and achieve identification with the source from which this potential arises. A third common feature is that one passes through a number of interconnected levels of consciousness on the way to this identification. The clearest explanatory system of these developmental levels is that of the *Advaita Vedanta* school of Hinduism, and set out by the ninth-century CE philosopher Shankara (Fontana, 2000).

## The Advaita Vedanta Developmental Model of Consciousness

This system, which Wilber (1993) refers to as the most "spectacular and consistent" model of consciousness in existence, consists of six major levels (each, with the exception of the last, with many subdivisions). The six levels in ascending order of experience are as follows:

- *The material level*, at which consciousness is identified exclusively with sense data, and the self and the physical body are seen as synonymous. Failure to progress beyond this level is said to result in the loss of contact with the higher levels, even to the extent of rejecting their existence. The world and everything in it is seen as fundamentally physical, and there is no awareness of any underlying unity.
- *The vital level*, at which consciousness becomes aware of the self, of the distinction between life and death and of the mortality of the physical body, and experiences the will toward its preservation. Life is valued and death is seen as a threat and a mystery.
- *The discriminative level*, at which consciousness begins to categorize the objects and events presented by experience, and to recognize the important distinction between turning inwards toward the nonmaterial world of thoughts and intuitions and perhaps spiritual awareness, and outwards toward the material world.
- *The ratiocinative level*, at which consciousness acquires the capacity for analytical and rational thought, and becomes capable of abstract thinking, philosophical debate, and advanced theory building.
- *The causal level*, at which consciousness can experience pure contentless awareness, or pure consciousness in and of itself. At the previous levels, consciousness has always been aware *of* something, but now is conscious just of itself, a state almost impossible to describe to anyone who has not experienced it.
- *The Brahmanic level*, in which consciousness is aware of reality as a unified field of energy in which the material world, the individual, and the source of all phenomena, *Brahman* or the Absolute, are in essence identical with each other.

As children develop, they usually acquire at least the first three levels. The third of these has obvious similarities with Piaget's *formal operations*, just as the first two remind us respectively of his *sensori-motor* and *concrete operations* stages in child development (Piaget and Inhelder, 1969), but unlike Piaget's stages these levels are not progressively left behind as the individual moves up the hierarchy. Each is carried throughout life (as Bruner insisted is the case with his proposed stages of cognitive development – Bruner, Goodnow, and Austin, 1966). Thus it is possible to operate at more than one level at the same time. For example a thinker may be operating at the *ratiocinative* level in terms of reasoning and analysis, but may be simultaneously so located at the *material* level in other areas of his thinking that his theory building is devoted exclusively to explaining every discovery in material terms. All descriptions of reality that introduce nonphysical concepts are firmly rejected. The opposite example, that of someone operating simultaneously at the *ratiocinative* and the *causal* levels and rejecting materiality, is also likely to occur less frequently, simply because even if one is convinced that the physical world is not ultimate reality, there is no denying its present existence. (Nevertheless, there are accounts of Hindu saints such as Ramakrishna and Ramana Maharshi who on first experience of the *causal* level were quite unable for a time to function at the material level, and had to be cared for virtually like babies.)

This *Advaita-Vedanta* developmental model recognizes that as our consciousness progresses through the various levels we gain the potential to see reality in different ways, even though we may not put this potential to full use. The gross consciousness that operates at the *material* level only allows us to see the world in gross terms, but as consciousness becomes more refined our capacity to see beyond this grossness increases. However, there is nothing necessarily spiritual about the first four levels, although a sense of the spiritual may be present from level two onwards, as the individual discovers and begins to question and ponder the existence of death and its relationship to life. The spiritual nature of one's being is only fully realized at level five, although few people catch more than occasional glimpses of the states concerned. Only very rare individuals such as Christ, the Buddha, Mohammed, and the Hindu *Avatars* (said to be direct incarnations of divine consciousness) are regarded in *Advaita-Vedanta* as having reached the highest level of all, that of *Brahmanic* consciousness.

A sustained attempt has been made by Wilber (e.g. 1998, 2000) to link the developmental levels recognized by the *Advaita-Vedanta* model (together with many other aspects of Eastern thought) to Western science. The resulting model has it that the developing consciousness spirals progressively upwards from the impulsive state of the small child with his or her archaic and instinctual worldview, the egocentric state in which the worldview becomes magical and animistic, the conformist state with its mythic, symbolic worldview, the conscientious state with its formal, rational worldview, the individualistic state with a worldview that is pluralistic and relative, and the autonomous state where the worldview becomes integral and holistic. Development can be arrested at any one of these states, and few reach that of autonomy. This model has the virtue of seeing development from an all-embracing, self-identity standpoint. Thus the manner in which we think, feel, behave, plan, and react is shaped by the particular way we look at the world through the prism of who we take ourselves to be.

Wilber also draws attention to the concept of the "great chain of being" which is recognized in the great traditions as central to both individual and social development. Best described as a holarchy running from matter to life to mind to soul to spirit, mistakes arise if this holarchy is seen as a *hierarchy*, with each level superior to the ones below. Wilber tells us they are more properly thought of as nested together, with each level (or, better still, each state) interacting with each of the others. For example mind (which is nonphysical) and brain (which is organic and material) are intimately connected. In addition, each of the states in the great chain of being has its own attendant discipline, namely physics (for the exploration of matter), biology (for the exploration of life), psychology (for the exploration of mind), theology (for the exploration of soul), and mysticism (for the exploration of spirit). And far from being exalted and other-worldly, the final state, "spirit," is in fact the causal factor from which all the other states arise, and thus comprises the foundation as well as the culmination of the great chain.

The idea of "spirit" as the "cause" of everything else seems strange to the ears of the Western scientist, but it is in keeping with the beliefs of all the great traditions, whether they refer to spirit as God (as do the theistic traditions), as Emptiness (as in Buddhism), or as the Tao (as in Taoism). But it is also in keeping with the theories of modern physicists such as those of Goswami (Goswami, 1993) which start from the premise that at the quantum, subatomic level consciousness, as expressed through the behavior of the observer, appears able directly to interact with and influence the activity and perhaps even the form of manifestation of the energetic forces that constitute matter (and thus actually to alter the physical world). If this is indeed the case, then far from being independent of consciousness, the material world appears in some sense to be influenced by it, even perhaps partly subject to it (for some of the background to quantum mechanics in layman's language see Gribbin, 1991, 1995, 1998). This extraordinary idea derives further support from the argument that since the universe appears to have had a beginning in the Big Bang, and since the intricate complexity of the mathematical relationships without which the universe as we know it would have destroyed itself in the first nanosecond of this cataclysmic event, we are faced with believing either that mathematics was created by chance in the first instant of the Big Bang, or that the consciousness – without which we cannot understand mathematics – was at a cosmic level somehow involved in (even perhaps the cause of) this act of primal creation. If the latter is the preferred belief, then both consciousness and matter emerged from some higher reality, such as Bohm's implicate order (Bohm, 1980). Furthermore, as a belief it accords with Sir James Jeans well-known conclusion that:

. . . substantial matter [resolves] itself into a creation and manifestation of mind. We discover that the universe shows evidence of a designing or controlling power that has something in common with our own individual minds . . . the tendency to think in the way which, for want of a better word, we describe as mathematical (Jeans, 1931, p. 138).

For Jeans' "designing or controlling power", and for the consciousness that Goswami and others consider appears able directly to affect the form of manifestation of matter, we can it seems substitute Wilber's "spirit," the first cause from which he argues that not only each of the states in his holography but also the whole of the phenomenal world arises. Such an idea, together with theories like those of Goswami and Jeans on the role of consciousness, is emphatically rejected by scientists who prefer materialist–reductionist models of reality, and who maintain that the idea that consciousness influences matter at the subatomic level is still under dispute, and that until the physics of the Big Bang is more fully understood what are in effect metaphysical speculations on the genesis of the mathematics involved are premature to say the very least.

Nevertheless, any theories commensurate with ideas from theoretical physics and from other branches of science that bring consciousness and spirit back into the reckoning after their supposed dethronement by materialist–reductionist philosophy are of great significance to religion. Without such nonmaterial realities religion, as anything more than a set of teachings about desirable social behaviors, collapses. In addition to possible support from theoretical physics and astronomy, on what else therefore does Wilber base his models of self and spirit and the great chain of being, and what does he have to say about the relevance of his model to our understanding of human behavior?

## Wilber's Models

Firstly, he recognizes the significant coherence of beliefs in the great chain across all the great traditions. This suggests that such beliefs are based upon the direct experiences of the sages who first gave them voice, experiences that embraced both the inner and the outer worlds. True the great chain becomes progressively more metaphysical as it moves from the objectivity of the outside world to the evident (but mysterious) fact of life and to the subjectivity of mind and spirit, but both of the latter are nevertheless said to be accessible to our own personal experience. The former is self-evident when we look into ourselves, while the latter is available to those who embark upon developmental practices laid out in great detail by some of the sages concerned such as Patanjali

(Prabhavananda and Isherwood, 1953) in the fourth-century BCE and in modern times by Aurobindo (1957), and reviewed and commented on extensively from a modern scientific perspective by Ravindra (2000). And as Wilber makes clear, although claims for the existence of spirit in the great chain of being are strongly rejected by many scientists, they are not in fact contradicted by scientific knowledge itself.

Secondly, Wilber surveys the history of Western thought and identifies two distinct groups within it, one of which relates to inner aspects of knowledge and experience and the other to the outer aspects. These two groups each have two facets, giving us what he terms four areas – or quadrants as he calls them – in all. The quadrants in the first group consist of the inner aspects respectively of the individual and of the collective, while those in the second group consist of their outer aspects. Wilber calls the two quadrants in the first or inner group "The Left Hand Path," and the two quadrants in the second or outer group "The Right Hand Path" (terms unconnected with the two so-called left and right hand paths in tantric and occult practices).

The inner individual quadrant (the "I" quadrant) he regards as concerned with mind, intention, subjectivity, truthfulness, and sincerity, and the inner collective quadrant (the "we" quadrant) with culture, ethics, morals, worldviews, justice, and understanding. By contrast the outer individual quadrant (the "it" quadrant) is concerned with behavior, objective truth, and representation, and the outer collective quadrant (the "they" quadrant) with society, objective nature, and empirical forms generally. The two outer quadrants refer to material located in space – and therefore to material that is directly observable and quantifiable – while the two inner ones, which are concerned with mind, refer to domains that are non-spatial. The two outer quadrants are accessed through perception and studied through observation, measurement, science, and the articulation of propositional truth, while the two inner ones are accessed through interpretation and explored through introspection, self-expression, art, aesthetics, common context, and intersubjective meaning.

All four, Wilber insists, are of equal importance to humankind's attempt to understand the totality of creation and to advance human knowledge, and all four are expressions – the first two covert and the second two overt – of what he insists is spirit. However, each of the four carries its own truths and is revealed by its own methods of investigation, and no one of them is reducible to any of the others. Indeed, it is our attempt to do so, whether we are arguing in favor of the inner quadrants or of the outer, that has led to much of the confusion in thinking across the centuries, and which now is represented as a conflict between religion and science.

Wilber illustrates the distinction between the inner individual quadrant ("I") and the outer individual quadrant ("it") by the study respectively of mind and brain. Mind is "I" and brain is "it". No matter how many correlations we find between the two they are not one and the same, and should never be treated as such by those interested in truth. Mind is studied by the reports people give of their own inner world of thought, dreams, concepts, valuations, etc., while brain is studied by the exploration of electrochemical activity in the cortex.

Wilber illustrates the difference between the inner collective quadrant ("we") and the outer collective quadrant ("they") by discussing a group activity such as the Hopi Rain Dance. In the context of the dance, the "we" quadrant is explored by questioning the dancers as to the meaning the dance has for them, and by attempting to interpret this meaning, while the "they" quadrant is studied by observing the function that the dance appears to have for the Hopi social system. In answer to the "we" quadrant questions, the dancers will say that the dance celebrates for them the sacredness of nature, and is a way of asking nature to bless the earth with rain. By contrast, the observation of social behavior will suggest that the dance assists group cooperation and cohesion. Both methods of investigation and both sets of findings are correct and interesting in their own right, and neither should be seen as dominating or devaluing or capable of replacing the other.

Wilber thus emphasizes the need to respect the different methodologies of the four quadrants, and to see each of them as concerned with valid aspects of how spirit expresses itself in the created world. In his view the four quadrants have the potential to express between them the good, the true, and the beautiful. The good arises from the ethics and morals created through culture (through "we"), the true through the quantifiable, objective approach of science (through "it" and "they"), and the beautiful from the artistic expression and quality of being created through the individual (through "I"). For Wilber, the good, the true, and the beautiful make up "The Big Three," the qualities that define humanity at its best.

Thirdly, having explained and justified the four quadrants as areas of knowledge and as expressions of spirit, Wilber then looks back to see how each of them has fared through history. In his view, the distinction between them was not in fact properly recognized before the eighteenth-century Enlightenment, with the result that attempts to study the Right Hand Path of the two outer quadrants and to develop perceptual science were seen as heresy by the Church, which wrongly regarded all such knowledge as the exclusive preserve of the Left Hand Path of the two inner quadrants. Followers of the right-hand quadrants were in consequence victimized by the arrogant intolerance of an authoritarianism Church. Anyone who sought to follow the methods of what was then called natural philosophy and is now known as science, such as Copernicus,

Galileo, and Brahe, lived in constant danger within a society where the highly organized machinery of the Church (equivalent in many ways to a modern secret police) was constantly seeking out those who could be accused of heresy. The Enlightenment and the Age of Reason corrected this imbalance, but then proceeded to create an equally damaging imbalance of its own in that attempts at studying the two inner quadrants were dismissed as impossibly subjective, and thus as unscientific and unworthy of serious consideration. Those who sought to follow the methods of the left-hand quadrants were thus, in a quite different and more humane but nevertheless equally efficient way, labeled as heretics to orthodox canons of belief.

Wilber argues that the dichotomies between the left-hand quadrants and right-hand quadrants arise not from within the design of reality itself, but from our interpretation of this design and our stubborn belief that the methods and the knowledge associated with our preferred quadrant carry a monopoly of the truth. On the strength of the damage done to our understanding of the world and of ourselves by the Church before the Enlightenment and by science in subsequent years, Wilber insists that both extremes, whether of the Left Hand or of the Right Hand Path, are equally dangerous. And despite the fact that something of a balance is currently being restored by the paradigm shift that started in the last decades of the twentieth century, there is a risk that the respective followers of the two Paths will remain polarized, disregarding or actively devaluing the other Path instead of recognizing the important and specific role it has to play. Each of the quadrants has variously contributed to and impeded material and spiritual progress, and a sickness in any one of them reverberates through them all.

Fourthly, Wilber surveys the form that spiritual beliefs and behaviors have taken within the two Paths. Those who approach religion with an orientation toward the Left Hand Path have traditionally focussed on the transcendence of spirit, on God external to His creation, and on the consequent human need to ascend in order to approach the Divine, while those orientated toward the Right Hand Path have preferred to focus upon the imminence of spirit, and the need to descend in order to realize it. Followers of the Left Hand Path have emphasized wisdom, male gods or God, deity mysticism, and the need to rise above the "evils" of the natural world. Those adhering to the Right Hand Path have emphasized compassion, female gods or God, nature mysticism, and the need to repudiate the "evils" of the artificially created cultural world. Throughout recorded history, either the ascenders of the Left Hand Path or the descenders of the Right Hand Path have tended to dominate spiritual thinking in the West, again leading to imbalance and negative consequences.

Wilber points out that even today, within the so-called "New Age" philosophies which draw from an eclectic mix of spiritual teachings from East and West, a polarization is still apparent between those who adhere to the Left Hand Path and emphasize primarily the need to find our "Higher Self," and those who follow the Right and emphasize the need to contact "Gaia" and Earth energies. The first group denigrates objectivity, the second denigrates subjectivity. Genuine spiritual insights, which Wilber considers can come to those on both Paths, are accepted and rejected by those concerned solely on the basis of whether or not they accord with existing preferred spiritual beliefs (and prejudices). As a consequence, further spiritual development remains largely inhibited, and the crucial importance of all four quadrants for this development is overlooked. Every aspect of creation, from atoms to human beings, contains facets of all four because each of them has both an inner and an outer reality in that each of them is both an entity in itself, an amalgam of smaller entities, and an integral part of a larger whole.

Wilber's four-quadrant model provides us with a self-evident description of how reality is arranged. (Wilber has his critics – e.g. de Quincy, 2000 – though few dispute the accuracy and usefulness of this model.) Inner and outer, individual and collective form the pattern for existence. Furthermore, a recognition of these four quadrants allows us to understand many of the problems, misunderstandings, and intolerances of the past. It is evident also that all four quadrants have a contribution to make to Wilber's Great Chain of Being, and that it is crucial for our understanding of the psychology of religion and spirituality that we do not confuse their respective roles. The investigation of the first two levels of the Chain, matter and life, belongs, with their attendant disciplines of physics and biology, primarily to the right-hand quadrants. Investigation of the third level, mind, belongs with its attendant discipline of psychology to both quadrants, while investigation of the remaining two levels, soul and spirit and their attendant disciplines of theology and mysticism, belongs predominantly to the left-hand quadrants.

However, the term "primarily" is important here, because it indicates that the investigations concerned are not the sole prerogative of right- and left-hand quadrants respectively. For example matter, the investigation of which belongs primarily to the right-hand quadrants, nevertheless profoundly influences personal and social development in the left-hand quadrants, and provides the context within which mind builds its picture of external reality. Life, which is also investigated primarily through the methods of the right-hand quadrants, is nevertheless fundamental to sentient existence and therefore to all quadrants, and is an experiential reality for the left-hand quadrants. Soul, which is investigated by direct experience within the left-hand quadrants, is investigated indirectly by the methods of the right-hand quadrants through the outer behavior of those professing to have realized its reality. The workings of Spirit, if Spirit is indeed the culmination and source of all things, is experienced as culmination through inner experience in the left-hand quadrants, and as source through an investigation of the mysteries and complexities – Sir James Jeans' "designing and controlling power" – of the natural world in the right-hand quadrants, with discoveries in the one set of quadrants feeding, informing, and stimulating discoveries in the other.

Of most immediate relevance to psychology is the mind–brain relationship, with mind accessible directly only to the methods of the left-hand quadrant, and brain only to those of the right-hand, and it is to the critical mind–brain relationship that we turn in the next section.

## The Mind–Brain Relationship

The distinction between mind and brain is most easily drawn, as we said earlier, by asking how you can directly experience your brain, and how you can physically probe your mind. The answer – obviously enough – is that you can do neither of these things. Your brain is the gray matter inside your skull, and your mind is your inner world of thoughts, ideas, memories, dreams, intuitions, and so on. The former can only be experienced from outside, the latter only from inside. No matter how many advances we make in brain research, this will never change. Brain and mind remain functionally separate, the one objective and the other subjective. Because of this functional separation, the methods for investigating brain and mind respectively – right-hand quadrant methods for the brain and left-hand quadrant methods for the mind – will forever remain distinct. Nevertheless, there are those who argue that in spite of this unavoidable distinction, it should become possible to establish the nature of the relationship between brain and mind, and that science is already well on the way to doing so.

Two sets of competing theories as to this relationship, monism (the brain creates mind) and dualism (the mind works through brain) have been argued over from the time of Descartes onwards, with first one and then the other preferred by Western science. Currently, monism is the preferred theory. The mind, it is argued, is the product of electrochemical activity within the gray physical matter of the brain and is – as we said earlier in relation to consciousness – a kind of epiphenomenon in that the brain could handle the problems of survival perfectly well without its mental activity. Let us make no mistake, this theory is deeply threatening to religion and spirituality. If the brain does generate mind, then when the brain dies the mind dies, and along with it beliefs in the soul, the spirit,

God, salvation, life after death, and all the other notions that make of religion something more than a set of rules for personal and social conduct.

The question of how justified is the monist theory of brain and mind is thus of crucial interest to religion. And not only to religion but also to psychology, to philosophy, and indeed to the very fabric of our understanding of what it means to be human and who and what, as humans, we actually are. Supporters of the theory argue strongly that the recent advances in brain-mapping to which we referred in chapter 7, advances which allow us to identify clearly which parts of the brain are identified with which kind of mental activity, demonstrate that the parts of the brain thus identified are responsible for – probably by implication actually initiate – the mental activity. We referred in chapter 7 to work by Persinger (1996) and by Ramachandran and Blakeslee (1998) into the so-called "God Spot," an area in the frontal lobes of the cerebral cortex which may be involved in mystical experiences. Newberg and d'Aquili (2000) report findings which suggest that religious and spiritual experiences are associated particularly with activity in the right posterior superior parietal lobe (PSPL), an area involved in the analysis and integration of higher order sensory information. This leads them to conclude that the right PSPL is therefore "the neurological substrate" which, together with structures in the left cerebral hemisphere, is responsible for the states of undifferentiated unity associated with mystical experience. Dennett (1991) is even bolder, arguing that once we have described the way the brain works in every detail, then we have given a full description of the consciousness of man and nothing more is required. Even the higher emotions such as love, truth, and beauty (Wilber's "Big Three") are nothing more than patterns of electrical activity traversing different areas of the brain. Francis Crick, Nobel Prizewinner for the discovery of the double-helix structure of DNA (1994) takes a largely similar view.

Dualists would respond to these monist arguments by emphasizing again that the presence of correlations between mental events and brain events does not demonstrate that the latter are the cause of the former. The existence of correlations does not justify conclusions as to causality. One could as readily suggest that it is the mind working through the brain that causes the correlated changes in brain function. The purpose of the brain is to mediate between the nonphysical mind and the physical world, receiving impressions from this world which are then interpreted by the mind, and receiving impressions from the mind which are then related to the physical world. (Benson, 1996, refers to these two processes respectively as "bottom-up" and "top-down," and comments that "only recently has brain research revealed that the latter is possible.")

Monists reply that quite apart from the difficulties associated with the theory of the existence of a nonmaterial substance which can affect anything in the physical world, there is the problem that there appear to be no "gaps" in the neural causal chains within the brain where nonmaterial causes can operate. The brain appears to be a causally closed system. In addition, causation by a nonmaterial entity of some kind appears to contravene the principle of the conservation of energy, one of the basic principles of science. It makes much more sense to work from the known principles of brain function than to speculate on unknown and unseen metaphysical causes.

This argument has always carried particular weight, but the findings from quantum physics mentioned earlier that suggest consciousness may be able directly to interact with and influence the activity and perhaps even the form of manifestation of the energetic forces that constitute matter now provides a possible, if highly speculative and contentious response to it. Every cell in the brain, just as every cell in the body, is made up of atoms, each of which in turn is reducible to subatomic, quantum events. This being the case – and if consciousness can indeed exert an influence at the quantum level – it may be that it is at this level that a nonphysical mind interacts with a physical brain. It is unclear how such a possibility can be subjected to scientific test or how a mind–brain interaction at the quantum level would actually work, but at least, as a possibility consistent with some propositions from theoretical physics, it provides dualism with a model which has some explanatory power. Furthermore, no such model as yet exists to support the monistic argument. As Velmans (2000) puts it "no discovery that reduces consciousness to brain has yet been made." We have no idea how the brain's electrochemical energy can produce mental events such as thoughts, that is, we have no model based upon scientific discoveries that explains how thoughts arise.

This point was strongly emphasized by Sir John Eccles (1980, 1989), who after many years of brain research concluded that "Regardless of the complexity of electrical, chemical, or biological machinery" in the brain there is in "natural laws" no statement as to how the mind can emerge. "The 'self-conscious mind' must have some nonmaterial existence." The mind influences the body through the exercise of freewill, and the body influences the mind by providing sensory information, which the mind integrates into perceptual experience. Eccles' conclusion supports in effect what is sometimes called the "substance dualism" position enunciated by Plato in the fourth/third century BCE and by Descartes in the seventeenth century CE, namely that the universe consists of two fundamental kinds of stuff, material stuff and the stuff of consciousness, the latter associated with soul and spirit.

So-called "property dualists" such as Sperry (1985) and Libet (most recently 1996) also take the view that the self-conscious mind is nonphysical, but unlike the substance dualists see it as actually emerging from physical systems once the latter have attained a certain level of complexity (see Velmans, 2000, for an excellent survey of these and other models relevant to the nature of consciousness). Libet's work is of particular interest as he has discovered that there is a 200-millisecond delay between the *arrival* of stimuli at the cerebral cortex and the *arousal of conscious awareness* of the stimuli. In other words, conscious awareness appears fractionally to lag behind brain activity.

This discovery seems at first sight as if it might support the monist position that brain gives rise to consciousness, but the position is more complex in that a mismatch between actual stimulus arrival and experienced stimulus arrival is avoided by the fact that the mind somehow *judges* that the stimulus was received at the correct time. Thus a time mismatch between the brain receiving the stimulus and the mind becoming aware of this stimulus is avoided. Commenting upon Libet's findings, Eccles (1984) makes the point firstly that this ante-dating procedure by the mind is not explicable in terms of neurophysiological processes in the brain *per se*, and secondly that the delay in recognition time is due to the fact that the brain has to build up "an immense and complex patterned modular activity before it is detectable by the scanning self-conscious mind." The ante-dating procedure is thus "presumably a strategy learnt by the self-conscious mind . . . so that all experienced events can be corrected in time so that their time sequence corresponds to the actual initiating stimuli." The self-conscious mind makes these slight temporal adjustments (in effect it plays tricks with time) "in compensation for the tardy development of weak neuronal spatio-temporal patterns up to the threshold level for conscious recognition. In this way all experienced events are corrected in time so that their time sequence corresponds to the initiating stimuli, whether they be strong or weak." But for this adjustment, "a sequence of weak and strong taps, as in playing a percussion instrument, would be experienced in a distorted time relationship."

The monist may then argue that nevertheless, the mind can be influenced by electrical stimulation of the brain – as for example in the quasi mystical experiences that result from stimulation of the so-called "God Spot" in the frontal lobes (chapter 7). This seems to provide a strong argument for brain as the seat of the mind. However, this can be countered by the observation that in such cases of altered consciousness the stimulation (as with the stimulation provided by drugs) comes from *outside* the brain rather than from within the brain itself. Thus it still cannot be said that the brain initiates these altered states. It might also be pointed out that before the experiences consequent upon stimulation of the God Spot can be compared with genuine mystical experiences, we need research that is carried out on those who have had these genuine experiences; only in this way can valid comparisons between the two states of awareness be attempted. (It is also worth the dualist pointing out that in any case mystics don't go around with electrodes plugged into their frontal lobes in order to stimulate the God Spot.) Further, the argument that finding a brain state associated with mystical experiences somehow demonstrates there is no spiritual dimension associated with the initiation of these experiences is illogical. You will be having a succession of brain states at this very moment that are associated with reading these words, but the existence of these states does not demonstrate that the words have no existence. Both words and brain states have their own reality.

The monist may then attack the dualist argument that the electro-chemical activity of the brain does not appear capable of generating a conscious mind from a slightly different direction. We can produce computers capable not only of mimicking but also of vastly outperforming the intelligent behavior of the human mind. In the future new generations of computers may even be able to take their own decisions and so demonstrate freewill and apparent self-consciousness, and to design new computers cleverer than themselves. We may even have a computer that will pass a version of the famous Turing Test in which a judge is asked to interview a computer and a human down separate computer terminals; if he cannot identify which is the computer, the computer will have passed the test and convinced us it is conscious. What then will be the difference, if any, between the human mind and the mind of a computer? And what will have become of the argument that material objects working on electrical energy cannot generate mind?

The dualist may answer this question by saying that I know I am not a computer, but a computer does not know that it isn't me (or an elephant or a straw hat) unless at some point I first put this information – or ways of testing for this information – into the software. Even a small child, without being told, knows the difference between a human being and a computer, thus outsmarting the latter on one of the most basic of tests. (An even simpler answer might be that we can switch off the computer's brain by unplugging it from the current that feeds it, but it can't do the same thing to us.) A further answer the dualist might offer is that even if we can build a computer which is modeled on the neural networks of the human brain but operating trillions of times faster, we still could not program into it the subjective feeling of what it is like to be alive and to experience color, beauty, music, art, love, painting, architecture, nature, parenthood, happiness (even drunkenness) – all the things in fact that go to make us human. Thus although it may be that there are persons somewhere out there who would prefer to be computers rather than humans – who would prefer to be clever machines rather than flesh and blood – they are probably relatively few in number.

And so the debate goes on, with arguments and counter-arguments on either side. The monist may choose to remind the dualist of the changes in thinking, memory, and affect consequent upon brain damage, to which the dualist can reply that if the brain is indeed the point of contact between the nonphysical mind and the material world, then any damage to it will inevitably affect the ability of mind to function in this material world, much as a fault in a television will interfere with the reception of the program. The dualist may add that when quite massive brain damage occurs in young children, whether through accident or surgery, the child may still grow up normally or virtually normally, with other parts of the brain somehow "knowing" that they must take over the functions of the missing parts. How does this "knowing" arise if not from a nonphysical mind able, if we use Eccles' term, to "scan" the brain and find new ways of working with and through it?

To this the monist will reply that even in these cases some part of the brain still existed. We have no evidence that mind can exist if there is no brain function at all. Surely if the mind is nonphysical it would give some indication that physicality is not essential for its operation. At which point the dualist may choose to bring up the subject of near-death experiences (NDEs), to which we turn in the next section. NDEs have great potential relevance both to psychology and to religion because, if the evidence for them is genuine, they do suggest that the mind may indeed be able to operate other than in association with the physical brain. And if this suggestion turns out to be correct, then the NDE may help us solve at long last the problem of the mind–body relationship, and also provide some support for the religious belief that consciousness survives the demise of the physical body.

## Near-Death Experiences

Experiences in which the subject has been apparently clinically dead but on resuscitation returns not only to tell the tale but also to report the continuation of consciousness during this intermission have been reported since antiquity. One of the earliest accounts is by Plato at the end of *The Republic*. A soldier, Er, was apparently killed on the battlefield, but revived when placed on the funeral pyre (in the nick of time one might think) and described a journey out of his body to a place of judgment where souls were divided into those destined for heaven and those destined for punishment. Er had been "sent back" to Earth in order to tell others what he had seen. We have, of course, no way of knowing the actual state of Er's health during his experience of apparent death, but modern resuscitation methods now result in the revival of more and more people after incidents such as cardiac arrest, and a significant percentage of them report experiences not dissimilar in some ways to that of Er.

Brought to popular attention by Moody in 1983 (drawing upon his medical experience), earlier and more extensive collections of such experiences were published by Crookall (1961, 1978), while a range of subsequent studies conducted by medical doctors, neuropsychiatrists, and psychologists (e.g. Sabom, 1982, 1998; Ring, 1984; Ring and Valarino, 1998; Ring and Cooper, 1999; Fenwick and Fenwick, 1995), indicate variously that between 12 and 40 percent of those at or near clinical death report going through NDEs prior to resuscitation. Reports typically suggest that during the NDE consciousness appears to be located outside the body, and that sometimes details of the medical procedures carried out on the body during the NDE are observed and later accurately reported, even though these procedures would not have been visible from where the body was lying at the time even had it been conscious. Sometimes there are also accounts of traveling to "paradise" conditions and of meeting deceased relatives or "beings of light" who are instrumental in sending the wandering consciousness back into the physical body. Usually re-entry into it is said to occur with great reluctance and even repugnance. Most people claim they would prefer not to return, and only do so either because they are given no choice or because they have responsibilities in physical life that they cannot abandon.

Drawing upon findings into brain function by neurologists and neuropsychiatrists, Fenwick (Fenwick and Fenwick, 1995) concludes from his study of 300 NDE cases that attempts to explain the NDE as generated by the chaotic activity of the dying brain, by oxygen starvation, by a build-up of carbon dioxide in the blood, by hallucinations consequent upon the action of medical drugs, or of the body's release of endorphins do not appear to be adequate for the following reasons.

1.  Subjects report that the NDE becomes more coherent as it progresses, rather than less coherent as it would if the dying brain or oxygen starvation was responsible.

2.  No Intensive Care Unit of any standing would tolerate the build-up of carbon dioxide (hypercarbia) in the blood of a patient who has had a heart attack. In addition hypercarbia produces convulsive muscle movements – these have never been reported in patients with NDEs.

3.  Although anoxia has been induced in experimental conditions thousands of times in thousands of people – at one time artificially induced anoxia was part of the training of many medical students – there are no reports of any consequent NDEs.

4.  On the question of medical drugs, Fenwick reports that only 14 percent of his sample were being given such drugs at the time of

their NDEs, and that people who are so disorganized by any drugs that consciousness is lost do not produce coherent hallucinations. And loss of consciousness is of course inseparable from the absence of vital signs in those experiencing NDEs.

5.  Although endorphins can lead to feelings of euphoria, athletes who sometimes produce high levels during competition do not report NDEs. More pertinently, recent research has shown that sufferers from grand mal seizures have very high endorphin levels, which persist even after the termination of their seizures, yet they do not report NDEs.

Fenwick's reasons for rejecting the above natural explanations accord with those advanced in medical detail by Morse and Perry (1990), by Griffin (1997) and others, and supported by Dossey (2000). Griffin further points out that although some commentators have suggested that the so-called "tunnel effect" (the experience reported by some that their NDE involved passing through a dark tunnel on their way to "paradise conditions") is evidence of abnormal brain conditions consistent with the theory that NDEs are no more than the hallucinations of the dying brain, 62 percent of those experiencing NDEs make no mention of this effect. To this we can add that in some of the cases quoted by Crookall (1961, 1978), movement through a tunnel was reported not only when supposedly leaving the body, but also on the way *back into* it as well. It seems unlikely that the brain would be dying at the commencement of the NDE, recover during it (on some occasions while experiencing "paradise" conditions), begin to die again as it comes to an end, and then recover once more when normal consciousness is restored.

If normal explanations for the NDE appear on the above submissions to be unlikely, it can still be argued that as those experiencing NDEs are subsequently successfully resuscitated they cannot be said actually to have died, and that therefore their experiences do not in fact tell us anything about life after death. This is undeniable. The medical profession accepts that the exact moment of death is becoming more and more difficult to establish. However, by all the currently accepted criteria of death, many of the patients reporting NDEs appear to qualify. But in a sense whether they have died or not, our main concern when assessing the relevance of NDEs to our understanding of mind is whether or not the brain shows any vital signs during them. Certainly we can never be sure that we know how to detect all these signs; unknown to us there may be cellular processes related to consciousness going on within the brain even when it appears moribund. But the lack of any of the recognized vital signs of brain activity would seem at the very least to indicate it unlikely, and that in consequence we would not expect on a physical basis reports of NDEs or of anything else upon resuscitation. Thus one recent and well-documented case (the Pam Reynolds' case) where there is indisputable medical evidence that the brain showed no vital signs over a relatively long period is of particular interest.

The case centers upon a pioneering and very risky operation to correct an hemolysis (ballooning) of an artery at the base of the patient's brain. The blood supply to the brain had first to be shut off and the brain drained completely of blood in order to collapse and deal with the artery. As the operation was a lengthy one and irreparable brain damage takes place if the brain is deprived of oxygen for more than eight minutes or so, the patient's body temperature had also to be lowered to a level of suspended animation. Thus all the vital signs in the brain were deliberately switched off by the medical team. Yet on recovering consciousness after the operation was successfully concluded and the vital signs restored, the patient reported an NDE and even proved able to give an accurate description of some of the clinical procedures carried out on her brain during her "death" (Sabom, 1998). Even though we cannot be sure of the exact moment at which the reported NDE commenced, the fact that it persisted far enough into the operation to allow the patient to give these details suggests (some would say demonstrates) that lucid consciousness continued even during the complete absence of any detectable brain activity.

In addition to suggesting that consciousness may persist in some cases when the brain is apparently dead, a further significant feature of the NDE from the psychological perspective is its life-changing impact upon the individuals undergoing the experience. Ring (1984) found that as a consequence of their NDEs his sample had typically lost their fear of death, worried less about past grievances and future problems, had increased feelings of self-worth together with increased acceptance of others and concern for their welfare, had often changed their life goals and values in less material and more spiritually attuned directions, had come to place more emphasis upon the overriding importance of values such as love and compassion, and tended to seek a deeper understanding of life, particularly at the spiritual and religious level. Even those who had had their experiences many years previously reported that the experiences still remained fresh in their minds, as did the firm conviction that they had died during the NDE and now knew the reality of survival.

Drawing upon Ring's samples and his own investigations, Wilson (1997) presents a number of case studies further illustrating the effects of NDEs upon recipients' subsequent behavior. In some instances the effects are dramatically life changing, extending from giving up everything and establishing a spiritual retreat center to abandoning atheism and becoming an ordained minister (a personal account of the latter case is given by Storm, 2000). The fact that an event is life changing does not, of course, mean that it is what it seems. It may have been misinterpreted. Memory and subsequent imaginings may have played tricks. Exaggeration may creep in during the telling and retelling. Nevertheless, otherwise sane and well-balanced people do not lightly give up successful careers to follow what they regard as a more spiritually orientated path – sometimes in the face of incomprehension and even active opposition from friends and family. Their testimony at least deserves our close attention. If we fail to provide it, psychology abandons data which, whatever our ultimate conclusions in relation to it, provide us with valuable information about the workings of the human mind.

One of the best-known first-hand comments on the NDE is by Carl Jung, who himself experienced a near-fatal heart attack in 1944 and wrote afterwards that:

> What happens after death is so unspeakably glorious that our imagination and our feelings do not suffice to form even an approximate conception of it. . . . The dissolution of our time-bound form in eternity brings no loss of meaning (Jung, 1960, p. 6).

Jung felt such peace and fulfillment during his NDE that he had no wish to return to normal life. However, not all NDEs are pleasant. Greyson and Bush (1996) comment that although most are accompanied by profound feelings of peace or bliss, joy, and a sense of cosmic unity, a small number are reported as distressing. The initial experience of leaving the body may be experienced as frightening, or as it develops there may be a feeling of moving into nothingness or a featureless void, or even of a sense of falling into a dark pit containing hellish images. Interestingly enough, expectation seems to play no part in whether individuals have pleasant or unpleasant NDE experiences. Nor, for that matter, does expectation play any part in whether or not individuals near death have an NDE. They are as likely to occur to those without religious belief and/or belief in life after death as to those with these beliefs, a finding that substantially weakens the argument that NDEs are purely imaginary experiences brought on by wishful thinking.

Further evidence against the expectation scenario is provided by pediatrician Morse (1990), who studied NDEs reported by a sample of 12 children after cardiac arrest, many of whom he considers too young to have absorbed cultural beliefs on death and dying. Morse found striking similarities between the accounts of NDEs given by his sample of children and those given by adults. In addition, in a follow-up study 10 years later, his sample had become in his words "special teenagers with excellent relationships with their families. They share a wisdom that is humbling." There was a "conspicuous absence of drug abuse and even experimentation" in the group, little rebelliousness, no excessive risk taking, and no pregnancies. They had good educational grades, and in spite of having undergone cardiac arrest early in life they showed no evidence of "the brain damage and retardation that usually result from such a traumatic event."

Morse compared his sample with 121 child patients who had been seriously ill and in receipt of a wide range of medication, but who had not suffered cardiac arrest. In his interviews with them, none of them reported NDEs. Morse's sample was of course very small (it took a trawl through 10 years of medical records to identify even this number of children who had suffered cardiac arrest) but his study was meticulously conducted. The children in both the sample and in the comparison group were only asked what it was like to be very sick, and no mention was made to them of NDEs. Yet the sample gave spontaneous accounts of NDE experiences and the comparison group, though many times larger, did not. If young children, with few or no culturally prompted expectations, nevertheless report NDEs similar to those of adults, we can at least hypothesize that prior mind-set does not play a significant part in these experiences.

We need of course more data from both adults and children reporting NDEs before we can arrive at firm conclusions as to their meaning. Jansen (1996) claims that ingestion of ketamine, a drug used primarily in veterinary medicine, can reproduce the NDE experience, and if this is the case it obviously offers possibilities for controlled experiments. Jansen is incorrect to say that anything, other than the near-death state itself, can "reproduce" the NDE, but it is possible that ketamine (or some other substance) may facilitate a so-called out-of-body experience (an OBE), a frequently reported state in which it is maintained that the consciousness leaves the body for a short time and one which may be comparable in some relevant respects to the NDE. In order to establish whether anything – mind, soul, call it what you like – really does leave the body during an OBE these experiments would assess whether or not those claiming the OBE experience can, under carefully controlled conditions, gain knowledge of objects or events out of visual range from the position occupied by their bodies.

In a groundbreaking experiment Tart (1968, 1996) invited a subject who claimed to have spontaneously occurring OBEs to attempt to do just that. On each of the four nights that the subject spent in his sleep laboratory, Tart placed a five-figure random number on a shelf near the ceiling and well out of sight from her position on the bed. On the first three nights she reported that she was unable, even though reportedly out of her body, to locate the position of the number, but on the fourth night she proved not only able to do so, but also to read it correctly. The odds against getting a five-digit random number right on a single reading by chance alone are 100,000 to one. Wired up as she was each night to electrodes designed to measure any changes in brain waves, it was impossible for her to leave her bed undetected. In any case, even from a standing position, the number was too high up to be visible. Further interest is added by the fact that Tart found that during the OBE her brain exhibited a highly unusual set of rhythms, further evidence that something extraordinary was taking place. The presence of these unusual rhythms renders less credible the claim that she may have read the number using other supposed psychic abilities instead of leaving her body. Furthermore, some credence should be attached to the subject's own insistence that she obtained results through an OBE rather than through these other hypothesized abilities, particularly in light of the fact that she reported her experience of OBEs was extensive and consistent from childhood onwards.

## The Function of Prayer

Like mystical experiences, NDEs may provide some support for that conscious nonphysical element within the material body without which religion and spirituality have no real meaning for the vast majority of their followers. And discussion of NDEs takes us into another area regarded with extreme misgivings by many scientists, yet one which is crucial to any scientific assessment of the reality of claimed religious experiences, namely prayer. Prayer is central to all the theistic religions in the belief that it offers a channel for direct communication with God. Islam in particular stresses the necessity to pray five times a day, facing always toward Mecca, the burial place of the prophet Mohammed and the holiest place in the religion. Regular prayer, it is claimed, ensures that the mind turns toward God at set times during the day, reminding the worshipper always of his or her responsibilities to God, and ensuring that direct contact is maintained between God and the soul. Although the details of observance vary, Judaism and Christianity place equal emphasis upon prayer, as do many of the sects within Hinduism. Even two of the non-theistic religions – Buddhism and Jainism – also employ prayer, though here it is considered that ultimately there is no distinction between inner and outer, between one's own true nature and the source from which that nature arises, with the result that prayer is addressed as much to one's inner potential as to any outside spiritual forces.

Prayer can be formal, following a set form of words, or individual and spontaneous. It can express praise and gratitude, or it can be supplicatory, asking for guidance, support, forgiveness, healing, spiritual strength, wisdom, or anything else thought to be compatible with a loving and omniscient God. Those who pray believe that it works, that prayers are indeed answered. Materialists reply that any benefit that seems to arise from prayer comes in fact from a psychological feel-good factor consequent upon the illusory belief that there is a power outside and greater than oneself that listens to one, intervenes miraculously in human life in response, and improves the quality of that life for the faithful.

Clearly it is important to know whether there is anything more to prayer than a feel-good factor. If prayer really does work on a level other than the purely psychological, it provides potential support for non-physicality, for some form of contact between a nonphysical mind and energies unknown to science. In theory it should be possible to put prayer to scientific test, but the difficulties are formidable in that we have to disentangle the individual's own psychological resources from these hypothesized spiritual energies. However, there is a way around these difficulties. Many supplicatory prayers are not for oneself but for others, and this is particularly true of prayers asking for healing. Thus experimental focus can be placed not upon the effects apparent in those who are doing the praying, but upon the effects observable in those for whom the prayers are offered – provided of course that the latter are not aware that prayers are being said on their behalf.

Byrd (1988), a medical doctor, set up just this kind of experiment at San Francisco General Hospital. With the full and necessary consent of the medical ethics committee at the hospital, Byrd divided a sample of 393 coronary care patients randomly between an experimental group who were to receive prayers for healing from a number of home prayer circles (totaling more than 2,000 individuals) in addition to normal medical treatment, and a control group who were not. The prayer circles were given no details of the experimental group beyond patients' first names and a brief description of their medical conditions and prognosis, and in keeping with usual double-blind procedures patients were not told to which of the two groups they belonged. During the 10-month experimental period, a panel of medical doctors, also blind to the membership of the two groups, assessed patients for medical outcomes.

Results, summarized from those given by Byrd, are shown in Table 11.1. In addition, the need for diuretics was 5 percent less in the experimental than in the control group, the incidence of pneumonia was 5 percent less, and the incidence of cardiopulmonary arrest 6 percent less. Added to this, 85 percent of the experimental group were assessed by the medical panel to have "a good hospital course" as compared to 73 percent judged to have a good hospital course in the control group.

These various differences between the two groups may seem relatively small, but compared to studies in other areas of medicine this level of advantage in experimental as compared to control group is regarded as

**Table 11.1**   Results for experimental and control groups showing differences in medical status during a 10-month prayer period (based on Byrd, 1988)

| Medical variable | Experimental group % | Control group % |
|---|---|---|
| Need for antibiotics | 3 | 16 |
| Edema (fluid in the lungs) | 6 | 18 |
| Mechanical ventilation | 0 | 12 |
| Death | 13 | 17 |

First three findings significant at .05 level (odds greater than 20:1 against chance).

nothing short of sensational. Some differential results between experimental and control groups in medical trials are minuscule in comparison with the results of Byrd's study, yet are heralded as important breakthroughs. For example, of the 25 studies demonstrating that therapeutic doses of aspirin help prevent heart attack (a result described at the time as "a major advance in preventative medicine") only five reached statistical significance. It was only when all the results were combined and subjected to a meta-analysis (i.e. treated as if the 25 studies were separate trials within the same experiment, and could therefore all be added together) that aspirin was seen to be of real benefit.

## Effects of Distant Healing

Due to the double-blind nature of the study, Byrd's results cannot be put down to expectancy on the part of those receiving help through prayer. Other reports (Benson 1996) suggest that prayer and intention may also have beneficial effects when the subjects are animals – or even microbes or yeast cells – rather than human beings. Further evidence for the effects seen in these prayer studies come from investigations into distant healing. Sicher *et al.* (1998) report in one of America's most prestigious medical journals the results of a triple-blind study in which 20 AIDS patients who received distant healing for one hour a day for 10 weeks from 40 healers were found to show significantly less severe illnesses and fewer AIDS related illnesses, and to require fewer medical visits, fewer hospitalizations, and fewer overnight stays during each hospitalization than a matched group of 20 controls. Subjects receiving distant healing also showed what was medically described as significantly "better mood." Healers were given only the first name and a photograph of each patient to whom healing was to be directed.

An earlier study by Bentwich and Kreitler at Kaplan Hospital found similar benefits in a group of hernia patients receiving distant healing when compared with controls on four medically assessed post-operative variables – scar healing, elevated body temperature, intensity of pain, and patient attitude. Healers were informed only of the time of operation of subjects in the experimental group (reported in Targ and Katra, 1999). Controlled laboratory experiments by Braud (1990) also appear to show that even unskilled individuals may produce something of a healing effect, although in Braud's study the task was directed toward protecting by visualization blood cells from being destroyed in a saline solution. The use of blood cells rather than human subjects means that contaminating variables such as the patient's own mind-set can be ruled out, and Braud's results yielded odds against chance reported as 5,000 to one.

It could be argued that prayer and distant healing, even if both shown to work by further studies, are not comparable from a religious perspective in that the former claims to call upon the help of a Divine Being while the latter uses only the power of the healer's mind. Healers reject this argument, however, emphasizing repeatedly that it is not they who heal but some spiritual power that works through them. Their function is simply that of a channel for this power (e.g. Targ and Katra, 1999).

The above results do not demonstrate conclusively the efficacy of prayer and distant healing. More studies are needed. But the scientists responsible for these results can reasonably argue that findings of the order reported by them and under the same carefully controlled conditions and subject to the same supervision by medical ethics panels would be readily accepted as demonstrating a genuine effect in other areas of investigation. Nevertheless, extreme claims require extreme levels of proof. The problem for much of science remains that there are no theories consistent with scientific understanding that explain how prayer and distant healing can work. There is no measurable exchange of energy between those who pray and those who receive the benefit of prayer, or between those who heal and those who are healed. Nothing physical passes between the respective groups. Science relies heavily upon measurement for its results, and here there is nothing to measure between alleged cause and alleged effect. Some scientists accept in private that the results of studies such as these cannot be discounted. No fault can be found with the methodology used, which follows standard practice in medical research. In their view, the effect must therefore be explicable in terms of physical energies that remain to be discovered, but which will be found to be in accordance with the known laws of science. Other scientists dismiss the findings as examples of the quirky, coincidental things that occasionally turn up in research, only to be dismissed when further studies fail to replicate them. Time will tell. But supporters of religion can be content that researchers are at last able to put some of their claims for the efficacy of prayer and of spiritual healing to the test.

## Evidence from Parapsychological Research

The charge that extreme claims require extreme levels of proof applies to another area where properly conducted research suggests that nonphysical effects may be at work. If such effects are genuine, they provide further potential support for the idea of a nonphysical quality present in the human mind which operates outside the known laws of science. The evidence for such effects certainly bears close inspection, and once more those involved claim that in any other area of science results of the magnitude reported by them would be accepted without much demur as reliable. The area concerned is that of *parapsychology*. The term is disliked by many psychologists because it implies a relationship with their own subject, but it is a fact that from the foundation of the first parapsychology unit at Duke University in North Carolina in 1927 under the leadership of the eminent William McDougal, parapsychology has mainly found its home in university psychology departments. Headed by J. B. Rhine and Louisa Rhine, the unit at Duke initially produced impressive results for so-called telepathy (direct mind-to-mind contact between individuals), clairvoyance (direct contact between mind and environment), precognition (direct contact between mind and future events), and psychokinesis (direct contact between mind and physical objects).

However, the history of the subject has been very much up and down since this time. Charges of fraud, of poor experimental procedures, of incorrect statistical analysis have all been made not only against the Rhines' findings but also against the relatively impressive array of positive results produced in subsequent years in a number of laboratories worldwide. These results are too extensive to be summarized here, and would in any case take us too far from our main subject matter. Those who wish to know more will find excellent surveys in Broughton (1991), Beloff (1993), Stokes (1997), and especially Radin (1997), who also summarizes and attempts to answer all the criticisms leveled at the methodologies used in parapsychology. The important point is that if the abilities said to be revealed in telepathy, etc. are indeed demonstrated as veridical, the case for a form of dualism, for a mind that can operate outside the constraints of the time–space continuum which constrains the brain and the physical body, would be much harder to resist. It is perhaps primarily for this reason that many scientists are singularly uneasy over the findings of parapsychological research. If one starts from the unshakable conviction that nonmaterial realities do not and cannot exist, then one will always prefer alternative explanations, however unlikely, to accepting as genuine the results yielded by parapsychological research, no matter how respectable the laboratories from which these results come. And if arguments such as fraud, experimenter error, and faulty statistical analysis fail to stand up, then resort can be made to the argument that there must nevertheless still be something wrong with the research somewhere if only one can find it.

Just such an argument was used by Hyman (1996), a well-respected critic of parapsychological research data, in his comments upon the findings of the supervising committee set up by US government agencies to assess the results of the so-called *Stargate* project funded to the tune of some 20 million dollars by the CIA, the US Defense Intelligence Agency, the US military, and NASA. Briefly the project, which ran from 1970 to 1994, was designed principally to ascertain whether or not it was possible to obtain information about distant locations by paranormal means (specifically by clairvoyance to use the old terminology, by anomalous cognition to use the new). Hyman, who was a member of the supervising committee accepted that the experiments were "well-designed . . . and eliminated the known weaknesses in previous parapsychological research," and that the results "probably cannot be dismissed as due to chance," but went on to say:

> . . . I cannot provide suitable candidates for what flaws, if any, might be present. Just the same it is impossible in principle to say that any particular experiment or experimental series is completely free from possible flaws (pp. 39–40).

Hyman's last sentence is true of course, but it apples in principle to all scientific research, and says little more than that there might be something wrong with the results under scrutiny even though we can't find what it is and don't know what it might be. Analysis of the results of the Stargate data yielded odds against the observed effects being due to chance of $10^{20}$ (one in a hundred billion billion). Utts, the professor of statistics on the supervising committee, wrote in her conclusions (Utts, 1996) that:

> It is clear that anomalous cognition is possible and has been demonstrated. This conclusion is not based on belief, but rather on commonly accepted scientific criteria (p. 30)

The Stargate project is probably the most extensive (and certainly the largest funded by public money) study into parapsychology yet attempted, and the strength of the results and the quality of the methodology demand we at least pause before dismissing its findings as no more than a scientific oddity, explicable enough by normal means at some indeterminate time in the future when we possess knowledge not readily to hand at the moment. Its positive findings are by no means unusual, as acquaintance with the published literature (summarized by Radin and the other commentators mentioned earlier) reveals. However, parapsychology remains stubbornly banished to the fringes of modern scientific respectability, and until and unless it receives more institutional funding it is difficult to see the issues that it raises being more extensively explored, and the data that it yields either being accepted as established beyond sensible doubt, or finally dismissed as of no consequence to science. Thus its relevance to religion is still unclear. If demonstrated as fact, it provides powerful potential support to the whole mind/soul/spirit concept. If dismissed, it makes the argument that men and women are more than their physical bodies more difficult to sustain.

Before leaving the subject of parapsychology three further points are worth making. Firstly, among the Eastern spiritual traditions (and to some extent among those of the West) it has long been accepted that as the individual develops spiritually – particularly through practices such as intensive meditation – paranormal powers akin to those mentioned above (and known in the East as the *siddhis*) arise spontaneously. The argument seems to be that as the mind is stilled through meditation, it becomes more aware of the subtle information received by telepathy, etc. and usually drowned out by the mind's mental chatter. However, one is warned that spiritual progress becomes impeded if these powers are allowed to strengthen the ego, or are used for anything other than the benefit of other people. They are simply one of the signs that mind training is having an effect, nothing more.

Secondly, it is frequently said that just as belief in religion is wishful thinking, so is belief in the paranormal. Men and women, like children, enjoy mystery and the frisson of the unknown. However, wishful thinking can also feature among those who dismiss religion and among those who dismiss the findings of parapsychology. Discussing the existence of entrenched prior belief – and by implication the wishful thinking that such belief will prove triumphant – Griffin (1988) puts it that "Probably the most powerful force motivating our desire to protect our beliefs – from others' attacks, from our own questioning, and from the challenge of the new evidence – is commitment." Once committed to a belief, we may cling to it as tenaciously in science as elsewhere. The desire to do so, as Griffin goes on to say, "is especially strong when the belief has led to public commitment." Once we are identified with a particular position, whether it is in religion or science or anything else, we hate to admit we were in the wrong. In science and in religion this resistance to admitting we are in error may arise not just from fear of losing face, but from the prospect of having to relinquish some of the important parameters that define life and its laws for us.

The third point is that if there is a nonphysical element to the human mind, as both religion and parapsychology seem to suppose, this in no sense threatens what we know about physical science. The whole of science does not collapse, as some scientists seem to fear. If there are two realities, material and nonmaterial, neither necessarily invalidates the findings of the other. Each is concerned with a different order of being. The two may interact at various points (as perhaps at the brain–mind interface), but their respective roles may be complementary rather than antagonistic toward each other. Wilber (1998) argues the point particularly persuasively, and in recent years there have been a number of encouraging dialogues between leading figures in religion and in science in an attempt to find more common ground such as the Harvard Mind Science Symposium (e.g. Goleman and Thurman, 1991). Several notable attempts have also been made by individual authors to make the same attempt (e.g. Wallace, 1996; deCharms, 1998). The initiative in most cases seems to come more from those approaching things from a religious perspective than from those coming from the direction of hard science. Scientists would argue that this shows religion has far more need to accommodate itself to science than the other way around. At one level this is true. Scientific knowledge has yielded innumerable and highly visible benefits to humankind in terms of relieving physical suffering and in making life materially more comfortable. Religious knowledge and spiritual experience, concerned as they are with states of mind and ultimate meaning, have to do with much less obvious things. And the popular view is that science has – or knows how to find – most of the answers.

But this popular view is not necessarily correct. As Wallace (1996) points out, even mathematical axioms that at one time were thought to be self-evident truths are now recognized as no more than conventions (comparable points are made by Kline, 1980 and by Davis and Hersh, 1986, making reference among other things to the work of Gödel and to the Lowenhein–Skolem theory). And if a system as comparatively rational as mathematics is not self-contained – i.e. is found to contain statements that belong to it but cannot be proved by it and that therefore rely upon nonformal arguments from outside the system – it seems optimistic to suppose that any grand unified theory of physics (of natural phenomena) could have a self-contained quality. Wallace considers that metaphysical reasoning – a form of reasoning which calls upon nonphysical argument – may therefore be necessary to account for certain physical truths, just as metamathematical reasoning is needed to establish certain mathematical truths. These and other considerations lead Wallace to conclude that "the meaningfulness of scientific and contemplative knowledge is . . . complementary. In the absence of either, the world is impoverished."

This suggests a support for dualism rather than for monism, a support for the notion that a self-contained physical system such as the brain cannot fully understand itself, and therefore requires some metaphysical element to supplement this understanding. Many will disagree with such a suggestion, but at least the subject remains open for debate.

# CHAPTER 12

# Religion, Health, and Well-being

## Religion and Physical and Psychological Benefits

The importance of studying behavior in order to assess the psychological importance of religious and spiritual belief and practice has been stressed at various points throughout the book. In the case of the NDEs discussed in the last chapter, the evidence suggests that what are taken by many of those involved to be spiritual experiences of an afterlife can lead to profound changes in value systems, long-term goals, and close relationships. How true is this of other experiences interpreted as religious or spiritual by recipients – indeed how true is it of religious and spiritual beliefs in general? Are people who share these beliefs happier, healthier, better adjusted socially, more at peace with themselves than those who do not? We saw in the last chapter that evidence suggests prayer and distant healing may have beneficial effects upon the well-being of others. Is there evidence they have similar effects upon those who pray and those who give healing?

These issues are clearly of primary importance. If religious and spiritual beliefs appear to bring psychological benefits, then irrespective of their truth or not, it can be said that these beliefs are of value, even perhaps of therapeutic value. Some of these benefits may come from membership of a generally supportive group such as a church community. Others may come from the raised self-esteem that arises from the belief that one is loved by God or by other higher powers. Yet others may arise purely from the fact that religion and spirituality provide avenues of interest. The literature generated by both is vast, as is the art and the architecture and the poetry. And the thought of other worlds, of higher levels of being, is certainly an attractive one to many people. Other benefits may come from the welcome changes that individuals may observe in themselves consequent upon belief. They may feel to have become better people, more loving and compassionate, more open to the beauties of creation, less selfish and self-centered, more charitable and drawn towards good works, more in tune with life, and of more value as community members.

As yet, insufficient research has been done into the precise changes in self-concepts consequent upon the acquisition of religious and spiritual beliefs. But irrespective of the details, if religious and spiritual beliefs and practices appear generally to bring measurable physical and psychological benefits, this is of particular interest to the scientist. Conversely, if religious and spiritual beliefs are associated with negative effects upon physical and psychological well-being, this is of equal interest. Not surprisingly, these issues have attracted considerable research in recent years, and in their mammoth review of this research Koenig, McCullough, and Larson (2001) conclude that "there is ample evidence to demonstrate that religious belief and practice are associated with positive health behaviours," and agree that this belief "is likely a major pathway by which religion affects physical health." We'll start looking at this evidence by summarizing some studies that suggests an association between religion and physical health.

## Religion and Physical Health

Estimates vary, but it has been suggested even conservatively that one-third of physical illness may be due to psychological factors. Thus the intimate connection between religious belief and states of mind may mean that the former has some significant bearing upon the incidence of sickness and health. Disentangling religious and spiritual beliefs from a host of other relevant variables is not easy, however. Those who follow religious and spiritual paths may for example indulge less in alcohol, tobacco, and other possibly harmful drugs than nonbelievers. They may indulge less in promiscuous and risky sex, and may be less inclined to enter potentially stressful extramarital relationships. They may be less prone to overeating and other physical indulgences, and more inclined to spend time in enjoying nature and thus in taking regular physical exercise. They may relax more on Sundays, and thus prove better able to combat the stresses of modern living, and may be more inclined to keep pets – another known antidote to stress. They may enjoy more harmonious relationships with family and friends, may choose less risky and hectic occupations, and may be less prone to suffer from or inflict domestic violence. And they may keep more regular hours, be more inclined to avoid confrontation, and be less frustrated by the absence of material success. Religion may thus prompt people generally to take better care of themselves, and perhaps to seek medical help more promptly than the norm. Without religious belief those concerned might lead very different lives. Religion also lays a number of behavioral responsibilities upon its followers, both explicit and implicit. Concern to avoid the disapproval of fellow believers may impose even more.

Materialists who reject any intrinsic value in religion would argue that these lifestyle variables are the sole reason for any benefits accruing from religious beliefs, and some studies do indeed show that a link with life-style variables appears to be present. For example Troyer (1988) found that in the United States many cancers (including lung, breast, cervical, urinary, and gastrointestinal tract) are less prevalent among Seventh Day Adventists, Mormons, Hutterites, and the Amish Community than among the population at large. Religious sects such as these are known to provide strong directives for personal behavior, and thus to encourage lifestyles that may positively affect health in additive and multi-implicative ways. A number of other studies (e.g. Gardner and Lyon, 1977; Fraser, Beeson, and Phillips, 1991) support Troyer's findings, and it seems clear from them that the abstinence from cigarette smoking and from over-indulgence in alcohol together with the better diets and safer sexual practices apparent in these highly disciplined religious communities all contribute to lower cancer risk.

Lifestyle variables may also play a part in findings by Ogata, Ikeda, and Kuratsune (1984) that a sample of 4,352 Japanese Zen priests (the term should perhaps be "monks" rather than "priests") show significantly lower mortality rates than the general population for cerebrovascular diseases, pneumonia, bronchitis, peptic ulcer, cirrhosis of the liver, and cancer of the respiratory organs. Japanese Zen monks smoke less than other Japanese men, consume less meat and live in less polluted parts of the country – although the researchers found there was little difference in alcohol consumption between the two groups (a finding that may surprise some readers and be a source of reassurance for others).

However, supporters of religion are likely to argue that lifestyle variables are not the only reason why people gain health benefits from following a religious path. Religious people believe that God actually gives them the strength to live up to the responsibilities that religion lays upon them, and rewards them for their self-discipline with inner peace and spiritual growth. They also argue that God – or spiritual energies – can influence their lives directly, rather as the absent prayer and absent healing discussed in the last chapter appear on the evidence to influence the welfare of hospital patients. One of the most thorough and extensive attempts to hold lifestyle variables constant (Strawbridge et al., 1997) suggests that such arguments cannot be easily dismissed. In a 28-year follow-up study of 5,286 individuals in the United States, the researchers found that among women weekly church attendance during the baseline year of 1965 was associated with a 34 percent reduction in mortality even when adjustments were made for health conditions, perceived health, education, ethnicity, religious denomination, marital status, close social contacts, smoking, exercise, alcohol consumption, and body mass. Although the figures for men lost statistical significance when no adjustment was made for the last four variables, a number of studies starting from more recent baseline dates (e.g. Oman and Reed, 1998; Koenig *et al.*, 1999) have produced positive findings for both sexes, again after allowing for lifestyle and other health-promoting variables. On the strength of these studies, the protective effect of weekly or more frequent church attendance and/ or of the belief systems that prompt this attendance seems to be equivalent to that of wearing car seat-belts, with approximately a 25 to 33 percent reduced risk of death, and with the effect apparent in both sexes, even if rather more marked for women than for men.

The largest study currently available, that by Hummer *et al.* (1999), using a random national US sample of 21,204 adults over the years 1987 to 1995, reports the average age at death of nonchurch attenders as 75.3 years as compared to 81.9 for weekly attenders and 82.9 for those attending more than once a week. Among African Americans, the figures are even more remarkable, with an average age of 66.4 at death for nonattenders and 80.1 for attenders. Controlling for health at entry into the study and for exercise levels and socioeconomic factors failed to remove this sizeable and consistent relationship between church attendance and longevity.

What of those professing to be religious but without necessarily attending church? Oxman, Freeman, and Manheimer (1995), carrying out a prospective study of 232 middle-aged patients subjected to elective cardiac surgery, found that the risk of death was 14 times greater for those without both social and religious support than for those with. Helm *et al.* (2000) in a six-year follow-up of nearly 4,000 subjects found that lack of private religious practice (meditation, prayer, or Bible study) was a significant predictor of mortality in previously healthy individuals, even when controlling for social support and health behaviors. Thus private religious and spiritual practice as well as regular church attendance appears to be associated with positive health outcomes, which suggests that it is not merely the social support provided by church membership that is the effective factor. However, more comparative studies between churchgoers and those who practice their religiosity and spirituality privately are clearly needed.

If lifestyle variables can be eliminated as the sole reason for the greater longevity enjoyed by those following religions and spiritual paths, are there any other incidental factors that may play a part? One of these has already been mentioned, namely interest. People who have an interest in life tend to be healthier and to live longer than those who do not. Glass *et al.* (1999) at the School of Public Health at Harvard University, discovered that even after controlling for a wide range of variables (sex, age, race, marital status, body mass, smoking, income, functional disability, and health history), a number of interest-related activities correlate positively with reduced mortality. Productive activities such as gardening, community work, preparing meals, and even frequent shopping reduce the death rate by 23 percent; social activities reduce it by 19 percent, and fitness activities by 15 percent. Church attendance was lumped in with social activities in the Glass study, so it is difficult to separate it out as an effect, but it seems clear that many things that give life some focused meaning and purpose, and that involve excitement and commitment, help people to live longer. Optimism and a positive, hopeful, and respectful attitude towards life may also do so. Carson, Soeken, and Grimm (1988) found that both spiritual well-being and – even more so – existential well-being are associated with both optimistic personality traits (i.e. with long-term aspects of personality) and personality states (i.e. with short-term moods). However, whether in the case of religious people optimism and hope arise from actual spiritual experience or simply from the belief that there is a spiritual dimension to life that somehow takes account of individuals and provides the necessary support and direction is unknown, and in any case difficult to assess.

It has also been suggested that the "proxy" effect may be the actual determinant of better health and longevity in religious people. This effect refers to the fact that people may gain benefit not from an activity itself but from the things they have to do in order to engage in that activity, and from the fact that such engagement may in any case presuppose a certain degree of health. Thus religious people may benefit for example from the walk to church, and their presence at church may be an indication of good physical health. However, the proxy effect receives no support from work by Idler and Kasl (1997), who found that on entry into their longitudinal study frequent church attenders had in fact *more* rather than less mobility problems than infrequent attenders.

Are there other studies that support the notion that it is religion and spirituality *per se* that appear positively to affect health rather than incidental factors? One possibility is to look at research into how well people adapt to illness should it actually occur, and there are a number of studies which attempt to do just this. In their investigation in the United States, Johnson and Spilka (1991) established that 85 percent of the women with breast cancer in their survey reported that religion helped them cope with their ailment. The authors also looked at whether or not there was any difference in coping behavior between those whose religion was *intrinsic* as opposed to those for whom it was *extrinsic*. The *intrinsic–extrinsic* distinction was first described by Allport (Allport and Ross, 1967), and the intrinsically religious person defined by him as one who finds major motivation in religion, and regards other needs as of less ultimate significance. He or she endeavors to internalize religious belief, so that it becomes central to life. By contrast, Allport defined extrinsically religious people as those who tend to use religion for their own ends – for example for security, sociability, distraction, or self-justification. In theological terms, the intrinsically religious person turns towards God and away from self, while the extrinsically religious person turns to God while remaining orientated towards self.

In the event, Johnson and Spilka found that coping benefits accrued exclusively to those whose religion was intrinsic. Intrinsically-orientated people seemed to have a depth of faith that allowed them to believe that God was involved in the cancer (as in all things), and therefore that their illness carried meaning. The authors felt able to conclude that "religion is an extremely important resource for the majority of these breast cancer patients." In another relevant study, Jenkins and Pargament (1988) established, even after controlling for education level and for Lie Scale scores, that among their sample of cancer patients, perceived control by God over the disease was significantly related to higher levels of self-esteem and to lower levels (as rated by nurses) of behavioral upset. Roberts *et al.* (1997) report similar findings with a group suffering from gynecological cancer, 79 percent of whom indicated that religion had a "serious place" in their lives. Interestingly, 49 percent of their sample claimed they had become *more* religious since the onset of their illness, whereas none indicated that they had become less religious. This finding may be attributed to a tendency to take refuge in religion when facing a life-threatening condition, but one would have predicted that at least some of the sample would turn away in anger from any such belief on the grounds that it had failed to protect them from serious disease. The fact that they did not do so would seem to suggest the recognition that religious belief confers real experiential benefits at a time of crisis.

Nevertheless, it could be argued that these various coping benefits may simply be a consequence of normal psychological processes. The very belief that there is a loving God who plans things and cares for the faithful may in and of itself be the cause of enhanced coping behaviors, with no spiritual dimension necessarily involved. One way to assess this would be to look more deeply into the actual experiences of those reporting that religious belief helps them cope with disability. Does this help consist only of a generalized feeling of comfort, or is something more profound involved, perhaps analogous to certain of the experiences discussed in chapter 10, or even to the unexpected healing effects reported as arising from absent healing? Data such as these would give us useful pointers to what may be happening. Religious experiences and unexpected healing effects would both support the idea that something more than normal psychological processes are at work.

Research of this kind has yet to be attempted. If it is carried out, it may be found that those whose religion is intrinsic report more in the way of direct spiritual experience than those whose religion is extrinsic, and it is regrettable that studies such as that of Ringdal (1996), which demonstrated that religious belief appears positively correlated with a 14 percent better survival rate in cancer patients and with general satisfaction and fewer feelings of hopelessness, do not include a measure for this experience. Were these studies to do so, it is possible that not only would further light be thrown upon the actual mechanisms through which religion confers benefits, but also that the figures for those receiving benefit would be augmented in the case of the intrinsically religious group. It is also regrettable that a third measure of religious orientation, labeled by Batson (Batson and Schoenrade, 1991a, and 1991b; Batson *et al.*, 1993) *quest orientation* has not been more widely used in research. Batson uses the term to refer to those who view religion as an endless process of questioning prompted by the ongoing tensions, contradictions, and tragedies evident in their personal lives and in the world as a whole. Such people apparently actually value their religious doubts and uncertainties, see questions as more central to their religious experience than answers, and accept that their view of religion is fluid and open to change. Edwards (2001) considers that quest orientation is a form of religious liberalism, and draws attention to its possible association with mysticism. The assumption here may be that the very act of constant questioning and uncertainty prompts the arrival of answers in the form not of words but of direct inner experience (an assumption which perhaps receives particular support from accounts of the enlightenment experiences of Zen practitioners, who are encouraged to develop what is called "great doubt," i.e. a great *desire to know*, see e.g. Sheng Yen, 1982).

Religious belief appears to assist the coping behavior of cancer patients in countries other than the United States. In Switzerland, Kesseling *et al.* (1986) found that 38 percent of their sample indicated that faith in God and prayer were important sources of experienced help. In Canada, Ginsburg *et al.* (1995) found a similar percentage (44 percent) of lung cancer sufferers reported finding support in religion. The figures for such support are even higher in an Islamic country. The same investigators found that in Egyptian patients the percentage reporting that God or Allah was important in their coping was as high as 92 percent.

Many of the above studies are concerned with the relationship between religious belief and cancer rates/coping with cancer. What of the relationship between religion and the other major Western killer, coronary heart disease? Friedlander, Kark, and Stein (1986) compared a sample of 454 Israeli men and 81 women suffering from their first experience of this disease with healthy controls, and found that only 49 percent of the men and 50 percent of the women in the first group defined themselves as religious as compared to 79 percent of the men and 84 percent of the women in the control group. Still in Israel, Goldbourt, Yaari, and Medalie (1993) established that the risk of death from coronary artery disease was 20 percent less for orthodox Jews than for those who were less orthodox or unbelievers, even after controlling for age, blood pressure, blood cholesterol, smoking, diabetes, and body mass index.

A further finding in support of the value of religious belief came from Oxman, Freeman, and Manheimer (1995), who investigated six-month mortality rates after coronary bypass surgery among a sample of 232 older adults and found that only 5 percent of those who attended religious services at least every few months died as compared to 12 percent of those who never or very rarely attended. None of the sample who described themselves as deeply religious died compared with 11 percent of the rest of the sample. Six percent of those who received strength and comfort from religion died as compared to 16 percent of those who did not. When variables such as previous cardiac surgery, severity of artery impairment, age, and social participation were all controlled, it emerged that those who did not derive strength or comfort from religion were thee times more likely to die than those who did.

In sum it seems that religiosity is independently associated with a lower risk of heart attack, a lower death rate from heart attack, and a longer survival rate after surgery for coronary artery problems. However, as the number of studies is small, more work is needed before we can arrive at firmer conclusions on the value of religion to coronary health and coronary care. The same is true for another potentially valuable area of investigation, namely the influence of religious belief upon the functioning of the immune system. The immune system is the body's primary defense against infectious diseases and possibly other illnesses. As an autonomic system it lies outside conscious awareness; thus if religious belief is found to be associated with system enhancement, it may be indicative of some direct link between the two – though once again lifestyle factors could also be involved. Very few studies have so far investigated the presence of this association, but those that have lead Koenig et al. (1999) to conclude cautiously that religious faith and religious practices such as prayer and meditation may be associated with lower serum cortisol levels (one of the signs of good immune system function). Findings also suggest tentatively that these variables are linked to better immune function in the elderly, in those who are HIV-positive, and in AIDS sufferers.

On the strength of these various studies, there seems little doubt that religion and spirituality are quite strongly associated with better physical health and increased longevity. In fact in a meta-analysis of 29 studies involving some 125,000 individuals, McCullough *et al.* (2000) conclude that the association between religiosity and increased survival rates is in fact significant at odds of over 1,000 to one against chance. On the strength of a review of the available studies, it is reasonable to conclude that a similar meta-analysis of the correlation between religion and a lower incidence of such diseases as cancer and heart disease would yield similar findings, as would a meta-analysis of the observed relationship between religion and coping behavior and outcomes among the physically ill.

## Negative Effects of Religion upon Physical Health

However, there are a few studies that suggest religion may be negatively correlated with physical health in certain circumstances. Using a broad definition of spiritual beliefs rather than traditional religious activity, King, Speck, and Thomas (1999) found worse health outcomes on selected variables among the experimental than the control group. However, the definition was so broad that there proved to be no correlation between it and measures of traditional religious involvement, which casts doubt on the implications of their results. Nevertheless, it is true that groups with certain fundamentalist religious beliefs reject some important medical interventions such as blood transfusions, prenatal care, and childhood vaccinations. They may also prefer to rely upon their religious faith than upon orthodox medical care in some instances, and in extreme cases may even refuse surgery on principle. The numbers involved in these groups are relatively small, and it is not known what the overall effect their beliefs have upon mortality and upon other health-related variables.

A small number of studies have failed to find any connections, positive or negative, between religion and health. Idler and Kasl observed no relation between the two variables in their 1992 Yale Health and Aging study, although in their follow-up in 1997 a significant correlation between church attendance and survival did emerge. Koenig *et al.* (1998) found no correlation over a nine-year period between the use of religion as a source of coping behavior and all-cause mortality in a sample of just over 1,000 men hospitalized for medical conditions. However, their unusual finding that there was also no connection between survival and psychosocial variables led them to suggest that age, medical diagnosis, and severity of health problems in their sample may have overwhelmed the weaker positive effects of both social and religious factors.

## Religion, Spirituality, and Psychological Health

Of the 100 studies identified by Koenig, McCullough, and Larson (2001) as yielding statistical data on the relationship between religious involvement and well-being (a broad term variously said to cover such things as happiness, life satisfaction, positive affect, optimism, and hope), 79 report at least one positive correlation between the two, and only one reports a negative correlation. These figures are interesting, but to what extent do lifestyle variables, as with the relationship between religious/spiritual beliefs and physical health, confuse the issue?

Even when variables such as age, education, and income are taken into account, people involved in religious activities tend to have more stable marriages than the general population (Call and Heaton, 1997), with the difference between stable and unstable marriages most marked for couples who share a religious affiliation on the one hand and couples with no religious affiliation on the other (unstable marriages are defined as those with high levels of communication problems, disagreements about parenting or about gender roles, financial difficulties, untrustworthiness, infidelity, and drug abuse – e.g. Bloom et al., 1985). In addition, as seen earlier, people with religious affiliations tend to have more reliable systems of social support. Both marital stability and social support are known to correlate with life satisfaction and other well-being variables, so marital stability and social support rather than religious affiliation could be the reason for higher levels of well-being. However, when it comes to religion and lifestyle variables, the difficulty is also how to identify which is cause and which effect, as the major religious traditions all teach greater commitment to the male–female bond, to parenthood, and to the community. A more general difficulty is to decide whether people with higher levels of well-being turn to religion, or whether those with religious affiliations tend to develop higher well-being. Another possibility is that religiosity and well-being simply develop together, with a complex interaction between the two. Do feelings of happiness and life-satisfaction prompt some people to conclude there must be a beneficent creator responsible for existence, or does a belief in (and perhaps experiences thought to be associated with) a beneficent creator lead to enduring feelings of happiness and life-satisfaction?

Such questions are best addressed by looking at prospective studies which follow subjects over a sufficient period of time for changes in well-being to occur and for the developmental factors apparently associated with them to be assessed. Such studies present considerable difficulties (researcher commitment and sample attenuation over the length of time necessary for their completion being two of the most obvious), and of those attempted none has focused particularly on these factors. In a

37-year prospective study of 2,009 subjects (1,650 at follow-up), Willits and Crider (1988) found that church attendance and well-being were significantly related at odds of over 1,000 to one against chance in 1984, and that once gender and income and other variables known to be related to religiosity were controlled, adolescent religious participation and parent religious attendance in 1947 were not related to well-being in 1984. This suggests that a developmental process rather than simple adherence to parental example may indeed have been involved in religiosity over the intervening years. Blazer and Palmore (1976), in a 20-year prospective study of 272 volunteers, found that significant correlations between religious activities and measures of usefulness and happiness increased over the length of the study, which also suggests the growing importance of religion for well-being as subjects grew older, though dropouts from the sample over the 20 years of the study possibly weakens this suggestion.

Significant correlations between religiosity and various well-being measures over periods of time were also noted by Markides (1983) and by Musick (1996), while Francis (Francis and Robbins, 2000) reports significant correlations between a positive attitude towards Christianity and scores on the Oxford Happiness Inventory (Argyle, Martin, and Crossland, 1989) among a sample of 295 individuals with ages ranging from late teens to late seventies. Importantly, this relationship held good even when the variables of sex, extraversion, neuroticism and psychoticism (as measured by the Eysenck Personality Questionnaire) were taken into account. These findings are consistent with the results of studies using the same measures with samples of undergraduates in the UK and in the United States, and with samples of adults across the age range. Francis concludes that these results "suggest that a consistent positive relationship between happiness and religiosity emerges over a range of different populations" when happiness is defined in the terms of the constructs refined by Argyle Martin, and Crossland (i.e. absence of negative feelings such as depression and anxiety; the frequency and degree of positive affect or joy; and a significant average level of satisfaction over a period of time). Such findings do not of course tell us whether happy people have better attitudes towards religion than unhappy ones, or whether people become happier as their attitudes towards religion become more positive, but the existence of the relationship is clearly of potential psychological importance.

In sum, these and the other studies summarized above all point to a significant association between religiosity and the variables associated with well-being. Such an association appears to hold good for both sexes and for all age groups from adolescence through to retirement. What is lacking – apart from a clearer idea as to why these associations exist – are studies designed to look at the effects of religious conversion. Are people who suddenly "find" religion higher in well-being as a result? With many young people in Europe and America turning towards Buddhism and other Eastern traditions, the identification of samples experiencing conversion is unlikely to be particularly difficult. How enduring are these conversions? What is their effect upon lifestyle, upon occupation, upon life goals, and upon relationships? And what leads people to become converted? Is it primarily the charisma of a particular teacher irrespective of tradition? Is it the attraction of joining an admired social group? Is it study of relevant scriptures and other literature? Or is it an internal process, such as a form of direct religious experience?

## Mysticism and Psychological Health

Some insight into at least the last of these possibilities is possible if we look at research into mysticism and psychological health. Mystical experience might be considered by some as resembling in many ways the visions and inner voices of the mentally ill. What do we know of the mental stability of the mystic? As we saw in chapter 10, mysticism can involve alternations between periods of great pain and suffering (as in the so-called dark night of the soul when the mystic feels abandoned by the divine) and ecstatic levels of spiritual joy. Extreme mystics also sometimes manifest *ligature*, a state in which will-power disappears, bodily functions slow down, and sense perceptions are diminished, and this is comparable in some ways with experiences reported by the mentally ill. However, while accepting that some of the lesser mystics of extreme type may show evidence of mental disorder, Pratt – who as a graduate student studied under William James and subsequently wrote a study of religious experience second only in extent and importance to James' *Varieties of Religious Experience* (Pratt, 1920) – argued that generally mystics show marked differences from psychotics. Outstanding among these differences are the mystics' strength of will, and their determination to direct their activities consistently and with total dedication to what they see as the divine purpose. Far from seeing mysticism as confined to a chosen few, Pratt considered all intensely religious people possess it to some degree, as evidenced by the strength of their aspiration, insight, and powers of contemplation.

Was Pratt correct in assuming the ubiquitous nature of mystical experience? And was he correct in differentiating this experience from mental disorder? Greeley (1975) attempted to answer both these questions by researching a carefully selected sample of 1,460 Americans. His findings were in many ways amongst the most remarkable in the psychology of religion in that 35 percent of his sample reported that at least once or twice in their lives they had had experiences of being "very close to a powerful, spiritual force that seemed to lift [them] out of themselves." Twelve percent of the total sample claimed to have had such experiences several times, and 5 percent that they happened often. If Greeley's sample was as representative of the total population as he supposed, his findings suggest that no less than 87 million Americans at the time of his research had had a spiritual sense of presence, and that 12 million Americans had had so frequently.

Thus Pratt's first assumption seems correct. What of the second? Greeley's results support that too. Those in his sample reporting mystical experience produced scores correlating positively with the Positive Affect Scale developed by Bradburn (1969) and measuring psychological well-being, and negatively with the Negative Affect Scale, which correlates consistently with traditional indicators of poor mental health. Overall, the mystics emerged as notably happier, and notably more free from mental disorders than the norm. Replicating Greeley's work with 1,865 subjects in the UK, Hay and Morisy (1978) produced remarkably similar results in terms of the frequency of mystical experience, and also found correlations between mystical experience and well-being, though the latter were less strong than in the American study.

It is not clear from these findings whether it is mystical experience that leads to enhanced happiness and lower levels of mental disorder, or whether people who are already in possession of these characteristics tend to have mystical experiences more frequently than those who are not. But the findings make it clear that what individuals regard as mystical experience is widespread, and does not appear to be linked to mental disorder.

## Negative Effects of Religion upon Psychological Health – Wars and Violence

The most obvious of the negative psychological consequence associated with formal religion must surely be the wars, violence, and intolerance perpetrated by its followers in its name. Of all areas of the psychology of religion this is one that most demands careful research, yet it remains the one that has been most neglected, probably because of the enormous difficulties involved. However, much can be said about it at a theoretical level.

The first and most obvious point is that none of the founders of the great traditions preached intolerance and violence. The teachings of the founder of Christianity, a tradition which has had more warfare and bloodshed associated with it than any other, was particularly clear on this issue, notably in the Gospel of St. Matthew: "Love your enemies, bless them that curse you, do good to them that hate you, and pray for them which despitefully use you, and persecute you" (Matthew 5:44). "Blessed are the peacemakers, for they shall be called the children of God" (Matthew 5:9). ". . . resist not evil: but whosoever shall smite thee on thy right cheek, turn to him the other also" (Matthew 5:39). The only reference that might be taken to the contrary occurs in Matthew 10:34, where the words "Think not that I am come to send peace on earth: I came not to send peace, but a sword" appear. However, the context makes it clear that this refers to the family divisions that may arise when individuals become converted to his teachings against the wishes of their kinsfolk, and to the broader religious persecutions from which many converts may suffer.

The doctrine of *ahimsa*, nonviolence, mentioned in chapter 5 is even more intrinsic to the great traditions of Hinduism, Buddhism, and Jainism born in India. The conversion of Tibet to Buddhism led to an extraordinary metamorphoses by the population from near barbarism to one of the most pacific cultures known at the time or subsequently. In China the Taoist doctrine of *wu wei* – literally inaction or noninterference but better translated as "pure effectiveness" (Smith, 1994) also emphasized nonviolence. The Taoist bible, the *Tao Te Ching*, makes it clear that pure effectiveness in Taoism amounts to "wisdom action," that is action which reduces friction in any of its forms to an absolute minimum – friction with individuals, with other groups and cultures. The Taoist is informed that "One who will guide a leader in the use of life will warn him against arms. An army's harvest is a waste of thorns." Confucianism, the other major strand in the religious and ethical life of China, also emphasized nonviolence through its teaching that the task of becoming fully human involves turning one's attention progressively away from oneself to one's family (thus transcending egoism), away from one's family to the community (thus transcending nepotism), away from one's family to one's nation (thus transcending parochialism), and away from one's nation to all of humanity (thus transcending chauvinistic nationalism). Having done so, and in the process explored deeper and deeper into oneself, one is in a sense able to embrace both Earth and Heaven, for one must never forget that "he who offends the gods has no-one to whom to pray."

Islam also emphasizes peace. The word Islam derives from *salam*, meaning "peace" and in a secondary sense "surrender" – surrender to Allah and to the service of one's fellow beings. The name of the last of the prophets, Mohammed, is never mentioned without adding "blessings and peace be unto him." Succoring others – the giving of alms even to strangers – is one of the five pillars of Islam (chapter 2). Allah's compassion and mercy for his creation is mentioned no fewer than 192 times in the Koran. Islam teaches great respect for Allah's world and for one's fellow beings (it is this respect for material reality that helped give rise to Islamic science, which flourished during the so-called Dark Ages in Europe and which gave us among many other things the priceless gift of mathematical computation). As Allah's creation, all men and women are seen as irrevocably good by nature. There is thus no doctrine of original sin in Islam. If we fall from grace it is because we forget our divine origin, not because we are fundamentally evil.

Islam also teaches peace through its doctrine of racial equality. The power of this doctrine is witnessed by the fact that in 50 years Arabia under Islam witnessed a moral advance that is probably unmatched elsewhere in such a short time and among so many people. Before Muhammad intertribal violence in Arabia was the norm rather than the exception. Women had no rights and female infanticide was widespread. Gambling, the abuse of alcohol, and glaring social inequalities were part of the natural order of things. In half a century all this changed. If we take the treatment of women as an example, we find that Islam transformed their status in a manner far ahead of that prevailing in seventh-century non-Islamic Europe. Infanticide was forbidden, and women were given the right of inheritance (set at half that of their brothers, on the grounds that unlike men, women were not called upon to assume financial responsibility for their households). The possibility of women enjoying equal rights with men to education, suffrage, and vocation was established if not specifically enjoined. Sexuality was sanctioned only within marriage, and marriage without the full and free consent of the female partner was forbidden. At marriage, husbands were required to provide wives with an amount of property agreed by her and which she retained in its entirety even in the event of divorce. Divorce proceedings could be initiated by wives as well as by husbands, and although the latter were given the right to acquire up to four wives, it was made clear that this could only be done if the husband was able to deal equitably and justly with each of them (a stipulation which in effect enjoins monogamy, as in practice it is impossible to divide affection and attention equally). Far from insisting on the veiling of women, the Koran merely tells them "to draw their cloaks closely round them when they go abroad" – a sensible precaution in times that were dangerous for unaccompanied women.

Unlike Christianity, Islam does not teach that one should turn the other cheek, but it does insist on forgiveness and the return of good for evil when circumstances allow. War is only sanctioned – as in the Canon Law of Catholicism within the Christian religion – when it is either defensive, or designed to right a terrible wrong. Even in warfare Mohammed left a tradition of rules for conduct far ahead of anything then current in Europe. Agreements were to be honored, treachery avoided, the wounded were to be protected, the dead were to be left in peace, and women and children, the elderly, and crops and sacred objects were all to be spared. And Mohammed practiced what he preached, forgiving his enemies when he returned to Mecca in triumph after 10 years of fighting against attempts to annihilate himself and his followers.

I have given more space to Islam than to the other traditions because Islam provides us with a modern example of how a religion can be accused by outsiders of being the direct cause of violent conflict, whereas when one studies the teachings upon which it is based it becomes clear that such an accusation is unfounded. The question is then why, if their founders taught peace, certain of the great traditions are so associated historically with wars, bloodshed, and conquest? One possible answer is that religion can be misrepresented in order to provide the perfect excuse for exercising the violence and intolerance that seem to be such an intrinsic part of human nature. Most human societies (or influential members of most human societies) have been territorial, both when it comes to the possession of land and to the possession of ideas, and have not scrupled to use war as a way of achieving their territorial ends. And what greater excuse can be given to followers for pursuing warfare than the argument that in so doing one is pleasing an almighty divinity – and perhaps booking a place for oneself in heaven?

For example, before the so-called Albigensian crusades against the Cathar heresy in thirteenth-century France, Pope Innocent III gave absolution in advance to the crusaders for any sins they might commit (with predictable results in terms of the most horrifying barbarity). In fact the formal religious philosophy behind all the many crusades from the eleventh century onwards was that violence was not evil in itself but morally neutral (Riley-Smith, 1991). Everything depended upon the intentions of the perpetrator, which in turn depended upon the justice of the cause concerned – and the justice of a cause could not be decided by individual moral responsibility but only by a legitimate God-given authority, in practice the pope or the emperor. God was seen as a political god, whose intentions for mankind are reflected in a particular political structure whose nature is determined or approved by the same legitimate authority. If such a structure is threatened, God's intentions are placed at risk, and must be defended, if necessary by military means. Stated in various ways, this still remains the justification for violence in the name of religion.

The argument that religion provides the ideal excuse for humankind's innate propensity for violent behavior suggests that the actual message of the founders of the major religions, with its emphasis upon peace, forgiveness, and compassion, actually has had little real effect upon many of those who profess to follow it. Critics of religion might then question whether religious beliefs, whatever their foundation, have psychological value if they can so readily – albeit falsely – be used to justify violent behavior. In particular, it might be said that the religious teaching of an afterlife, with special privileges reserved for the faithful, is a potent weapon in persuading men and women to throw their lives away in a so-called just war.

The counter-argument to this is that even without religion the violence would probably take place, albeit under a different banner. The headiest mix of all is race and politics, with religion serving as little more than a kind of tribal totem, rather like the colors brandished by football fans. In addition, in neither of the two world wars was religion an overt precipitating factor, though both camps predictably claimed that God was on their side.

## Negative Effects of Religion upon Psychological Health – Personal Difficulties

Freud was one of the first psychologists to claim that religious teachings can lead to excessive levels of guilt, primarily through the emphasis of these teachings upon sin and divine punishment – even for unexpressed immoral thoughts and fantasies (Freud, 1927). In his view this guilt, particularly when associated with the body and its sexuality, can be one of the causes of neurosis, especially when generated in childhood through stern parenting and an emphasis upon the need to rid children of the burden of original sin which some Christian teachings claim they bring into the world. Emphasis upon hell fire and eternal damnation and upon the dangers of incurring the wrath of God can raise the levels of guilt and fear still further.

Freud based his association between religion and guilt upon his clinical work, but experimental findings by Spellman, Baskett, and Byrne (1971) found that this association appears to hold good more significantly for individuals who have undergone recent religious conversion than for those who have become religious gradually over time. Zeidner and Hammer (1992), working with a cross-sectional sample of northern Israelis subject to missile attacks during the Gulf War, also found a positive relationship between spirituality as a coping mechanism and increased anxiety. In their view the association was explained either by the tendency of anxious people to turn to religion and spirituality at a time of crisis, or by the fear among the more spiritually inclined that the missile attacks posed a direct threat to Jewish religion and culture.

These conclusions highlight the difficulty of distinguishing cause and effect in research of this kind, and also in identifying what it is about religious belief that may help prompt anxiety in certain circumstances.

Baker and Gorsuch (1982), using a sample of Christian participants at a religious wilderness camp in southern California, discovered in fact that anxiety scores correlated *negatively* with intrinsic religiosity and *positively* with extrinsic. The intrinsically religious therefore were less anxious then the norm, and the extrinsically religious more anxious. Other characteristics symptomatic of psychological problems such as lack of self-sentiment (poor social integration), ego weakness (inability to balance emotions), and paranoia (suspicious insecurity) also correlated negatively with intrinsic religion and positively with extrinsic.

These findings suggest that those whose religion is a more deeply felt experience are more aware of spirituality as a source of protection and comfort, whereas those whose religion is more superficial are inclined to focus on religious teachings that appear to highlight the sinfulness of human failings. Alternatively, those with existing psychological problems such as ego weakness and paranoia may find it more difficult to penetrate deeply into religion and its meaning. However, whatever the reason, this disparity in anxiety levels between those whose religion is intrinsic and those for whom it is extrinsic has been confirmed by other studies (e.g. Sturgeon and Hamley, 1979; Bergin, Masters, and Richards, 1987). It also seems to hold good across traditions. Tapayana and colleagues (1997) found a negative correlation between intrinsic religiosity and anxiety in samples of both Christians and Buddhists, although a difference emerged in that Buddhists whose religion is extrinsic appear to experience even higher levels of anxiety than do extrinsic Christians. In the view of the researchers this difference is due to the fact that whereas Christianity teaches that redemption is possible from a loving God at any time, Buddhism generally considers that if one fails to achieve enlightenment during earthly life one is condemned to repeat the weary cycle of birth and death. (Results for Buddhists might have been different had the researchers looked at a sample from Pure Land Buddhism, since here the belief is that calling upon Amitabha, the Buddha of Boundless Light, can secure rebirth in the Western Paradise rather than back here on Earth.)

A number of other studies have looked at the relationship between frequency of church attendance and anxiety, and consistently found that frequent attendees score significantly lower on anxiety than infrequent attendees and those who do not attend church at all (Hertsgaard and Light, 1984, Williams *et al.*, 1991; Koenig *et al.*, 1993). These findings, by inference, seem to support the fact that the more intrinsic one's religion becomes the more it leads to reduced anxiety, while if religion remains extrinsic (or is absent) anxiety may even be enhanced. Furthermore, the findings again support the notion that the more one enters into religion and the more deeply felt the religious experience becomes, the more one is likely to be aware of religion as a source of strength and support.

However, none of the above studies throws direct light upon Freud's belief that religion is a source of neurosis. As we saw earlier in the chapter, there is significant evidence that, speaking generally, religious people are less subject to neurotic disorders than the rest of the population. However, Freud may have been correct in supposing that in certain of his clients early religious fears did predispose towards neurosis. But before we can be categorical about this we would need to know the extent to which the stern religious parenting that had been shown towards his clients was embedded in a generally authoritarian and punitive parental style. Anything that induces extreme fear in children, whether it be through fantasies of hell fire, separation anxiety, withdrawal of affection, physical abuse, sexual abuse, excessive anger, constant criticism, or unrealistic expectations is likely to lead to long-term psychological damage.

We need also to take into account changing social and cultural attitudes towards the raising of children, and changing patterns of religious belief. Fundamentalist groups and fundamentalist teachings still persist among some groups. Koenig *et al.* (1993) for example found that anxiety disorder was more frequent among the younger adults in their sample who were members of fundamentalist Pentecostal Christian groups. But generally Western thinking on religion has moved towards a more liberal view, which lays stress upon divine love rather than upon divine punishment (upon an all-merciful God rather than upon a vengeful God intent on consigning elements of his creation to eternal punishment). Thus the pattern identified by Freud may be much less apparent now than it was in his time a century ago.

## Health and the Clergy

Levels of physical and psychological health associated with religiosity have also been widely explored among the clergy (for convenience the term "clergy" is used here to cover all ordained ministers and not just those in certain traditions). Assuming that ordination doesn't attract significant numbers of those who are more physically delicate or psychologically unstable than the norm, then one would expect that findings reporting a positive association between religion and physical and psychological health for the laity will be reflected in the clergy, and results tend to bear this expectation out. King and Locke (1980), following on from a number of earlier studies by King, found a 37 percent lower incidence of cancer deaths among a sample of over 28,000 clergy from five Protestant Christian denominations when compared with the United States as a whole. In fact clergy, monks, and nuns all appear to live longer than the norm, and to suffer less from other serious illnesses such as heart disease. They are also less likely to commit suicide than the norm, and less likely to die from accidents.

Social factors may play a significant part here. Clergy and certainly monks and nuns may live more sheltered lives than the norm, and where married may have more stable relationships. The importance of these relationships is perhaps illustrated by the fact that, as pointed out by Argyle and Beit-Hallamhi (1997), Protestant clergy enjoy better health than Catholic priests, who are celibate. Overall, the longevity of the clergy is comparable to that of university teachers, whose mortal span in the Western world appears to be second only to that of the judiciary among professional groups. A factor here would seem to be that of continuing usefulness. Many members of the clergy, of academia, and of the judiciary continue working in ways deemed valuable by the community long after the recognized age of retirement, something that seldom happens in other walks of life where the advance of technology renders most skills, no matter how laboriously acquired, obsolete in a few short years.

As with physical health, there is no evidence that clergy suffer from more psychological disorders than the norm. Francis (1991) tested 252 individuals studying for ordination in the Anglican Church and found that the 155 males scored no more highly on either Eysenck's Neuroticism or Psychoticism Scales than the general population, and scored lower on the Lie Scale. Unlike the males, who emerged as more introverted than the norm, the 97 females emerged as more extraverted and slightly higher than the norm on the Psychoticism Scale, but lower than the norm on the Neuroticism and Lie Scales. These results led Francis to suggest that, as males are normally more extraverted than females and less neurotic, female ordinands tend to be more masculine than the average for their sex while males tend to be more feminine.

These sex-related differences are interesting. Wolf (1989) concludes that some 40 percent of American Roman Catholic priests are homosexual, though Sipe's interviews with 1,000 Catholic priests (Sipe, 1990) revealed that as many (20 percent) were in stable covert relationships with women as with men. However, it may be that if the relationship between the male priesthood and introversion holds good across the traditions and sects, it has more to do with the higher levels of thoughtfulness, study, and sensitivity in those drawn to a clerical life than with sexual orientation and femininity. And the link between female clergy and masculinity may be connected more with the determination, assertiveness, and intellectuality necessary in female clergy who have to survive in a largely masculine-dominated profession than with any aspect of sexuality.

On the strength of these findings, the clergy do not emerge as having more problems of psychological adjustment than the norm, but what of attempts to find particularly positive characteristics among them? If religiosity bring psychological benefits for the laity, one might expect these benefits to be more marked among the clergy, given that their lives are particularly focused upon religion. Work by Webster and Stewart (1973) shows that their sample of New Zealand clergy scored above the norm on the Personal Orientation Inventory (POI), a measure of self-actualization, self-acceptance, maturity and personal integration. However, the liberally orientated members of the sample scored more highly on these measures than did the conservative-minded, a finding which agreed with that of Kennedy *et al.* (1977) who found 271 American Catholic priests were lower on the POI than the norm, with 57 percent emerging as "underdeveloped" psychologically, particularly in their relationship with others, and in their faith. The lesson here would seem to be that it is liberal rather than conservative religiosity that is most likely to prompt psychological benefit in the clergy. This supposition receives some support from Ferder's findings (quoted by Wulff, 1997) that 211 Catholic women who would choose ordination if this was allowed emerged as more psychologically developed than the female norms. The rejection by these women of the convention that Christ's teachings only sanction ordination for men suggests a liberal and reforming orientation.

Investigations into stress among the clergy show that generally levels are below the norm, although the pressure to please others, the low tangible rewards, and the absence of sanctions to exclude those who cause problems are acknowledged as causing difficulties (Fletcher, 1990; Argyle, 1996). Job satisfaction also appears higher among the clergy than is generally the case. Fletcher found that only 3 percent of his sample of 230 clergy in the UK are considering leaving the profession, while as many as 53 percent profess they "would not dream of doing anything else."

## Negative Effects of Religion upon Attitudes to the Natural World

Another area said to be influenced negatively by religious beliefs – in particular those associated with the Judeo-Christian tradition – is the exploitation of our natural environment. First advanced in a serious form by White in 1967 and by Pruyser in 1971, the criticism is that the ecological crisis facing the planet today owes much to the biblical teaching (Genesis 1:26) that man is given "dominion" over every living thing, and thus has a God-given right to conquer and transform the material world. This exploitative ethic has permeated Western man's attitude towards natural resources, and has been largely taken over by our materialistic science and technology. Man is the measure of all things, and has divine permission to do as he pleases with the animal, vegetable, and mineral kingdoms that sustain and feed him.

However, there is some doubt as to whether or not the biblical teaching was intended to indicate that humankind was given this kind of license, as it is debatable if the word "dominion" is a correct rendering of the original Hebrew terms *kivshuah* and *redu*. The Hebrew seeks rather to express the concept of "to cultivate," "to engage with," and therefore "to be responsible for," rather than that of suzerainty, usage, and exploitation. This point of "cultivation and responsibility" rather than "dominion" is further emphasized in Genesis 2:15, where the Hebrew makes it clear that God put man in the Garden of Eden "to serve it and guard it" rather than to "dress and keep it" as in the authorized translation. A suspicion exists that the misunderstandings over the exact meaning of the Hebrew, which seem to have originated during the translation of the Old Testament into Latin in the fourth-century CE, may have arisen from an attempt to legitimize the burgeoning powers assumed by humanity over the natural world. Be this as it may, there is some truth in the notion that the superiority assumed by Western man over the material world, and perpetuated in the philosophies and practices of modern science and technology, has its origins in the idea that everything is given to man to do with as he wills. Only recently have the major Christian denominations turned proper attention to ecology, and begun to form effective environmentalist movements (Fowler, 1995), though whether or not this is going to have much effect upon modern attitudes towards the planet remains to be seen.

The association between religion and environmental issues (including comparisons between the views of Christians and those of professed agnostics and atheists on these issues) has been explored by a number of social scientists with largely inconclusive results. What does seem relatively clear, however, is that the more theologically conservative an individual is, the less likely is he or she to be concerned by environmental issues (a finding which incidentally also holds good for political conservatism). In a study with particularly clear-cut results, Guth *et al.* (1993) found that 47 percent of Protestants and liberal Catholics listed the environment as the most important issue facing the United States, while only 3 percent of what Guth and his colleagues term the Christian Right (Fundamentalist Protestants, evangelicals, and charismatic Christians) did so. Among Fundamentalists, a belief in the imminent end of the world also appears to contribute to an indifference towards environmental issues. The biblical injunction to "be fruitful and multiply," appropriate to an early agrarian community with high rates of infant mortality, also appears to contribute to an indifference towards one of the greatest challenges facing the modern world, namely overpopulation. The Vatican teaching against contraception is thought to be a factor in overpopulation (Howard, 1994), as is the worldwide subjugation, sexual educational and social, of women.

Other religions do not share the relative indifference to the environment shown by the Christian Right and by Western science. The Shamanic traditions of the Americas and Asia and once present in the pagan religions of the West recognize the sacredness of the natural world, as does Taoism and Jainism, as did the mystery cults of ancient Egypt, Greece, and the Eastern Mediterranean basin, and as does Hinduism with its belief that all is *Brahman*. Islam and Judaism also recognize that the world is God-given, and that a special duty of responsibility for its welfare is placed upon the human race. Individuals in the West with a mystical sense of the transcendence of the divine also recognize the sacredness of nature (Wulff, 1997), and emphasize that the need for harmony between humanity and the environment is as pressing as the need for harmony within humanity itself.

Thus as in many areas of religion, we find an anomaly, with some of those professing religious and spiritual beliefs showing the most passionate concern for the environment, and others showing the least concern. Explaining this propensity of religion for bringing out extremes in human behavior remains a major challenge to psychological research.

# Conclusion

A book on the psychology of religion and spirituality has to end, in some ways, as it began, by acknowledging that the urge to religious and spiritual experience and belief, and the consequences of this urge for human behavior, are among the greatest mysteries facing psychology. In spite of the countless words written over the centuries, we are still a long way from finding answers to these mysteries. On the basis of the research summarized in the preceding chapters, it seems clear that religion and spirituality cannot be explained away simply as attempts to counter the fear of death, as the expression of a need to find in God or the gods fantasy substitutes for earthly parents, as a neurotic escape from the realities of life, or as symptoms of incipient or real psychosis. As we have seen, a large percentage of the population even in the Western world believes in a spiritual dimension of one sort or another, and a sizeable percentage report actually having experiences which they interpret as mystical and religious. Far from declining in the West, the measure of such belief may even be increasing. The most recent pole in the United States (Princeton Religion Research Center, 1996) reveals in fact that 96 percent of those sampled now express a belief in God or a higher power, 90 percent a belief in heaven, 79 percent a belief in miracles, and 73 percent a belief in some form of hell. Ninety percent pray, and 43 percent have attended church in the last seven days. Few other areas of human belief and behavior are likely to reveal this kind of consensus.

The evidence reviewed in the foregoing chapters also shows that religious belief and spiritual experiences appear to enhance well-being and positive relationships, and generally to assist in the development of psychological health. In addition, such belief and experiences potentially influence self-concepts, moral values, human relationships, life-style, life goals, life philosophies, creative expression, and social affiliations and group membership.

In fact the association between religion and a very wide range of human concerns is clearly apparent throughout the material we have been covering. On the negative side religion, by becoming linked to political movements, has frequently been used to authorise or excuse acts of conquest and barbarity, as a means toward bolstering the power of those in various forms of authority, and as a way of engendering guilt and anxiety. However, the fact that none of these activities finds any real justification in the teachings of the founders of the great traditions seems to indicate that they arise more from other areas of human individual and social psychology than from religious or spiritual inclinations *per se*.

It seems clear that the psychology of religion and spirituality raise issues that are of such importance to psychologists that in spite of the imprecisions and disagreements that face us in the area, it will remain central to much of our understanding of human thought and behavior. The pressing need for further research, and the avenues that such research might take, are clear enough from much that has been said throughout the book. Such research, of necessity, must take into account not only the outer but also the inner aspects of the subject, and the main barrier to it remains the prejudice with which much of science still regards the whole question of religion, neglecting in so doing the role that religion continues to play in thought and behavior, both in the lives of individuals and of society as a whole. Whatever our views on the transcendent dimension of religion and spirituality may be, men and women appear to have an innate propensity to find in these experiential systems a meaning and purpose for their existence, and a code of beliefs and values that give psychological strength and that inform and guide their actions. The coming decades will prove testing times for religion as new advances in science appear on the one hand to threaten its position and on the other to lend support to some of its beliefs. But one thing remains certain. Those psychologists who wish to study the role that religion and spirituality have played and continue to play in the lives of their fellow men and women need not be deterred by fears that their work will lack either relevance or excitement.

# References

Aaronson, B. S. (1970). Some hypnotic analogues to the hypnotic state. In B. Aaronson and H. Osmond (eds.), *Psychedelics*. New York: Anchor.

Abe, M. (1995). *Buddhism and Interfaith Dialogue*. Basingstoke: Macmillan (Library of Philosophy and Religion).

Abhayananda, S. (1996). *History of Mysticism: The Unchanging Testament*. Olympia, WA: Atma (3rd edn.).

Akhilananda, Swami (1948). *Hindu Psychology: Its Meaning for the West*. London: Routledge & Kegan Paul.

Alexander, F. (1931). Buddhistic training as an artificial catatonia. *Psychoanalytic Review*, **18**, 129–45 (original German version published 1923).

Allport, G. W. (1961). *Pattern and Growth in Personality*. New York: Holt, Rinehart, & Winston.

Allport, G. W. and Ross, J. M. (1967). Personal religious orientation and prejudice. *Journal of Personality and Social Psychology*, **5**, 432–43.

Altemeyer, B. (1988). *Enemies of Freedom: Understanding Right-Wing Authoritarianism*. San Francisco: Jossey-Bass.

Altemeyer, B. (1994). Reducing prejudice in right-wing authoritarians. In M. P. Zanna and J. M. Oslos (eds.), *The Psychology of Prejudice: The Ontario Symposium Vol. 7*. Hillsdale, NJ: Erlbaum.

Anderson, J. R. (1990). *Cognitive Psychology and its Implications*. New York: Freeman (3rd edn.).

Anderson, W. (1979). *Open Secrets: A Western Guide to Tibetan Buddhism*. New York: Viking Press.

Andresen, J. (2000). Meditation meets behavioural medicine. In J. Andresen and R. K. C. Forman (eds.), *Cognitive Models and Spiritual Maps: Interdisciplinary Explorations of Religious Experience*. Bowling Green, OH: Imprint Academic (Special Issue of *Journal of Consciousness Studies*, 7, 11–12).

Argyle, M. (1996). *The Social Psychology of Leisure*. Harmondsworth: Penguin.

Argyle, M. and Beit-Hallahmi, B. (1975). *The Social Psychology of Religion*. London: Routledge & Kegan Paul (rev. ed. Argyle 1958).

Argyle, M. and Beit-Hallahmi, B. (1997). *The Psychology of Religious Belief and Experience*. London: Routledge.

Argyle, M., Martin, M., and Crossland, J. (1989). Happiness as a function of personality and social encounters. In J. P. Forgas and J. M. Innes (eds.), *Recent Advances in Social Psychology*. Amsterdam: Elsevier.

Assagioli, R. (1975). *Psychosynthesis*. Wellingborough: Turnstone (new edn.).

Atwater, P. M. H. (1994). *Beyond the Light: Near Death Experiences – The Full Story*. London: Thorsons.

Aurobindo, Sri (1957). *The Synthesis of Yoga*. Pondicherry: Sri Aurobindo Ashram (2nd edn.).

Austin, J. J. (2000). Consciousness evolves when the self dissolves. In J. Andresen and R. K. C. Forman (eds.), *Cognitive Models and Spiritual Maps*. Bowling Green, OH: Imprint Academic.

Bailey, L. W. and Yates, J. (eds.) (1996). *The Near Death Experience: A Reader*. New York: Routledge.

Baker, M. and Gorsuch, R. (1982). Trait anxiety and intrinsic–extrinsic religiousness. *Journal for the Scientific Study of Religion*, 21, 119–22.

Barber, R. (1979). *A Companion to World Mythology*. Harmondsworth: Penguin-Kestrel.

Batson, C. D. and Schoenrade, P. (1991a). Measuring religion as quest: 1. Validity concerns. *Journal for the Scientific Study of Religion*, 30, 416–29.

Batson, C. D. and Schoenrade, P. (1991b). Measuring religion as quest: 2. Reliability concerns. *Journal for the Scientific Study of Religion*, 30, 430–7.

Batson, C. D., Schoenrade, P., and Ventis, L. (1993). *Religion and the Individual*. Oxford: Oxford University Press.

Bear, D. and Fedio, P. (1977). Quantitative analysis of interictal behaviour in temporal lobe epilepsy. *Archives of Neurology*, 34, 454–67.

Behe, M. J. (1996). *Darwin's Black Box*. New York: Simon & Schuster.

Beit-Hallahmi, B. and Argyle, M. (1997). *The Psychology of Religious Behaviour, Belief and Experience*. London: Routledge.

Beloff, J. (1993). *Parapsychology: A Concise History*. London: Athlone Press.

Benson, H. B. (1996). *Timeless Healing*. London: Simon & Schuster.

Bergin, A. E., Masters, K. S., and Richards, P. S. (1987). Religiousness and mental health reconsidered: A study of an intrinsically religious sample. *Journal of Counselling Psychology*, 34, 197–204.

Bibby, R. W. (1995). *Beyond Headlines, Hype and Hope: Shedding Some Light on Spirituality*. Presentation to Annual Conference of the Society for the Scientific Study of Religion, October, St. Louis, USA.

Blakney, R. (1941). *Meister Eckhart: A Modern Translation*. New York: Harper & Row.

Blazer, D. G. and Palmore, E. (1976). Religion and ageing in a longitudinal panel. *Gerontologist*, 16, 82–5.

Bloom, B. L., Hodges, W. F., Stern, M. B., and McFadden, S. C. (1985). A preventive intervention program for the newly separated: Final evaluations. *American Journal of Orthopsychiatry*, 55, 9–26.

Bloom, W. (1991) (ed.). *The New Age: An Anthology of Essential Writings*. London: Rider.

Bock, D. C. and Warren, N. C. (1972). Religious belief as a factor in obedience to destructive commands. *Review of Religious Research*, 13, 185–91.

Bockmeuhl, K. (1990). *Listening to the God Who Speaks*. Colorado Springs: Helmers and Howard.

Bohm, D. (1980). *Wholeness and the Implicate Order*. London: Routledge.

Brabbins, C. J. (1992). Dementia presenting with complex visual hallucinations. *International Journal of Geriatric Psychiatry*, 7, 455–7.

Bradburn, N. M. (1969). *The Structure of Psychological Well-being*. Chicago: Aldine.

Brasic, J. R. (1998). Hallucinations. *Perceptual and Motor Skills*, 86, 851–77.

Braud, W. (1990). Distant mental influence of rate of hemolysis of human red blood cells. *Journal of the American Society for Psychical Research*, 84(1), 1–24.

Braud, W. and Anderson, R. (1998). *Transpersonal Research Methods for the Social Sciences*. London: Sage.

Brinkley, D. and Perry, P. (1994). *Saved by the Light*. New York: Villard Books.

Brook, S. (1987) (ed.). *The Oxford Book of Dreams*. Oxford: Oxford University Press.

Broughton, R. (1991). *Parapsychology: The Controversial Science*. London: Rider.

Bruner, J. S., Goodnow, J. J., and Austin, G. A. (1965). *A Study of Thinking*. New York: Wiley.

Bucke, R. M. (1923). *Cosmic Consciousness: A Study in the Evolution of the Human Mind*. New York: Dutton (first published 1901).

Bucke, R. M. (1991). *Cosmic Consciousness: A Study in the Evolution of the Human Mind*. Harmondsworth: Penguin/Arkana (first published 1901).

Budge, Sir A. W. (1972). *Egyptian Magic*. London: Routledge & Kegan Paul (first published 1899).

Bulkeley, K. (1995). *Spiritual Dreaming: A Cross-Cultural and Historical Journey*. New York: Paulist Press.

Burt, Sir C. (1962). The concept of consciousness. *British Journal of Psychology*, 53, 229–42.

Byrd, R. C. (1988). Positive therapeutic effects of intercessory prayer in a coronary care unit population. *Southern Medical Journal*, 81(7), 826–9.

Call, V. R. A. and Heaton, T. B. (1997). Religious influence on marital stability. *Journal for the Scientific Study of Religion*, 36(3), 382–92.

Campbell, J. (1968). *The Masks of God: Creative Mythology*. New York: Viking Penguin (3 Vols.) (Souvenir Press Edition 1973).

Campbell, J. (1973). *Creative Mythology: The Masks of God*. Harmondsworth: Penguin.

Campbell, J. and Moyers, W. (1988). *The Power of Myth*. New York: Doubleday.

Capra, F. (1975). *The Tao of Physics*. London: Wildwood House.

Capra, F. (1988). *Uncommon Wisdom*. London: Hutchinson.

Capra, F. (1996). *The Web of Life: A New Synthesis of Mind and Matter*. London: HarperCollins.

Carlton-Ford, S. L. (1992). Charisma, ritual, collective effervescence, and self-esteem. *Sociological Quarterly*, 33, 365–87.

Carson, V., Soeken, K. L., Shanty, J., and Grimm, P. M. (1988). Hope and its relationship to spiritual well-being. *Journal of Psychology and Theology*, 16(2), 159–67.

Chang, S. T. (1980). *Chinese Yoga: Internal Exercises for Health and Serenity of Body and Mind*. Wellingborough: Turnstone Press.

Child, I. L. (1985). Psychology and anomalous observations: the question of ESP in dreams. *American Psychologist*, **40**, 1219–30.

Christie-Murray, D. (1978). *Voices From the Gods*. London: Routledge & Kegan Paul.

Claridge, G. (1985). *Origins of Mental Illness*. Oxford: Blackwell.

Clark, W. H. (1977). The psychology of religious experience. In H. N. Malony (ed.), *Current Perspectives in the Psychology of Religion*. Grand Rapids, MI: Eerdmann.

Cohen, J. M. and Phipps, J-F. (1979). *The Common Experience*. London: Rider.

Conze, E. (1951). *Buddhism: Its Essence and Development*. Oxford: Bruno Cassirer.

Cook, C. M. and Persinger, M. A. (1985). Experimental induction of a "sensed presence" in normal subjects and an exceptional subject. *Perceptual and Motor Skills*, **85**(2), 683–93.

Cooper, J. C. (1978). *An Illustrated Encyclopaedia of Traditional Symbols*. London: Thames & Hudson.

Corbishley, T. (1973) (trs.). *The Spiritual Exercises of St. Ignatius Loyola*. Wheathampsted, Hertfordshire: Anthony Clarke.

Coward, H. (1992). Jung's commentary on the *Amitayut Dhyana Sutra*. In D. J. Meckel and R. L. Moore (eds.), *Self and Liberation: The Jung Buddhism Dialogue*. Mahwah, NJ: Paulist Press.

Cox, M. (1983). *Mysticism: The Direct Experience of God*. Wellingborough: Aquarian Press.

Crick, F. (1994). *The Astonishing Hypothesis*. London: Simon & Schuster.

Croog, S. H. and Levine, S. (1972). Religious identity and response to serious illness: A report on heart patients. *Social Science and Medicine*, **6**, 17–32.

Crookall, R. (1961). *The Supreme Adventure*. London: James Clarke.

Crookall, R. (1978). *What Happens When You Die*. Gerrards Cross: Colin Smythe.

Cupitt, D. (1980). *Taking Leave for God*. London: SPCK.

Cupitt, D. (1987). *The Long-Legged Fly*. London: SPCK.

Danto, A. C. (1976). *Mysticism and Morality*. Harmondsworth: Penguin.

Davidson, D. (1980). Mental events. In N. Block (ed.), *Readings in Philosophy of Psychology, Vol. I*. London: Methuen.

Davies, P. (1993). *The Mind of God*. Harmondsworth: Penguin.

Davis, P. and Hersh, R. (1986). *Descartes' Dream*. New York: Harcourt, Brace, Jovanovich.

Dawkins, R. (1979). *The Selfish Gene*. London: Paladin.

de Charms, C. (1998). *Two Views of Mind*. New York: Snow Lion.

de Quincy, C. (2000). The promise of integralism. In J. Andresen and R. K. C. Forman (eds.), *Cognitive Models and Spiritual Maps*. Thorverton: Imprint Academic.

de Riencourt, A. (1980). *The Eye of Shiva: Eastern Mysticism and Science*. London: Souvenir Press.

Deere, J. (1993). *Surprised by the Power of the Spirit*. Grand Rapids, MI: Zondervan.

Deere, J. (1996). *Surprised by the Voice of God*. Grand Rapids, MI: Zondervan.

Deikman, A. (2000). A functional approach to mysticism. In J. Andresen and R. K. C. Forman (eds.), *Cognitive Models and Spiritual Maps.* Thorverton: Imprint Academic.

Dennett, D. C. (1991). *Consciousness Explained.* Harmondsworth: Penguin.

Denney, F. M. (1985). *An Introduction to Islam.* New York: Macmillan.

DeSano, C. F. and Persinger, M. A. (1987). Geophysical variables and behaviour: XXXIX. Alterations in imaginings and suggestibility during brief magnetic field exposures. *Perceptual and Motor Skills,* 64, 968–70.

Dewhurst, K. and Beard, A. W. (1970). Sudden religious conversions in temporal lobe epilepsy. *British Journal of Psychiatry,* 117, 497–507.

Doblin, R. (1991). Pahnke's "Good Friday Experiment": A long-term follow-up and methodological critique. *Journal of Transpersonal Psychology,* 23, 1–28.

Dossey, L. (1999). *Reinventing Medicine: Beyond Mind–Body to a New Era of Healing.* New York: Harper Collins and Shaftesbury: Element Books.

Dossey, L. (2000). Immortality. *Alternative Therapies in Health and Medicine,* 6(3), 12–17 and 108–15.

Dulaney, S. and Fiske, A. P. (1994). Cultural rituals and obsessive-compulsive disorder: Is there a common psychological mechanism? *Ethos,* 22, 243–83.

Dundas, P. (1992). *The Jains.* London: Routledge.

Durkheim, E. (1915). *The Elementary Forms of the Religious Life.* London: Allen & Unwin (reissued 1976).

Eccles, Sir J. C. (ed.) (1976). *Brain and Conscious Experience.* New York: Springer-Verlag.

Eccles, Sir J. C. (1980). *The Human Psyche.* New York: Springer.

Eccles, Sir J. C. (1984). *The Human Mystery.* London: Routledge & Kegan Paul.

Eccles, Sir J. C. (1989). *Evolution of the Brain.* London: Routledge.

Eccles, Sir J. C. and Robinson, D. N. (1984). *The Wonder of Being Human: Our Brain and Our Mind.* New York: Free Press.

Edwards, A. (2001). Transpersonal experience and quest religious orientation. *Transpersonal Psychology Review,* 5, 34–40.

Eliade, M. (1977). *From Primitives to Zen: A Thematic Sourcebook of the History of Religions.* London: Fount.

Empson, J. (1989). *Sleep and Dreaming.* London: Faber & Faber.

Epstein, M. (1995). *Thoughts Without a Thinker.* New York: Basic Books.

Erikson, E. (1968). *Identity, Youth, and Crisis.* New York: Norton.

Evans, C. de B. (1924) (trs.). *Works of Meister Eckhart.* London: Watkins (2 vols.).

Eysenck, H. J. (1985). *Rise and Fall of the Freudian Empire.* Harmondsworth: Penguin.

Eysenck, H., Arnold, W., and Meili, R. (1972). *Encyclopaedia of Psychology.* London: Search Press.

Faulkner, R. O. (1985). *The Ancient Egyptian Book of the Dead.* London: British Museum Publications (rev. edn., ed. C. Andrews).

Feifel, H. (1974). Religious conviction and fear of death among the healthy and the terminally ill. *Journal for the Scientific Study of Religion,* 13, 353–60.

Fenwick, P. and Fenwick, E. (1995). *The Truth in the Light: An Investigation of Over 300 Near Death Experiences.* London: Headline.

Ferguson, M. (1982). *The Aquarian Conspiracy.* London: Collins.

Ferrucci, P. (1982). *What We May Be.* Wellingborough: Turnstone.

Fisher, S. and Greenberg, R. P. (1985). *The Scientific Credibility of Freud's Theories and Therapy.* New York: Columbia University Press.

Fletcher, B. (1990). *Clergy Under Stress.* London: Mowbray.

Fontana, D. (1989). *Managing Stress.* London: BPS Books.

Fontana, D. (1992). *The Meditator's Handbook.* Shaftesbury: Element Books/ Thorsons.

Fontana, D. (1993). *The Secret Language of Symbols.* London: Pavilion and San Francisco: Chronicle.

Fontana, D. (1994). *The Secret Language of Dreams.* San Francisco: Chronicle.

Fontana, D. (1995). *The Secret Power of Dreams.* Shaftesbury: Element Books.

Fontana, D. (1998). *The Meditator's Handbook.* Shaftesbury: Element Books.

Fontana, D. (2000). The nature and transformation of consciousness in Eastern and Western Psycho-Spiritual Traditions. In M. Velmans (ed.), *Investigating Phenomenal Consciousness.* Amsterdam: John Benjamins.

Forman, J. (1988). *The Golden Shore.* London: Robert Hale.

Forman, K. C. (1991). *Meister Eckhart: Mystic as Theologian.* Shaftesbury: Element Books.

Foss, L. and Rothenberg, K. (1987). *The Second Medical Revolution: From Biomedicine to Infomedicine.* Boston: New Science Library.

Fowler, R. B. (1995). *The Greening of Protestant Thought.* Chapel Hill, University of North Carolina Press.

Francis, L. J. (1991). The personality characteristics of Anglican ordinands: Feminine men and masculine women? *Personality and Individual Differences,* 12, 1133–40.

Francis, L. J. (1993). Personality and religion among college students in the UK. *Personality and Individual Differences,* 14, 619–22.

Francis, L. J. and Pearson, P. R. (1985). Extraversion and religiosity. *Journal of Social Psychology,* 25.

Francis, L. J. and Robbins, M. (2000). Religion and happiness: A study in empirical theology. *Transpersonal Psychology Review,* 4(2), 17–22.

Fraser, G. E., Beeson, W. L., and Phillips, R. L. (1991). Diet and lung cancer in California Seventh-Day Adventists. *American Journal of Epidemology,* 133, 683–93.

French, R. M. (1972) (trs.). *The Way of a Pilgrim.* London: SPCK.

French, R. M. (1973) (trs.). *The Pilgrim Continues His Way.* London: SPCK.

Freud, A. (1937). *The Ego and the Mechanisms of Defence.* London: Hogarth Press (1961).

Freud, S. (1900). *The Interpretation of Dreams.* London: Hogarth Press (1953).

Freud, S. (1907). *Obsessive Actions and Religious Experience.* London: Hogarth Press (in Vols. 4–5 of the Collected Works).

Freud, S. (1923). *The Ego and the Id.* London: Hogarth Press (in Vol. 19 of the Collected Works).

Freud, S. (1927). *Future of an Illusion.* London: Hogarth Press (in Vol. 21 of the Collected Works).

Freud, S. (1928). *A Religious Experience.* London: Hogarth Press (in Vol. 21 of the Collected Works).

Freud, S. (1930). *Civilization and its Discontents*. London: Hogarth Press (in Vol. 21 of the Collected Works).

Freud, S. and Pfister, O. (1963). *Psycho-Analysis and Faith*. London: Hogarth Press.

Friedlander, Y., Kark, J. D., and Stein, Y. (1986). Religious orthodoxy and myocardianl infaction in Jerusalem: A case-control study. *International Journal of Cardiology*, **10**, 33–41.

Fromm, E. (1965). *Socialist Humanism*. New York: Doubleday.

Gallemore, J. L., Wilson, W. P., and Rhoads, H. M. (1969). The religious life of patients with affective disorders. *Diseases of the Nervous System*, **30**, 483–6.

Gallup, G. (Jr.) and Proctor, W. (1983). *Adventures in Immortality*. London: Souvenir Press.

Gammond, P. (1997). *The A–Z of Classical Composers*. Godalming, Surrey: Bramley Books.

Gardner, J. W., and Lyon, J. L. (1977). Low incidence of cervical cancer in Utah. *Gynecologic Oncology*, **5**, 68–80.

Geschwind, M. (1983). Interictal Behaviour changes in epilepsy. *Trans-action* (May), 22–8.

Ghose, Sri Chinmoy Kumar (1970). *Yoga and the Spiritual Life*. New York: Tower Books.

Gillette, D. (1997). *The Shaman's Secret: The Lost Resurrection Teachings of the Ancient Maya*. New York: Bantam.

Ginsburg, M. L., Quirt, C., Ginsburg, A. D., and MacKillop, W. J. (1995). Psychiatric illness and psychosocial concerns of patients with newly diagnosed lung cancer. *Canadian Medical Association Journal*, **152**, 701–8.

Glass, T. A., Mendes de Leon, C., Marottoli, M. A., and Berkman, L. F. (1999). Population-based study of social and productive activities as predictors of survival among elderly Americans. *British Medical Journal*, **319**, 478–85.

Godwin, J. (1981). *Mystery Religions in the Ancient World*. London: Thames & Hudson.

Goldbourt, U., Yaari, S., and Medalie, J. H. (1993). Factors predictive of long-term coronary heart disease mortality among 10,059 male Israeli civil servants and municipal employees. *Cardiology*, **82**, 100–21.

Goleman, D. (1996). *Emotional Intelligence*. New York: Bantam.

Goleman, D. and Guerin, J. (1993) (eds.). *Mind Body Medicine*. New York: Consumer Reports Books/Fetzer Institute.

Goleman, D. and Thurman, R. A. F. (1991). *MindScience*. Boston: Wisdom.

Goodall, D. (1996). (ed. and trans.). *Hindu Scriptures*. London: Dent.

Goodwin, B. (1994). *How the Leopard Changed its Spots*. London: Weidenfeld & Nicolson.

Goswami, A. (1993). *The Self-Aware Universe: How Consciousness Creates the Material World*. New York: Tarcher/Putnam.

Govinda, Lama Anagarika (1969). *The Psychological Attitude of Early Buddhist Philosophy*. London: Rider.

Grant, J. (1984). *Dreamers*. Bath: Ashgrove Press.

Grant, P. (1985). *A Dazzling Darkness*. London: Fount.

Greeley, A. M. (1975). *The Sociology of the Paranormal*. London: Sage.

Grey, M. (1985). *Return from Death: An Explanation of the Near Death Experience*. London: Arkana.

Greyson, B. and Bush, N. E. (1996). Distressing near-death experiences. In L. W. Bailey and J. Yates (eds.). *The Near Death Experience*. London: Routledge.

Gribbin, J. (1991). *In Search of Schrödinger's Cat: Quantum Physics and Reality*. London: Black Swan.

Gribbin, J. (1995). *Schroedinger's Kittens*. London: Weidenfeld & Nicholson.

Gribbin, J. (2000). *Q is for Quantum*. London: Weidenfeld & Nicholson.

Griffin, D. R. (1988). Intuitive judgement and the evaluation of evidence. In D. Druckman and J. A. Swets (eds.), *Enhancing Human Performance: Issues, Theories and Techniques*. Washington, DC: National Academy Press.

Griffin, D. R. (1997). *Parapsychology, Philosophy, and Spirituality*. Albany, NY: SUNY Press.

Griffiths, B. (1982). *The Marriage of East and West*. London: Collins.

Griffiths, J. (1977) (ed.). *The Grace of Zen: Zen Texts for Meditation*. London: Search Press.

Grof, S. (1988). *The Adventure of Self-Discovery*. Albany: State University of New York.

Grof, S. (1998). *The Cosmic Game*. Dublin: Newleaf.

Grof, S. and Grof, C. (1989) (eds.). *Spiritual Emergency: When Personal Transformation Becomes a Crisis*. Los Angeles: Tarcher.

Grof, S. and Grof, C. (1990) *The Stormy Search for the Self*. New York: Tarcher.

Grossinger, R. (1987). *Planet Medicine: From Stone Age Shamanism to Post-Industrial Healing*. Berkley: North Atlantic Books (rev. edn.).

Grosso, M. (1997). *Soulmaking: Uncommon Paths to Self-Understanding*. Charlottesville, VA: Hampton Roads.

Guenther, H. V. (1976). *Buddhist Philosophy in Theory and Practice*. Boston: Shambhala.

Guerber, H. A. (1994). *Greece and Rome Myths and Legends*. London: Studio Editions (first published 1907).

Guerney, E., Myers, F. W., and Podmore, F. (1886). *Phantasms of the Living*. London: Trubner.

Guirdham, A. (1977). *The Great Heresy: The History and Beliefs of the Cathars*. Jersey: Neville Spearman.

Guntrip, H. (1969). *Schizoid Phenomena, Object Relations, and the Self*. New York: International Universities Press.

Guntrip, H. (1971). *Psychoanalytic Theory, Therapy, and the Self*. New York: Basic Books.

Gupta, M. N. (1978). *The Condensed Gospel of Ramakrishna*. Madras: Sri Ramakrishna Math.

Guth, J. L., Kellstedt, L. A., Smith, C. E., and Green, J. C. (1993). Theological perspectives and environmentalism among religious activists. *Journal for the Scientific Study of Religion*, **32**, 373–82.

Halifax, J. (1979). *Shamanic Voices: The Shaman as Seer, Poet and Healer*. Harmondsworth: Penguin.

Hall, C. and Nordby, V. J. (1972). *The Individual and His Dreams*. New York: New American Library.

Hampson, S. E. (1988). *The Construction of Personality.* London: Routledge.

Hansel, E. M. (1980). *ESP and Parapsychology: A Critical Re-evaluation.* Buffalo: Prometheus.

Hardy, J. (1987). *A Psychology with a Soul.* London: Routledge & Kegan Paul.

Hardy, Sir A. (1979). *The Spiritual Nature of Man.* Oxford: Oxford University Press.

Harner, M. (1990). *The Way of the Shaman.* San Francisco: Harper & Row (3rd edn.).

Hartsuiker, D. (1993). *Sadhus: Holy Men of India.* London: Thames & Hudson.

Harvey, A. (1996). *Light Upon Light: Inspirations From Rumi.* Berkeley, CA: North Atlantic Books.

Hawkes, J. (1965). *Prehistory in History of Mankind: Cultural and Scientific Development Vol. I.* London: UNESCO/New English Library.

Hay, D. (1982). *Exploring Inner Space.* Harmondsworth: Penguin.

Hay, D. (1990). *Religious Experience Today.* London: Mowbray.

Hay, D. and Heald, G. (1987). Religion is good for you, *New Society,* 17 April.

Hay, D. and Morisey, A. (1978). Reports of ecstatic, paranormal, or religious experience in Great Britain and the United States – a comparison of trends. *Journal for the Scientific Study of Religion,* **17,** 255–68.

Hayward, J. W. (1987). *Shifting Worlds Changing Minds: Where the Sciences and Buddhism Meet.* Boston: New Science Library.

Hearne, K. (1990). *The Dream Machine: Lucid Dreams and How to Control Them.* Wellingborough: Aquarian Press.

Helm, H., Hays, J. C., Flint, E., Koenig, H. G., and Blazer, D. G. (2000). Does private religious activity prolong survival? A six-year follow-up study of 3,851 older adults. *Journal of Gerontology,* **55A,** M400–5.

Herrigel, E. (1953). *Zen in the Art of Archery.* London: Routledge & Kegan Paul (trs. R. F. C. Hull).

Hertsgaard, D. and Light, H. (1984). Anxiety, depression, and hostility in rural women. *Psychological Reports,* **55,** 673–4.

Hjelle, L. A. (1975). Relationship of a measure of self-actualisation to religious participation. *Journal of Psychology,* **89,** 179–82.

Hoffman, E. (1992). *Visions of Innocence: Spiritual and Inspirational Experiences of Childhood.* Boston: Shambhala.

Hoge, D. R. (1974). *Commitment on Campus: Changes in Religion and Values Over Five Decades.* Philadelphia: Westminster.

Hoge, D. R. and Carroll, J. W. (1973). Religiosity and prejudice in Northern and Southern Churches. *Journal for the Scientific Study of Religion,* **53,** 581–94.

Hole, G. (1977). *Der Glaube bei Depressiven: Religions-pathologische und klinisch-statistische Untersuchung.* Stuttgart: Ferdinand Enke.

Hood, R. W. (1975). The construction and preliminary validation of a measure of reported mystical experience. *Journal for the Scientific Study of Religion,* **14,** 29–41.

Hood, R. W. (1995). The facilitation of religion experience. In R. W. Hood (ed.), *Handbook of Religious Experience.* Birmingham, AL: Religious Education Press.

Hopkins, C. J. (1971). *The Hindu Religious Tradition.* California: Wadsworth.

Horney, K. (1950). *Neurosis and Human Growth: The Struggle Towards Self-Realization.* New York: Norton.

Horowitz, M. J. (1975). Hallucinations: an information-processing approach. In R. K. Siegel and L. J. West (eds.), *Hallucinations: Behaviour, Experience and Theory*. New York: Wiley.

Horwitz, T., Kemmelman, S., and Lui, H. H. (1982). *Tai Chi Ch'uan: The Technique of Power*. London: Rider.

Housden, R. (1996). *Travels Through Sacred India*. London: Thorsons.

Howard, G. S. (1994). Reflections on change in science and religion. *International Journal for the Psychology of Religion*, 4, 127–43.

Hume, D. (1965). *A Treatise of Human Nature*. Oxford: Oxford University Press (ed. L. A. Selby-Bigge; original edition in three vols. 1739/40).

Hume, D. (1980). *Dialogues Concerning Natural Religion*. Indianapolis: Hackett (ed. R. H. Popokin; original edition 1779).

Hume, R. E. (1971) (trs.). *The Thirteen Principle Upanishads*. New York: Oxford University Press.

Hummer, R., Rogers, R., Nam, C., and Ellison, C. G. (1999). Religious involvement and U.S. adult mortality. *Demography*, 36, 273–85.

Hwa, J. T. (1980). *The Tao of Tai-Chi Chuan*. Taiwan: Tai Chi Foundation.

Hyman, R. (1996). Evaluation of a program on anomalous mental phenomena. *Journal of Scientific Exploration*, 10, 31–58.

Idler, E. L. and Kasl, S. V. (1992). Religion, disability, depression, and the timing of death. *American Journal of Sociology*, 97, 1052–79.

Idler, E. L. and Kasl, S. V. (1997). Religion among disabled and nondisabled persons: I Cross-sectional patterns in health practices, social activities, and well-being. *Journal of Gerontology*, 52B(6), 306–16.

Isherwood, C. (1963) (ed.). *Vedanta for the Western World*. London: Unwin.

Jacobi, J. (1968). *The Psychology of C. G. Jung*. London: Routledge & Kegan Paul (7th edn., trs. R. Manheim).

James, W. (1890). *The Principles of Psychology*. New York: Henry Holt (2 vols.).

James, W. (1902). *The Varieties of Religious Experience: A Study in Human Nature*. Cambridge, MA: Harvard University Press (reissued 1960 Fontana Books and 1961 Collier).

Jansen, K. (1996). Neuroscience, ketamine, and the Near Death Experience. In L. W. Bailey and J. Yates (eds.), *The Near Death Experience*. London: Routledge.

Jaynes, J. (1976). *The Origin of Consciousness in the Breakdown of the Bicameral Mind*. Boston: Houghton Mifflin.

Jeans, Sir James (1931). *The Mysterious Universe*. Cambridge: Cambridge University Press (2nd edn.).

Jenkins, R. A. and Pargament, K. I. (1988). Religion and spirituality as resources for coping with cancer. *Journal of Psychosocial Oncology*, 13, 51–74.

Johnson, R. (1963). *A Religious Outlook for Modern Man*. London: Hodder & Stoughton.

Johnson, R. (1971). *The Imprisoned Splendour*. London: Hodder & Stoughton (re-issued 1989 Pelegrin Trust/Pilgrim Books; original edn. 1953).

Johnson, S. C. and Spilka, B. (1991). Outcome research and religious psychotherapies: Where are we and where are we going? *Journal of Psychology and Theology*, 21, 297–308.

Jones, E. (1964). *The Life and Work of Sigmund Freud*. Harmondsworth: Penguin (abridged edn.; original edn. in 3 Vols. 1953–7).

Julian of Norwich (1966). *Revelations of Divine Love*. Harmondsworth: Penguin.

Jung, C. G. (1921). *Psychological Types*. London: Routledge & Kegan Paul (standard English translation 1971).

Jung, C. G. (1931). *The Spiritual Problem of Modern Man*. Princeton, NJ: Princeton University Press and London: Routledge.

Jung, C. G. (1932). *Psychotherapy or the Clergy*. London: Routledge (in Vol. 11 of the Collected Works, 1958, trs. R. F. C. Hull).

Jung, C. G. (1934). *The Soul and Death*. London: Routledge & Kegan Paul and Princeton, NJ: Bollingen Foundation.

Jung, C. G. (1938/40). *Psychology and Religion (The Terry Lectures)*. London: Routledge (in Vol. 11 of the Collected Works 1958, trs. R. F. C. Hull.)

Jung, C. G. (1943). *On the Psychology of the Unconscious*. London: Routledge (2nd edn. 1966; trs. R. F. C. Hull).

Jung, C. G. (1951). *Aion. Researches into the Phenomenology of the Self*. London: Routledge (2nd edn. 1968; trs. R. F. C. Hull).

Jung, C. G. (1952a). *Symbols of Transformation*. London: Routledge (2nd edn., Vol. 5 of the Collected Works, trs. R. F. C. Hull).

Jung, C. G. (1952b). *Answer to Job*. London: Routledge (2nd edn., Vol. 11 of the Collected Works, trs. R. F. C. Hull).

Jung, C. G. (1954). *Transformation Symbolism in the Mass*. London: Routledge (2nd edn., Vol. 11 of the Collected Works, trs. R. F. C. Hull).

Jung, C. G. (1955). *Letters*. London: Routledge & Kegan Paul (Vol. 2, ed. G. Adler).

Jung, C. G. (1956). *Symbols of Transformation*. London: Routledge (trs. R. F. C. Hull).

Jung, C. G. (1960). Psychological commentary on the Tibetan Book of the Dead. In W. Y. Evans-Wentz (compiler and ed.), *The Tibetan Book of the Dead*. London: Oxford University Press (4th edn., Jung's commentary trs. R. F. C. Hull; original edn. 1927).

Jung, C. G. (1963). *Memories, Dreams, Reflections*. London: Routledge & Kegan Paul (trs. R. and C. Winston, reissued 1967 Fontana).

Jung, C. G. (1964). *Man and His Symbols*. London: Aldus (1978 Pan).

Jung, C. G. (1966). *The Practice of Psychotherapy*. London: Routledge & Kegan Paul (2nd edn., Vol. 16 of the Collected Works, trs. R. F. C. Hull).

Jung, C. G. (1968). *Psychology and Alchemy*. London: Routledge (2nd edn., Vol. 12 of the Collected Works, trs. R. F. C. Hull).

Jung, C. G. (1969). *Psychology and Religion: East and West*. London: Routledge (2nd edn., Vol. 11 of the Collected Works, trs. R. F. C. Hull).

Jung, C. G. (1978). *Psychology and the East*. Princeton, NJ: Bollingen Foundation (edited publications from 1958–70).

Jung, C. G. (1984). *Dream Analysis: Notes of the Seminar given in 1938*. London: Routledge & Kegan Paul (ed. W. McGuire; first edn. privately printed 1934).

Kant, I. (1787). *Critique of Pure Reason*. New York: St Martin's Press 1965 (2nd edn., trs. N. K. Smith).

Kellehear (1996). *Near Death: Beyond Medicine and Religion*. New York: Oxford University Press.

Kennedy, E. C., Heckler, V. J., Kobler, F. J., and Walker, R. E. (1977). Clinical assessment of a profession: Roman Catholic clergymen. *Journal of Clinical Psychology*, **33** (Supplement), 120–8.

Kent, H. (1999). *Yoga: A Practical Approach to Achieving Optimum Health for Mind, Body and Spirit*. Shaftesbury: Element.

Kesseling, A., Dodd, M. J., Lindsey, A. M., and Strauss, A. L. (1986). Attitudes of patients living in Switzerland about cancer and its treatment. *Cancer Nursing*, **9**, 77–85.

King, H. and Locke, F. B. (1980). American white Protestant clergy as a low-risk population for mortality research. *Journal of the National Cancer Institute*, **65**, 1115–24.

King, M. B., Speck, P., and Thomas, A. (1999). The effects of spiritual beliefs on outcome from illness. *Social Science and Medecine*, **48**, 1291–9.

Kirkpatrick, L. A., and Hood, R. W. (1990). Intrinsic–extrinsic religious orientation: the boon or bane of contemporary psychology of religion. *Journal for the Scientific Study of Religion*, **29**, 256–68.

Kline, M. (1980). *Mathematics: The Loss of Certainty*. New York: Oxford University Press.

Koenig, H. G., Ford, S., George, L. K., Blazer, D. G., and Meador, K. G. (1993). Religion and anxiety disorder: An examination and comparison of associations in young, middle-aged and elderly adults. *Journal of Anxiety Disorders*, 7, 321–42.

Koenig, H. G., Hays, J. C., Larson, D. B., George, L. K., Cohen, H. J., McCullough, M., Meador, K., and Blazer, D. G. (1999). Does religious attendance prolong survival? A six-year follow-up study of 3,968 older adults. *Journal of Gerontology*, **54A**, M370–7.

Koenig, H. G., Idler, E., Kasl, S., Hayes, J. C., George, L. K., Musick, M., Larson, D. B., Collins, T. B., and Benson, H. (1999). Religion, spirituality, and medicine: A rebuttal to skeptics. *International Journal of Psychiatry*, **29**, 123–31.

Koenig, H. G., Larson, D. B., Hays, J. C., McCullough, M. E., George, L. K., Branch, P. S., Meador, K. G., and Kuchibhatla, M. (1998). Religion and survival of 1,010 male veterans hospitalized with medical illness. *Journal of Religion and Health*, 37, 15–29.

Koenig, H. G., McCullough, M. E., and Larson, D. B. (2001). *Handbook of Religion and Health*. Oxford: Oxford University Press.

Kris, E. (1952). *Psychoanalytic Explanations in Art*. New York: Schocken.

Krishna, G. (1970). *Kundalini: The Evolutionary Energy in Man*. Boston: Shambhala.

Krishnananda, Swami (1969). *The Philosophy of Life*. Sivanandanagar: Divine Life Society.

LaBerge, S. (1986). *Lucid Dreaming: The Power of Being Awake and Aware in Your Dreams*. New York: Ballantine.

LaBerge, S. and Rheingold, S. (1990). *Exploring the World of Lucid Dreaming*. New York: Ballantine.

Lagrand, L. (1997). *After Death Communications: Final Farewells*. St Paul, MN: Llewellyn.

Lagrand, L. (1999). *Messages and Miracles: Extraordinary Experiences of the Bereaved.* St. Paul, MN: Llewellyn.

Lambert, W. W., Triandis, L. M., and Wolf, M. (1959). Some correlates of beliefs in the malevolence and benevolence of supernatural beings: A cross-societal study. *Journal of Abnormal and Social Psychology,* **58**, 162–9.

Lazlo, I. (1993). *The Creative Cosmos.* Edinburgh: Floris.

Lee, S. G. and Herbert, M. (1970) (eds.). *Freud and Psychology.* Harmondsworth: Penguin.

Lehman, E. C. and Shriver, D. W. (1968). Academic discipline as predictive of faculty religiosity. *Social Forces,* **47**, 171–82.

Leonard, G. (1986). *The Transformation.* Los Angeles: Tarcher.

Leonard, G. (1991). *Mastery.* New York: Dutton.

Levy, J. J., Dupas, A., and Samson, J. M. (1985). Religion, death, and sexuality in Quebec. *Cahiers de Recherches en Science et de la Religion,* **18**, 243–51.

Libet, B. (1996). Neural processes in the production of conscious experiences. In M. Velmans (ed.), *The Science of Consciousness.* London: Routledge.

Liverziani, F. (1991). *Life, Death and Consciousness: Experiences Near and After Death.* Bridport: Prism Press, and Lindfield, Australia: Unity Press.

Lofland, J. (1978). *Doomsday Cult.* New York: Irvington.

Lu K'uan Yu (Charles Luk) (1971). *Practical Buddhism.* London: Rider.

Luk, C. (Lu K'Uan Yu) (1970). *Taoist Yoga.* London: Rider (reissued 1996).

MacCulloch, J. A. (1991). *The Religion of the Ancient Cults.* London: Constable (first published 1911).

Malony, H. N. (1977). The psychologist-Christian. In H. N. Malony (ed.), *Current Perspectives in the Psychology of Religion.* Grand Rapids, MI: Eerdmans.

Margenau, H. (1959). *The Nature of Physical Reality.* New York: McGraw-Hill.

Markides, K. S. (1983). Ageing, religiosity, and adjustment: A longitudinal analysis. *Journal of Gerontology,* **38**, 621–5.

Maslow, A. H. (1970a). *Motivation and Personality.* New York: Harper & Row (2nd edn.).

Maslow, A. H. (1970). *Religion, Values, and Peak Experiences.* New York: Viking.

Maslow, A. H. (1971). *The Farther Reaches of Human Nature.* New York: Viking (1976 Penguin).

Maslow, A. H. (1976). *The Farther Reaches of Human Nature.* Harmondsworth: Penguin.

Masters, R. E. L. and Houston, J. (1972). *Mind Games.* New York: Viking.

Matt, D. C. (1994). *The Essential Kabbalah.* San Francisco: Harper.

May, R. (1953). *Man's Search for Himself.* New York: Norton.

McClure, K. (1983). *The Evidence for Visions of the Virgin Mary.* Wellingborough: Aquarian Press.

McCreery, C. (1993). *Schizotypy and Out-of-the-Body Experiences.* Unpublished D.Phil Thesis, University of Oxford.

McCullough, M. E., Hoyt, W. T., Larson, D. B., Koenig, H. G., and Thoresen, C. E. (2000). Religious involvement and mortality: A meta-analytic review. *Health Psychology,* **19**, 211–22.

McDougal, W. (1928). *Body and Mind.* London: Methuen (7th edn.).

McDougal, W. (1950). *An Introduction to Social Psychology.* London: Methuen (30th edn.).

McLynn, F. (1996). *Carl Gustav Jung.* London: Black Swan.

Mead, G. W. (1934). *Mind, Self, and Society.* Chicago: University of Chicago Press.

Meckel, D. J. and Moore, R. L. (1992) (eds.). *Self and Liberation: The Jung/Buddhism Dialogue.* Mahwah, NJ: Paulist Press.

Meyer, M. W. (1987) (ed.). *The Ancient Mysteries: A Sourcebook.* San Francisco: Harper & Row.

Moody, R. (1983). *Life After Death.* New York: Bantam.

Moody, P. and Perry, P. (1988). *The Light Beyond: The Transforming Power of Near Death Experiences.* London: Macmillan.

Morse, M. and Perry, P. (1990). *Closer to the Light: Learning from Children's Near-Death Experiences.* New York: Villard (1991 Souvenir Press).

Moyer, B. D. (1993). *Healing and the Mind.* New York: Doubleday.

Murphy, G. (1947). *Personality: A Biosocial Approach to Origins and Structures.* New York: Harper.

Murphy, M. (1992). *The Future of the Body: Explorations into the Further Evolution of Human Nature.* New York: Tarcher/Putnam.

Murphy, M. and Donovan, S. (1990). *The Physical and Psychological Effects of Meditation: A Review of Contemporary Research.* Big Sur, CA: Esalen Institute (new edn. 1997 Institute of Noetic Sciences).

Murphy, M. and White, R. (1995). *In the Zone: Transcendent Experience in Sports.* Harmondsworth: Penguin/Arkana.

Musick, M. A. (1996). Religion and subjective health among black and white elders, *Journal of Health and Social Behaviour.* **37**, 221–37.

Myers, F. W. (1906). *Human Personality and its Survival of Bodily Death.* London: Longmans Green (2 vols.).

Nanamoli, Bhikku (1991). *The Path of Purification. Visuddhimagga, The Classic Manual of Buddhist Doctrine and Meditation.* Kandy, Sri Lanka: Buddhist Publication Society (5th edn., translated from the Pali text of Buddhaghosa).

Nelli, R. (1968). *Le Catharisme Vu a Travers les Troubadours.* Toulouse: Cahiers de Fanjeaux.

Nelson, L. D. and Cantrell, C. H. (1980). Religiosity and death anxiety: A multidimensional analysis. *Review of Religious Research*, **21**, 148–57.

Nelson, M. O. (1971). The concept of God and feelings towards parents. *Journal of Individual Psychology*, **27**, 46–9.

Nelson, M. O. and Jones, E. M. (1957). An application of the Q-technique to the study of religious concepts. *Psychological Reports*, **3**, 293–7.

Newberg, A. B. and d'Aquili, E. G. (2000). The neuropsychology of religious and spiritual experience. In J. Andresen and R. K. C. Forman (eds.), *Cognitive Models and Spiritual Maps.* Thorverton: Imprint Academic.

Nielsen, N. C., Hein, N., Reynolds, F. E., Miller, A. L., Karff, S. E., Cowan, A. C., McLean, P., and Erdel, T. P. (1988). *Religions of the World.* New York: St. Martin's Press (2nd edn.).

Nisbett, R. E. and Wilson, T. D. (1977). Telling more than we know: Verbal reports on mental processes. *Psychological Review*, **84**, 231–59.

Norman, W. T. (1963). Toward an adequate taxonomy of personality attributes: replicated factor structure in peer nomination personality ratings. *Journal of Abnormal and Social Psychology*, **66**, 574–88.

O'Shea, S. (2000). *The Perfect Heresy*. New York: Walker and London: Profile Books.

Ogata, M., Ikeda, M., and Kuratsune, M. (1984). Mortality among Japanese Zen priests. *Journal of Epidemiology and Community Health*, **38**, 161–6.

Oksanen, A. (1994). *Religious Conversion: A Meta-Analytical Study*. Lund: Lund University Press.

Oman, D. and Reed, D. (1998). Religion and mortality among the community-dwelling elderly. *American Journal of Public Health*, **88**, 1469–75.

Ornstein, R. E. (1972). *The Psychology of Consciousness*. San Francisco: Freeman.

Ornstein, R. E. and Sobel, D. (1989). *The Healing Brain*. New York: Macmillan.

Osis, K. and Haraldson, E. (1997). *At the Hour of Death: A New Look at Evidence for Life After Death*. Norwalk, CN: Hastings House (3rd edn.).

Oxman, T. E., Freeman, D. H., and Manheimer, E. D. (1995). Lack of social participation or religious strength and comfort as risk factors for death after cardiac surgery in the elderly. *Psychosocial Medicine*, **57**, 5–15.

Pagels, E. (1980). *The Gnostic Gospels*. London: Weidenfeld & Nicolson.

Pahnke, W. N. (1963). *An Analysis of the Relationship between Psychedelic Drugs and the Mystical Consciousness*. Harvard University: unpublished Ph.D. Thesis.

Pahnke, W. N. (1966). Drugs and mysticism. *International Journal of Parapsychology*, **8**, 295–314.

Palmer, E. H. (1984). *Oriental Mysticism: A Treatise on Sufism and Unitarian Theosophy of the Persians*. London: Octagon Press.

Papadopoulos, R. K. and Saayman, G. (1991). *Jung in Modern Perspective*. Bridport, Dorset: Prism Press.

Parrinder, G. (1987). *Encountering World Religions*. New York: Crossroad.

Pavlov, I. P. (1927). *Conditioned Reflexes*. New York: Oxford University Press.

Payne, P. (1981). *Martial Arts: The Spiritual Dimension*. London: Thames & Hudson.

Penfield, W. (1975). *The Mystery of the Mind: A Critical Study of Consciousness and the Human Brain*. New Jersey: Princeton University Press.

Persinger, M. A. (1987). *Neuropsychological Bases of God Beliefs*. New York: Praeger.

Persinger, M. A. (1996). Feelings of past lives as expected perturbations within neurocognitive processes that generate the sense of self: Contributions from limbic lability and vectorial hemisphericity. *Perceptual and Motor Skills*, **83**(3) (Part 2), 1107–21.

Piaget, J. (1967). *The Language and Thought of the Child*. London: Routledge & Kegan Paul.

Piaget, J. and Inhelder, B. (1969). *The Psychology of the Child*. New York: Basic Books.

Pickering, J. (1997). *The Authority of Experience: Essays on Buddhism and Psychology*. Richmond, Surrey: Curzon.

Poloma (1995). The sociological content of religions experience. In R. W. Hood (ed.), *Handbook of Religious Experience*. Birmingham, AL: Religious Education Press.

Powers, J. (1995). *Introduction to Tibetan Buddhism*. Ithaca, NY: Snow Lion.

Prabhavananda, Swami and Isherwood, C. (translators and commentators) (1953). *How to Know God: The Yoga Aphorisms of Patanjali*. New York: New American Library.

Pratt, J. B. (1920). *The Religious Consciousness: A Psychological Study*. New York: Macmillan.

Princeton Religion Research Center (1996). *Religion in America: Will the Vitality of the Church be the Surprise of the 21st Century?* Princeton, NJ: Gallup.

Pruyser, P. W. (1971). a psychological view of religion in the 1970s. *Bulletin of the Merringer Clinic*, **35**, 77–97.

Radin, D. (1997). *The Conscious Universe*. San Francisco: HarperEdge.

Ramachandran, V. S. and Blakeslee, S. (1998). *Phantoms in the Brain*. London: Fourth Estate.

Ravindra, R. (2000). *Science and the Sacred*. Wheaton, IL: Theosophical Publishing House.

Rechtschaffen, A. (1970). Sleep and dream states: An experimental design. In R. Cavanna (ed.), *Psi Favourable States of Consciousness*. New York: Parapsychology Foundation.

Regardie, I. (1972). *The Tree of Life*. New York: Samuel Weiser.

Reps, P. (1957). *Zen Flesh, Zen Bones*. New York: Charles Tuttle.

Rhodes, L. (1997). *Tunnel to Eternity*. West Chester, PA: Chrysalis Books.

Riley-Smith, J. (1991) (ed.). *The Atlas of the Crusades*. London: Times Books.

Ring, K. (1985). *Heading Towards Omega*. New York: Quill/William Morrow.

Ring, K. and Cooper, C. (1999). *Mindsight*. New York: William James Center for Consciousness Studies.

Ring, K. and Valarino, E. E. (1998). *Lessons From the Light*. New York: Insight Books.

Ringdal, G. I. (1996). Religiosity, quality of life, and survival in cancer patients. *Social Indicators Research*, **38**, 193–211.

Roberts, J. A., Brown, D., Elkins, T., and Larson, D. B. (1997). Factors influencing views of patients with gynecologic cancer about end-of-life decisions. *American Journal of Obstetrics and Gynecology*, **176**, 166–72.

Robinson, E. (1977). *Studies in Religious Experience*. Oxford: The Religious Experience Research Centre.

Rogers, C. (1961). *On Becoming a Person*. Boston: Houghton Mifflin.

Ryle, G. (1949). *The Concept of Mind*. London: Hutchinson.

Ryle, G. (1979). *On Thinking*. London: Hutchinson.

Sabom, M. B. (1982). *Recollections of Death*. London: Corgi.

Sabom, M. B. (1998). *Light and Death*. Grand Rapids, MI: Zondervan.

Sanella, L. (1987). *The Kundalini Experience*. Lower Lake, CA: Integral Publishing.

Sargant, W. (1974). *The Mind Possessed: A Physiology of Possession, Mysticism, and Faith Healing*. Philadelphia: Lippincott.

Schjelderup, H. and Schjelderup, K. (1932). *Uber Drei Haupttypen Der Religisen Erlebnisforam Und Ir Psychologische Grundlage*. Berlin: de Gruyter.

Schoeps, H-J. (1967). *An Intelligent Person's Guide to the Religions of Mankind*. London: Gollancz (trs. R. and C. Winston).

Scholem, G. (1974). *Kabbalah*. Jerusalem: Keter Publishing House.

Schrödinger, E. (1967). *What is Life?* New York: Cambridge University Press (original edn. 1944; includes *Mind and Matter* originally published 1958).

Schuhmacher, S. and Woerner, G. (1989). *The Rider Encyclopaedia of Eastern Philosophy and Religion.* London: Rider (trs. M. H. Kohn, K. Ready, and W. Wünsche).

Searle, J. (1989). *Minds, Brains and Science.* Harmondsworth: Penguin.

Shah, I. (1967). *Tales of the Dervishes.* London: Jonathan Cape.

Shah, I. (1968). *The Way of the Sufi.* London: Jonathan Cape.

Shah, I. (1972). *The Magic Monastery.* London: Jonathan Cape.

Shastri, H. P. (1971) (ed. and trs.). *World Within the Mind.* London: Shanti Sadan (5th edn.).

Sheldrake, R. (1988). *The Presence of the Past.* London: Collins.

Sheng Yen, Master (1982). *Getting the Buddha Mind.* New York: Dharma Drum.

Sicher, F. *et al.* (1998). A randomized double-blind study of the effect of distant healing in a population with advanced AIDS: Report of a small-scale study. *Western Journal of Medicine*, 169(6), 356–63.

Silbersweig, D. A., Stern, E., Frith, C. *et al.* (1995). A functional neuroanatomy of hallucinations in schizophrenia. *Nature*, 378, 176–9.

Simonton, C., Matthews-Simonton, S., and Creighton, J. (1978). *Getting Well Again.* Los Angeles: Tarcher.

Sipe, A. W. R. (1990). *A Secret World: Sexuality and the Search for Celibacy.* New York: Brunner/Mazel.

Slater, W. (1968). *Raja Yoga.* Wheaton, IL: Theosophical Publishing House.

Smart, N. (1968). *The Yogi and the Devotee: The Interplay Between the Upanishads and Catholic Theology.* London: Allen & Unwin.

Smart, N. (1989). *The World's Religions.* Cambridge: Cambridge University Press.

Smart, N. (1996). *Dimensions of the Sacred.* London: HarperCollins.

Smith, D. H. (1980). *The Wisdom of the Taoist Mystics.* London: Sheldon Press.

Smith, H. (1994). *The Illustrated World's Religions.* San Francisco: HarperCollins.

Smith, W. C. (1963). *The Meaning and End of Religion: A New Approach to the Religious Traditions of Mankind.* New York: Macmillan.

Solecki, R. S. (1971). *Shanidar.* New York: Knopf.

Solecki, R. S. (1977). The implications of the Shandar Cave: Neanderthal flower burial. *New York Academy of Science*, 293, 114–24.

Spellman, C. M., Baskett, G. D., and Byrne, D. (1971). Manifest anxiety as a contributing factor in religious conversion. *Journal of Consulting and Clinical Psychology*, 36, 245–7.

Spence, L. (1986). *Egypt Myths and Legends.* London: Bracken.

Spencer, S. (1963). *Mysticism in World Religions.* Harmondsworth: Penguin.

Sperry, R. W. (1985). *Science and Moral Priority.* New York: Praeger.

Spilka, B., Stout, L., Minton, B., and Sizemore, D. (1977). Death and personal faith: A psychometric investigation. *Journal for the Scientific Study of Religion*, 16, 169–78.

Spiro, M. E. (1978). Religious systems as culturally constituted defense mechanisms. In B. Kilborne and L. Langness (eds.), *Culture and Human Nature.* Chicago: University of Chicago Press.

Spiro, M. E. and D'Andrade, R. G. (1958). A cross-cultural study of some supernatural beliefs. *American Anthropologist*, 60, 456–66.

St. Theresa of Avila (1960). *The Life of Theresa of Jesus*. New York: Doubleday (trs. A. E. Peers).

St. Teresa of Avila (1974). *Interior Castle*. London: Sheed & Ward (trs. E. A. Peers; written in 1577).

St. Therese of Lisieux (1977). *Autobiography of a Saint*. London: Fount (trs. R. Knox).

Staal, F. (1975). *Exploring Mysticism*. Harmondsworth: Penguin.

Stace, W. T. (1960). *The Teachings of the Mystics*. New York: New American Library.

Stark, R. (1971). Psychopathology and religious commitment. *Review of Religious Research*, 12, 165–76.

Stevens, J. (1988). *The Marathon Monks of Mount Hiei*. London: Rider.

Stokes, D. M. (1997). *The Nature of Mind: Parapsychology and the Role of Consciousness in the Physical World*. Jefferson, NC: McFarland.

Stone, M. H. (1992). Religious behaviour in the psychiatric institute 500. In M. Finn and J. Gartner (eds.), *Object Relations Theory and Religion: Clinical Applications*. New York: Praeger.

Storm, H. (2000). *My Descent into Death*. London: Clairview.

Strawbridge, W. J., Cohen, R. D., Shema, S. J., and Kaplan, G. A. (1997). Frequent attendance at religious services and over 28 years. *American Journal of Public Health*, 87, 957–61.

Streeter, B. H. (1926). *Reality*. London: Macmillan.

Sturgeon, R. S. and Hamley, R. W. (1979). Religion and anxiety. *Journal of Social Psychology*, 108, 137–8.

Sulloway, F. J. (1979). *Freud, Biologist of the Mind: Beyond the Psychoanalytical Legend*. London: Andre Deutsch.

Suzuki, D. T. (1953). *Essays in Zen Buddhism*. London: Rider (3 vols.).

Suzuki, D. T. (1971). *What is Zen?* London: The Buddhist Society.

Suzuki, D. T. (1979). *Mysticism Christian and Buddhist*. London: Mandala.

Swenson, W. M. (1961). Attitudes towards death in an aged population. *Journal of Gerentology*, 16, 49–52.

Tapanya, S., Nicki, R., and Jarusawad, O. (1997). Worry and intrinsic/extrinsic religious orientation among Buddhists (Thai) and Christian (Canadian) elderly persons. *International Journal of Ageing and Human Development*, 44, 73–83.

Targ, R. and Katra, J. (1999). *Miracles of Mind*. Novata, CA: New World Library.

Tart, C. T. (1968). A psychophysiological study of out-of-body experiences in a selected subject. *Journal of the American Society for Psychical Research*, 62, 3–27.

Tart, C. T. (1988). *Waking Up*. Shaftesbury, UK: Element.

Tart, C. T. (1989). *Open Mind, Discriminating Mind*. San Francisco: Harper & Row.

Tart, C. T. (1994). *Living the Mindful Life*. Boston: Shambala.

Tart, C. T. (1996). Who might survive the death of the body? In L. W. Bailey and J. Yates (eds.), *The Near Death Experience*. London: Routledge.

Taylor, G. R. (1979). *The Natural History of the Mind: An Exploration*. London: Secker & Warburg.

Thich Nhat Hanh (1995). *Zen Keys: A Guide to Zen Practice.* New York: Doubleday, and London: Thorsons (2nd edn.).

Thomas, L. E. and Cooper, R. E. (1978). Measurement and incidence of mystical experience: An exploratory study. *Journal for the Scientific Study of Religion,* **17**, 433–7.

Thorndike, E. L. (1911). *Animal Intelligence.* New York: Macmillan.

Thouless, R. H. (1971). *An Introduction to the Psychology of Religion.* Cambridge: Cambridge University Press (3rd edn.).

Thun, T. (1959). *Die Religion des Kindes.* Stuttgart: Ernst Klett (2nd edn.).

Thun, T. (1963). *Die Religiose Entscheidung der Jugend.* Stuttgart: Ernst Klett.

Troyer, H. (1988). Review of cancer among four religious sects: Evidence that life-styles are distinctive sets of risk factors. *Social Science and Medicine,* **26**, 1007–17.

Ulanov, B. (1992). *Jung and the Outside World.* Wilmette, IL: Chiron.

Ullman, C. (1989). *The Transformed Self: The Psychology of Religious Conversion.* New York: Plenum.

Ullman, M. and Limmer, C. (1989) (eds.). *The Variety of Dream Experience.* New York: Continuum.

Ullman, M., Krippner, S., and Vaughan, A. (1989). *Dream Telepathy: Explorations in Nocturnal ESP.* Jefferson, NC: McFarland.

Underhill, E. (1942). *Mysticism: The Development of Humankind's Spiritual Consciousness.* London: Methuen (original edn. 1911, 14th edn. Bracken 1995).

Utts, J. (1996). An assessment of the evidence for psychic functioning. *Journal of Scientific Exploration,* **10**, 3–30.

Van de Castle, R. (1977). Sleep and Dream. In B. Wolman (ed.), *Handbook of Parapsychology.* New York: Van Nostrand Reinhold.

Van de Castle, R. (1994). *Our Dreaming Mind: The Role of Dreams in Politics, Art, Religion, and Psychology from Ancient Civilizations to the Present Day.* New York: Ballantine.

Van Eaden, F. (1913). A study of dreams. *Proceedings of the Society for Psychical Research,* **26**, 431–61.

Vardy, P. (1999). *The Puzzle of God.* London: Fount (revised edn.).

Vaughan, F. (1985). *The Inward Arc.* Boston: Shambhala.

Velmans, M. (2000). *Understanding Consciousness.* London: Routledge.

Vergote, A. and Tamayo, A. (eds.) (1981). *The Parental Figures and the Representation of God: A Psychological and Cross-Cultural Study.* The Hague: Mouton.

Vitz, P. C. (1988). *Sigmund Freud's Christian Unconscious.* New York: Guildford.

Vivekananda, Swami (1955). *Jnana Yoga.* Madras and New York: Sri Ramakrishna Math.

Von Arnim, B. (1810). *Letter to Goethe* (publisher unknown).

Wallace, A. F. C. (1966). *Religion, an Anthropological View.* New York: Random House.

Wallace, B. A. (1996). *Choosing Reality.* New York: Snow Lion.

Wallace, B. A. (2000). *The Taboo of Subjectivity: Toward a New Science of Consciousness.* Oxford: Oxford University Press.

Wallace, E. R. (1984). Freud and religion: A history and reappraisal. *Psychoanalytical study of society,* **10**, 115–61.

Wallace, R. K. (1970). Physiological effects of transcendental meditation. *Science*, **167**, 1751–4.

Wallace, R. K. and Benson, H. (1972). The physiology of meditation. *Scientific American*, **226**, 84–90.

Walsh, J. A. (1987). Myths, dreams, and divine revelation: From Abram to Abraham. In M. Ullman and C. Limmer (eds.) *The Variety of Dream Experience*. New York: Continuum.

Walsh, R. (1999). *Essential Spirituality*. New York: Wiley.

Walsh, R. and Vaughan, F. (1993) (eds.). *Paths Beyond Ego*. Los Angeles: Tarcher.

Walshe, M. (1979). *Meister Eckhart: German Sermons and Treatises*. London: Watkins (Vol.1).

Ware, Father K. (1979). *The Orthodox Way*. London: Mowbray.

Watson, J. B. (1919). *Psychology from the Standpoint of a Behaviorist*. Philadelphia: Lippincott.

Watson, J. B. (1930). *Behaviorism*. New York: Norton (rev. edn.).

Watson, L. (1986). *Supernature II*. London: Hodder & Stoughton.

Watts, A. W. (1957). *The Way of Zen*. New York: Pantheon.

Webster, A. C. and Stewart, R. A. C. (1973). Theological conservatism. In G. D. Wilson (ed.), *The Psychology of Conservatism*. London: Academic Press.

Wehr, G. (1987). *Jung: A Biography*. Boston: Shambhala.

Weil, G. M., Metzner, R., and Leary, T. (eds.) (1965). *The Psychedelic Reader*. New York: University Books.

Weimann, G. (1987). New religions: From fear to faith. *Canadian Journal of Sociology*, **12**, 216–28.

Weller, S. (1998). *Yoga Therapy: Safe Natural Methods for Healing and to Restore Health and Natural Well-being*. London: Thorsons.

Wellings, N. and McCormick, E. W. (eds.) (2000). *Transpersonal Psychotherapy*. London: Continuum.

Wesson, R. (1991). *Beyond Natural Selection*. Cambridge, MA: MIT Press.

West, L. J. (1975). A clinical and theoretical overview of hallucinatory phenomena. In R. K. Siegel and L. J. West (eds.), *Hallucinations: Behaviour, Experience and Theory*. New York: Wiley.

White, L. (1967). The historical roots of our ecological crisis. *Science*, **155**, 1203–7.

Whitehead, A. N. (1933). *Science and the Modern World*. Cambridge: Cambridge University Press.

Whitehead, A. N. (1974). *Religion in the Making*. New York: New American Library (first published 1926).

Whiteman, J. H. M. (1993). *Aphorisms on Spiritual Method: The Yoga Sutras of Patanjali in the Light of Mystical Experience*. Gerrards Cross: Colin Smythe.

Wiebe, P. H. (2000). Critical reflections on Christic visions. In J. Andresen and R. K. C. Forman (eds.), *Cognitive Models and Spiritual Maps*. Thorverton: Imprint Academic/Journal of Consciousness Studies.

Wilber, K. (1977). *The Spectrum of Consciousness*. Wheaton, IL: Quest.

Wilber, K. (1985). *Quantum Questions*. Boston: Shambhala.

Wilber, K. (1993). *The Spectrum of Consciousness*. Wheaton, IL: Quest (2nd edn.).

Wilber, K. (1998). *The Marriage of Sense and Soul: The Integration of Science and Religion*. Dublin: Newleaf.

Wilber, K. (1999). *One Taste*. Boston: Shambhala.

Wilber, K. (2000). *A Theory of Everything*. Boston: Shambhala.

Williams, P. (1989). *Mahayana Buddhism: The Doctrinal Foundations*. London: Routledge.

Williams, R. L. and Cole, S. (1968). Religiosity, generalized anxiety, and apprehensions concerning death. *Journal of Social Psychology*, **75**, 111–17.

Williams, D. R., Larson, D. B., Buckler, R. E., Heckmann, R. C., and Pyle, C. M. (1991). Religion and psychological distress in a community sample. *Social Science and Medicine*, **32**, 1257–62.

Willits, F. K. and Crider, D. M. (1988). Religion and well-being: Men and women in the middle years. *Review of Religious Research*, **29**, 281–94.

Wilson, I. (1997). *Life After Death*. Basingstoke: Sidgwick & Jackson/Macmillan.

Winnicott, D. W. (1953). Transitional objects and transitional phenomena. *International Journal of Psycho-Analysis*, **34**, 89–97 (see also Winnicott (1971) *Playing and Reality*, London: Tavistock, for an edited version).

Witelson, S. F. and Kristofferson, A. B. (1986) (eds.). McMaster–Bauer Symposium on Consciousness. *Canadian Psychology*, **27**, 123–82.

Wittgenstein, L. (1958). *The Blue and Brown Books*. Oxford: Blackwell.

Wittgenstein, L. (1963). *Philosophical Investigations*. Oxford: Blackwell.

Wolf, F. A. (1985). *Mind and the New Physics*. London: Heinemann.

Wolf, J. G. (1989) (ed.). *Gay Priests*. New York: HarperCollins.

Wood, E. (1962). *Yoga*. Harmondsworth: Penguin (rev. edn.).

Wulff, D. M. (1997). *Psychology of Religion: Classic and Contemporary*. New York: Wiley (2nd edn.).

Wundt, W. (1904). *Principles of Physiological Psychology*. New York: Macmillan (5th edn. trs. E. B. Titchener).

Zaehner, R. C. (1957). *Mysticism Sacred and Profane*. Oxford: Oxford University Press.

Zaehner, R. C. (1966) (trs.). *Hindu Scriptures*. London: Dent and New York: Dutton.

Zaehner, R. C. (1971). *Mysticism Sacred and Profane*. Oxford: Oxford University Press.

Zaleski, C. (1987). *Other World Journeys: Accounts of Near Death Experiences in Medieval and Modern Times*. Oxford: Oxford University Press.

Zeidner, M. and Hammer, A. L. (1992). Coping with missile attack: Resources, strategies, and outcomes. *Journal of Personality*, **60**, 709–46.

Zohar, D. and Marshall, I. (2000). *Spiritual Intelligence: The Ultimate Intelligence*. London: Bloomsbury.

Zukav, G. (1979). *The Dancing Wu Li Masters: An Overview of the New Physics*. London: Rider.

Zukav, G. (1991). *The Seat of the Soul*. London: Rider.

Zumm Brunn, E. and Epiney-Burgard, G. (1989). *Women Mystics in Medieval Europe*. New York: Paragon House.

# Index